To Jack Abbott with my
Compliments— Keep on drawing

Robert A. Hirsch

SCHNEIDER TROPHY *Racers*

Robert S. Hirsch

Motorbooks International
Publishers & Wholesalers ®

Hirsch, Robert S.
    Schneider Trophy racers/Robert S. Hirsch
      p. cm.
    Includes bibliographical references (p.) a
      index.
    ISBN 0-87938-616-9
    1. Schneider Trophy--History. 2. Airplane
      racing--History. 3. Seaplanes--History
  I. Title.
    GV759.2.S35H57   1993
    797.5'2--dc20   9213588

On the front cover: A painting of the Macchi M.52 by Uwe Feist.

On the back cover: Top left, Italian pilots in front of the M.52R at Calshot, England. Center left, from left to right, the M.52R, M.52, and S.6 are prepared for the contest at Calshot. Bottom left, the Supermarine S.5 being readied for flight at Calshot. Top right, a drawing of the French CAMS 36bis of 1923. Bottom left, a drawing of the American NAF Mercury racer of 1929.

On the frontispiece: Shown on October 15, 1926 are hopeful candidates for the Navy's 1926 Schneider Trophy team with one of the reserve F6C-3s. Third from left on the top row, is John J. Lenhart. *Ted Buckland*

On the title page: Italy's M.52R after being brought in to Ryde after a practice flight for the 1929 Schneider Trophy contest. *Hirsch Collection*

Printed and bound in Hong Kong

Contents

Chapter 1

To Fly from the Water

The First Hydroaeroplanes

The first attempts to fly off the water were not by powered flight but rather from a float glider, five years before Henri Fabre's successful flight. Built by Gabriel Voisin for Ernest Archdeacon, a Paris attorney and aviation enthusiast, it was an assembly of two sets of boxkites on floats.

Towed behind a motorboat the Voisin float glider did actually lift off from the surface of the Seine River in June 1905. It later underwent modifications and was tested on Lake Geneva, Switzerland, without any success. In 1905 Voisin also built another somewhat different float glider for Louis Bleriot. It had stubbier wings and less stability.

On July 18, 1905 Gabriel Voisin climbed into the Voisin-Bleriot (Bleriot II) and signaled the motorboat to pull out. The pull rope lifted, dripping water as it tightened, and the glider started moving. It lifted off the Seine rather suddenly, but then dropped a wing, started into a banking turn, and then sideslipped into the river. Voisin, seated on the center-section frame seat, nearly drowned extricating himself from the sinking wreckage. Moments later he was floundering in the river until the motorboat could reach him. He did not try again but later began building aeroplanes at Billancourt on the Seine.

The first person to devise a machine capable of lifting off and landing on water was Henri Fabre. Like many other Frenchmen trying to become pioneers of flight, he wasn't much of an aviator. Actually he was a marine engineer, which is probably why his floats were so successful. His craft, or as some called it, his contraption looked more like the top of some fancy fence than a flying hydrocraft. The engine was a Gnome rotary of 50hp and mounted at the rear, directly behind the main wing and rectangular fixed rudder. Jutting down from the wing mainspar on each side was a post attached to airfoil-like wooden floats.

Fabre sat about midway forward on top of the upper longitudinal post. Two forward horizontal elevators provided lateral control. Below this was a third float. Banking control was by foot pedals, which warped the wing tips downward similar to the Wright brothers' system. The hydrocraft in flight was remarkably stable, considering Fabre's limited knowledge of aerodynamics. His success with his embryo of a hydroplane was fantastic considering that several experienced flight pioneers failed in their attempts to fly off the water.

On March 28, 1910, in the Gulf of Fos at Martigues near Marseilles the strange contraption lifted off from the surface of the bay and remained in the air for several seconds, then landed without mishap on its three floats. Fabre was so encouraged by his success he continued making short flights until May 18, when he attempted to climb too steep, causing his hydroaeroplane to stall, and he came down into the Mediterranean with a splash. Although he was unhurt, his dignity was shattered, as was his machine. He chose to retire from aviation while still alive. The Fabre hydroaeroplane was salvaged, rebuilt,

Glenn H. Curtiss and Lt. T. G. Ellyson in a Navy A-1 Curtiss Triad at Hammondsport, by Keuka Lake. This plane had a 75hp Curtiss V–8 engine. By autumn of 1911, Curtiss had put the hydros on the open market, and those at Monaco had both the early 50hp and 75hp engines. *Hirsch Collection*

again flown about a year later, but by this time there were many more efficient flying machines putting on floats and flying from the water.

In 1911 most aeroplanes were still frail biplanes except for those designs following the Bleriot configuration. They were mostly constructed of wood, fabric, and piano wire. Pilots sat on the open framework of struts and braces. Most often they were not strapped in. By mid-1911 there were thirty recorded fatal flying accidents, which caused thirty-four deaths.

By 1912 the science of aviation was beginning to catch up with the aircraft development. Designs were becoming less and less an exercise in intuition and more of a systematic application of known science and theories. Teams of specialists instead of lone pioneers began to emerge. These specialists started companies that usually carried the originator's name. Each innovation brought on another until the stick-and-wire contraptions of early flight were replaced by the modern aircraft form. Streamlined fuselages and flight surfaces, as well as more sophisticated controls began to emerge.

In 1912 speed was king on both land and sea. With lift and controls better understood, the problems with power and engine reliability became the paramount thrust in research. This was also the year when women started capturing headlines in aviation, but not at Monaco or any of the Schneider contests. These were aero club sponsored, which was strictly dominated by the masculine gender.

It was considered premature to accept the new art of flying among the recognized branches of industry. But on examination, there was reason for those with ambition to do so. Aeroplanes were by then used in three distinct ways: sport or convenience of travel, postal service or for war, and for profit as in exhibitions, including racing. Flying schools were cropping up everywhere, and people exchanged money.

The market for aeroplanes was already of considerable magnitude, as noted by the volume of sales made by the various companies that built them. Louis Bleriot had already sold several hundred aeroplanes since 1909 at a cost of 24,000 francs for a single-seater and 28,000 francs for a two-seater. Voisin, Farman, Sommer, Breguet, and Nieuport were in the same ballpark. A Breguet cost $6,000 and an Antoinette was even more. In the United

Fabre getting ready to start his 50hp Gnome engine. This hydroaeroplane is of particular interest due to its unique blend of hydro and aviation designs. *Hirsch Collection.* Left, the Maurice Farman seaplane piloted by Gaubert at the Grand Prix de Monaco. Its motor is a 200hp Salmson. *H. Nowarra*

9

The Donnet-Leveque flying boat, piloted by Denhart. This type was entered in two of the 1912 Saint-Malo contests but not in any of the 1913 events. Below, the Voisin Canard seaplane at Monaco, 1912. It later carried No. 4 on the two outer side panels. This was the only successful canard type in the competition. *Hirsch Collection*

States Wright, Curtiss, and Burgess were the leaders of around a dozen or so builders. The average price ranged from $5,000 to $7,000 for a flying machine. But also the fatality rate dropped from nine out of fourteen pilots in accidents to one out of every twenty-nine. Many more pilots were flying, but they weren't killing themselves as fast. Dealers in secondhand machines also sprang up. They grew more slowly, though, since a secondhand aeroplane was a dangerous investment and an even more dangerous adventure.

Related industries (patent lawyers, maintenance, engines and accessories, gas, oil, spark plugs, and others) all contributed to the business of aviation. They still do. Metal had begun to replace wood, and offered more precise stress predictions and longer life. This added another industry to the list of support industries. Those companies building aeroplanes were beginning to consider safety in their designs.

Hugh Robinson in the Curtiss Triad crashing into the heavy sea at Monaco. *Hirsch Collection*

1912 Monaco Contests

There were three separate hydroaeroplane events held along the Riviera between Monaco and San Ramo. The first hydroaeroplane meet was held at Monaco and organized by The International Sporting Club of Monaco. It was called, Program D' Hydroaeroplane, or Aeroplane Marines, and was held from March 24–31, 1912. There were four prizes: 15,000, 8,000, 4,000, and 3,000 francs. Those listed as contestants were:

Aircraft	Motor/ Hp	Pilot
Voisin Canard	Salmson 110	Colliex
Voisin Canard Race No. 4	Anzani 60	Rugere
Maurice Farman	Renault 70	Renaux
Henri Farman	Gnome 70	Fischer
Curtis-Paulhan, Triad	Curtiss 75	Paulhan
Curtiss Triad	Curtiss 50	Robinson
Caudron-Fabre	Anzi 60	Caudron
Sanchez-Besa	Salmson 110	Benoist
Balliod Moteur 'X'		Balliod

The Riviera in spring was an ideal setting. The weather conditions were perfect and Monaco provided a permanent audience. Pilots competed in four categories: 1) takeoff from a calm port to circle buoys, 2) landing in calm port waters from the open-sea flight, 3) takeoff outside the port, and 4) landing on the open sea. There were some spills, including a spectacular dive into the sea by Robinson, yet he escaped injury. Fischer won, and Renaux was second. Jacques Schneider's nationalistic pride was aroused by Fischer, a German, flying a French Farman hydroaeroplane and winning the most contest points with ease. This patriotism could have prompted him into thinking of a trophy offer.

The first hydroaeroplane contest was followed by two other events during the summer of 1912. The first of the two was a contest for speed and was organized by the Automobile Club of France. It was held August 24–26, 1912, at Saint Malo, France. It was known as the Program Le Concours De Saint Malo. The contestants were:

Aircraft	Motor/ Hp	Pilot
Astra biplane	Gnome 80	Labouret
Borel monoplane	Gnome 80	Chambenois
Deperdussin	Gnome 80	Bussen
Donnet-Leveque biplane	Gnome 80	Beaumont
Maurice Farman	Renault 70	Renaux

Molla and crewman preparing to start the seaplane. Note the large, single float. This type of float was not easy to handle but the R.E.P. faired better in the two Saint-Malo races than the twin-float types.
H. Nowarra

Aircraft	Motor/ Hp	Pilot
Nieuport	Gnome 100	Weymann
Paulhan biplane	Curtiss 75	Barra
Paulhan biplane	Curtiss 50	Mesguich
R.E.P.	Gnome 80	Molla
Sanchez-Besa	Renault 100	Benoist
Sanchez-Besa	Renault 100	Rugere
Train-Astra	Gnome 80	unknown

Ten different models of hydroaeroplanes were entered. The R.E.P. outran all other competitors on the opening day. The rough sea and waves demonstrated that double-float aeroplanes had more stability than single-float and hull designs. The R.E.P. was an exception, riding the waves without difficulty. Charles Weymann on his Nieuport won the speed event showing that monoplanes were the fastest. Yet the final tally showed the Astra as the highest scorer and the Sanchez-Besa as the second highest. Both were biplanes.

The second of the two events held at Saint-Malo September 7–16, 1912, was known as the Program L'Hydroplane Colonial. It was sponsored by the Aero Club of Belgium. This was generally an extension of the previous gathering. Instead of speed, however, there were payload and nonstop-distance contests. King Leopold was present, and he donated an additional special trophy to the program. This contest was won by Conneau in a flying boat by Donnet-Leveque. The contestants for the main program were:

Aircraft	Motor/ Hp	Pilot
Paulhan-Curtiss Triad	Curtiss 85	Barra
Lanser biplane	Gnome 70	Lanser
Jero biplane	Gnome 70	Vershaeve
Sanchez-Besa	Renault 100	Benoist
Donnet-Leveque	Gnome 80	Beaumont
Aviatik-Autovia	Aviatik 100	Buchow
Nieuport	Gnome 100	Gobe
R.E.P.	Gnome 80	Molla
Borel	Gnome 80	Chemet
DeBrouckete	Gnome 100	Busso
Maurice-Parman	Renault 70	Renaux

Chemet's Borel monoplane scored the highest number of points. Benoist came in a reasonably close second. Renaux came in third , and Beaumont was fourth. All other competitors were far behind .

There were also paid passenger flights over water. Since these gatherings took place before the Gordon Bennett contest in Chicago, on October 18, 1912, Jacques Schneider witnessed some or all of the events, and he then resolved to create a hydroaeroplane trophy. He was one of the judges of the Program le Concours De Saint-Malo. The 1912 contests stimulated an immediate response, which was actually the kickoff for hydroaeroplane competition.

Early Speed Contests

The Schneider Trophy contests and attempts for world speed records are now well established in aviation history. No other contest has brought about the advance in speed as did the La Coupe d' Aviation Maritime Jacques Schneider. In a span of 18 years with four of them inactive due to World War I, the seaplane speed rose from 60.95mph (98.1km/h) to a world record of 407.5mph (655.79km/h). Then in 1934 the Italian challenger M.C.72 set a record of 440.68mph (709.5km/h), which still stands for propeller-drive seaplanes.

The Schneider Trophy competition was a series of contests for speed. It has been called the Schneider race by the press and writers in general. But the contestants were not racing

Roland Garros taxiing his Morane-Saulnier back into Monaco harbor. Roland Garros also had a De Marcay twin-float monoplane where a wing folded aft instead of warping for lateral control. It failed the water trials for the Grand Prix. *H. Nowarra*

each other, as they were on land, around pylons as we know it today. Instead they
were flying a given distance individually
against time. Therefore this book considers
the thirteen competitions a series of contests
to include other requirements besides speed.

Jacques Schneider was born near Paris on
January 25, 1879. He was the son of a wealthy
armament factory owner at La Creusot,
France. In carving out his own engineering ca-
reer he chose the unglamorous coal-mining industry. On August 8, 1908, Wilbur Wright
brought his Model B Aircraft to Le Mans,
France, for demonstrations. Aviation fever
spread quickly throughout France and some
parts of Europe.

As an engineer and having other engineering disciplines, Schneider became fascinated
with the operations and the mechanics of the
Wright flyer. As flying fever grew in 1909 his
fascination also grew. He joined the Aero Club
of France in 1910, where he gained his pilot
credentials. He built a machine with a 120hp
Salmson motor, which could reach speeds of
50mph (80km/h). Shortly thereafter he suf-

fered multiple fractures on one arm while
competing at a Monte Carlo seaplane event.
This left him handicapped for life, but it did
not stop him completely. In 1913 he established a balloon altitude record of 33,066ft
(10,081m).

Jacques Schneider became the undersecretary of state for aviation in the French government, but he never abandoned the Aero Club
of France's endeavors. On September 9, 1912,
at Chicago, Illinois, pilot Jules Vedrines won
the Gordon Cup. Schneider was there. As
Vedrines landed his tiny Deperdussin near his
hangar, Schneider ran out to meet him. There
Schneider kissed him on both his cheeks and
draped the French tricolor around his shoulders.

On October 18, 1912, Vedrines, Maurice
Prevost, and Armand Deperdussin were
guests of the Aero Club homecoming reception
in Paris. Schneider proudly turned over the
Gordon Bennett Cup to the club vice president. He expressed the hope that it would remain there permanently. He then announced
that he was to present and to support the La

Coupe d' Aviation Maritime Jacques Schneider, a cup that was valued at 25,000 francs. The contest for this was to be held between aero clubs rather than just between pilots.

The rules were carefully laid out by Schneider and his team of advisors. The team included Bleriot and Deperdussin. Like the rules of the Gordon Bennett contests, the cup would remain with the club that won it for that year. Not only that, but any three wins within a five-year period and then not challenged within a year of the last win would place the cup permanently with that club and end the contest. If the club that held the trophy was unable to organize a contest, the previous trophy winner would be asked to organize the contest. If all else failed, the contest would be held in France.

For the first three years there was a 25,000 franc prize for the winning pilot or club, whatever the contestant preferred. The contests were only open to seaplanes and to any club affiliated with the Federation Aeronautique International (FAI). The FAI had been formed in Paris in 1905 as a governing body for sport-flying events, four years before the first air race at Reims. Schneider had witnessed Henri Fabre's flight from the water on March 28, 1910. He reasoned that since about 70 percent of the earth's surface was covered by oceans, the seaplane should be developed. By the end of 1911 floats of various designs were being fitted to various aeroplanes with increasing success. It is surprising that Italy—being surrounded by water like England—did not become involved in seaplane racing until after World War I.

The majority of entries in the first two races were hastily converted from landplanes. These aircraft were unsuitable for water flying from the power-curve and airframe-stability aspects after the floats were installed. Float drag could be as much as 43 percent of total drag. But flying from water offered one great advantage: runway length was nearly infinite, which was very important for the low-powered aircraft of the era.

On May 1, 1928 Jacques Schneider died at the age of forty-nine, a resident of Beaulieu-sur Mer, not far from Nice and Monaco. This was where the course was laid out for the first two Schneider contests by the Aero Club of France. Schneider died in relative obscurity

while huge sums of money were being spent on machines to win the Schneider Trophy. He never knew the ultimate permanent winner, nor the effects it had on aviation.

By the end of 1927 it had been a long, yet interesting struggle from the tiny stick and wire boxkites of the 1913 and 1914 Schneider Trophy contests to the sleek, high-powered racers that traveled up to 300mph (482km/h) in the last contest Schneider could witness. This struggle was fraught with dangers and disasters, but Schneider did see them contribute beyond measure to the development of all phases of flying. Nothing worthwhile can be achieved without effort and some risk. Outstanding success such as in the Schneider contests required enthusiasm in addition to experience and ability.

The Schneider contests were to become the most important of all international aircraft speed events. The entrants were the pacesetters in the development of floatplanes. Through chronological accounting of designs of contenders and winners, one can trace the development up to 1931, when the last contest was flown. While the designs emphasized speed, benefits also were the development of testing facilities and methods for aerodynamic and hydrodynamic theories of aircraft form. Racing for the Schneider Trophy st' designers to ever-increasing va tios between engine-propeller thrust a...

Unlike other aeroplane races where pilots crowded each other in the turns, battling for the lead, the Schneider contests were run entirely against time. This might seem scarcely worth the effort watching the repetition of them rounding the course. Yet to those huge crowds that flocked to witness these speed contests over the years, these races were an ultimate thrill. As huge scoreboards announced the lap times, spectators eagerly compared lap speeds.

There were three basic periods of the Schneider contests:

First came the early period, or growth period, 1913–1922. This period produced the rotary engines known for their light weight and reliability. Their ease of cooling contributed to this reputation. Afterward, the Isotta-Fraschini water-cooled engines came about. This was followed by the development of the Napier Lion W-12, which was also water cooled.

lons mucii a
were flv:

The second period, 1923–1926, marked the appearance of equipment specially built for racing. American influence on seaplane racing development was extremely important. This is when governments developed an interest, and other countries began coveting the trophy. The Curtiss D-12 engine, Curtiss-Reed propeller, and the skin radiators were introduced, starting a whole new trend in floatplane development. By 1924 almost everyone was using Reed-type propellers.

During the third period, 1927–1931, the remainder of the contests were flown either in Italy or England. France now produced only half-hearted attempts for the trophy. However, some very interesting designs were developed in Europe. The Napier Lion, Rolls-Royce Kestrel and R engines—which later became the Merlin—and finally all the Fiat As. engines, from 2 through 5, were among these. They brought power up to 2,500–3,000hp. All the world speed records were held by seaplanes up to September 1939, eight years after the contests were officially ended. The specific power in this period had jumped to 0.85hp/ci (51.7hp/ltr) and the engine mass was lowered to 0.805lb/hp (0.366kg/hp). By 1931 these statistics rose to 1.18hp/ci (72.2hp/ltr) and a mass 0.615lb/hp (0.279kg/hp).

Such highly developed technology was mostly due to the Schneider contests and the speed the pilots attained while racing. Most of these breakthroughs were transposed into military machines for World War II. After 1926 the influence of the United States was less and less. Evidently this was why the United States trailed Europe in development of fast fighter aircraft during this era.

The Schneider Trophy itself was just another prize with almost any amount of monetary value, depending on who wanted it. After the 1919 prize of 25,000 francs, what other prizes were available is not clear. But rewards there were. Without any rewards the contests would certainly have faded out. Each nation's aero club and builders had a different approach based on their motivation at the time. France's failure to evaluate the importance of the contests became a major setback to its aspirations of leadership in aviation. The Schneider contests in the end were recognized as a valuable development ground for high-performance aircraft used in World War II.

Chapter 2

1913 Monaco

The Monaco Meet and the First Schneider Trophy Contest

The first competition for the Schneider trophy was held at Monaco on April 16, 1913. It was just one event of a large program of hydroaeroplane competition, the Grand Prix D' Hydroaeroplanes De Monaco, which began on April 3 and ended on April 16. There were four main competitions with thirteen days to complete them. The program listed them as: 1) Le Meeting De Monaco, with prize money of 50,000 francs; 2) Coupe Du Ministre De La Marine, with prize money of 50,000 francs; 3) Paris Alamer, with prize money of 50,000 francs; and 4) Coupe International Des Aeros Marines Coupe Jacques Schneider, with prize money of 25,000 francs.

The general arrangement of the moorings along the harbor for the seaplanes had them in six rows anchored along a line with machines facing the sea. They would exit to the right. All of the preliminary trials except the handling by crane took place outside the harbors. The assembled seaplanes attracted many visitors from other nations, especially England and Italy.

The schedule was continuous from the preliminary trials and the contests through the Schneider contest. The swell on the sea was much higher than the pilots were used to flying. The problem of hydroplaning was a very difficult one, which wrecked many of the assembled craft. Louis Gaudart died when his Artois biplane began to porpoise, then to lift at a high angle into the air. His plane stalled and dove into the sea, nose first. Gaudart was never found by rescue crews.

Of the twenty-six possible entries listed, only eighteen contestants underwent trials. Then by April 11, only seven had qualified for the Grand Prix for the April 12 event. Prevost had pancaked his Deperdussin from several feet above the sea. This accident left his tail section hanging from a point just forward of the horizontal stabilizer. It was repaired in time for the contests.

The rescheduled Grand Prix was a race of ten 31.07mi (10km) laps, or 310.69mi (500km) total. This proved too much for the four contestants: Bregi, Espanet, Gaubert, and Prevost, for none of them completed the course. Gaubert had the best effort with a total of 167.7mi (270km). Bregi was second with 161.56mi (260km). None of them had reached the 173.99mi (280km) minimum required for the Schneider course, so there was some doubt that the Schneider contest would go smoothly.

The Schneider Contest Begins

On Wednesday, April 16, the 174mi (280km) time-and-distance contest took place. The heavy seas, which had caused so many spills and disasters in the previous week, had subsided. Fortunately, that morning dawned clear and sunny and brilliantly blue. The wind was calm, with smooth water barely rippling enough to be visible from the harbor. The competitors were allowed to start anytime after 8:00am. All four contestants were at the harbor early, avoiding any afternoon breeze that could spoil their performance.

Charles Weymann in his Nieuport just before his engine quit. If it had not quit, he would have been the winner, and the 1914 contest might well have been in the United States. *France Report*

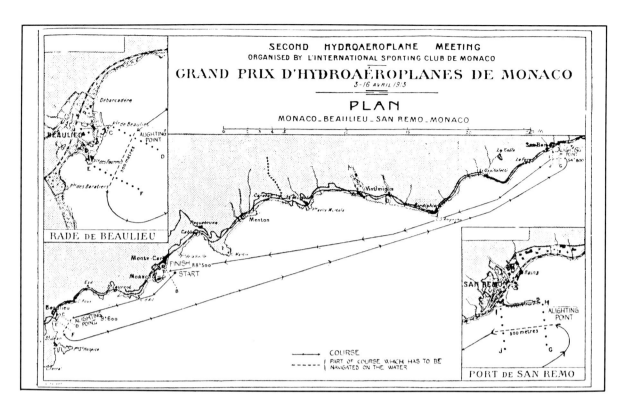

SECOND HYDROAEROPLANE MEETING
ORGANISED BY L'INTERNATIONAL SPORTING CLUB DE MONACO

GRAND PRIX D'HYDROAÉROPLANES DE MONACO
3-16 AVRIL 1913

PLAN
MONACO - BEAULIEU - SAN REMO - MONACO

RADE DE BEAULIEU

PORT DE SAN REMO

→ COURSE
----- PART OF COURSE WHICH HAS TO BE NAVIGATED ON THE WATER

The map of the Monaco hydroaeroplane race course.

There were seven registered starters for the contest; however, three were eliminated in the trials. Following is the list of contestants:

Race No.	Aircraft	Engine/HP	Pilot	Country
1	Borel Monaco	Gnome 160	Georges Chemet	France
—	Breguet	Salmson/Canton-Unne 110/115	Henri Bregi	France
—	Breguet	Salmson/Canton-Unne 200	Rene Moineau	France
19	Deperdussin	Gnome 160, 14cyl	Maurice Prevost	France
2	Morane-Saulnier	Gnome 80, 9cyl	Roland Garros	France
6	Nieuport	Gnome 100, 9cyl	Dr. Gabriel Espanet	France
5	Nieuport	Gnome 160, 14cyl	Charles Weymann	USA

Maurice Prevost in his Deperdussin No. 19 was first away at 8:08. He taxied smoothly to the starting line and then covered the first 3.1mi (5km) on the surface. He then opened to full power and the Deperdussin rose up on the step and planed smoothly over the water before lifting off.

Before Prevost completed his first lap, Roland Garros was sent to the starting line in his Morane-Saulnier, No. 1. After almost completing the taxi test, he accidentally let go of the blipper switch, and the motor went to full power throwing blinding sheets of water spray all over the cowling and fuselage. The tiny ma-

chine started into a series of up and down hops when it passed the takeoff line. So he stopped, taxied back, and tried again. The

drenching his machine received from the splashing fouled the ignition system, and on his second try he sloshed to a halt. Garros signaled for assistance and was soon in tow back to the harbor, where he went about getting ready again as quickly as possible.

Then at 8:50 Dr. Gabriel Espanet in his Nieuport, No. 6, got away onto the course. He was slower than Prevost on the compulsory 3.1mi (5km) surface run but got away without any apparent difficulty.

The last to taxi to the start line was Charles Weymann in his Nieuport, No. 5. He exercised extreme caution in negotiating the seaworthiness trial and lost considerable time. When he was finally well on the circuit, he was 7min behind Prevost.

Maurice Prevost skimmed across the water as he landed, crossing the finish line. Yet since the rules said "fly across the finish line," he was requested to go back out and do it over again. He hesitated until he saw Weymann land on the water, signaling for a tow since his engine was dead and he had two more laps to go. Prevost started up, taxied out, and flew another lap. This added 58min to his time, which reduced his final registered speed. Prevost was declared the winner. This exonerated him from his poor showing in the Grand Prix. So as Jacques Schneider happily watched, the first contest bearing his name was won by a Frenchman in a French machine with a French engine—an event that would not happen again. From 1929 on, Maurice Prevost headed the Esso Aviation marketing interests in France. He devoted his life to aviation. He was the only pilot to win two major speed contests in the same year, and the first to top 124mph (200km/h).

Roland Garros in his 80hp Morane-Saulnier had performed splendidly during the preceding days of the Monaco contests. He lost his chance during the Schneider races from a poor start and then his hesitation.

Flying his 100hp Nieuport, Dr. Gabriel Espanet dropped out after about 45mi (72.45km, or 4-1/2 laps) when his engine quit. He was towed in and soon withdrew from the race. Garros made a second attempt, but gave it up when he saw how well Prevost and Weymann were doing. His Morane-Saulnier proved difficult to handle, and he had already lost almost an hour since the starting bomb signaled the beginning of the race as well as the official times.

When Weymann's engine failed and could not complete the course and Prevost had not correctly completed it, Garros made a third try. He got off well enough and flew the course at about 60mph (96.54km/h). But he had lost so much time since his first try, that he was placed third in position on the board, and later was moved to second place because he finished. Weymann was moved to third.

The local newspapers made much of the accusations that Charles Weymann was born in Haiti of German and Russian parents. If the

committee was to pick up on this, then the "international" character of the contest would be lost. Therefore no one questioned Weymann's right to represent the United States. It turned out that Weymann was faster than Prevost. He had caught up with Prevost, and was in the lead by about 3.5–4sec on Lap 15. His start was slow, taking 18min on the first lap. By the 124.22mi (200km) point he was about 3min ahead of Prevost.

Of the three pilots who got airborne, a comparison at Lap 5 showed a sort of false picture of the pending outcome. The times were: Prevost, 34min, 49sec; Espanet 36min, 11sec; Weymann 40min, 13sec.

At this point both Weymann's and Espanet's Nieuports were lapping at a faster rate than Prevost's Deperdussin; Espanet was losing ground to Weymann. About halfway through the fourth lap Espanet's engine quit and he had to set down on the course and wait for a tow. Weymann then was lapping at about 70mph (113km/h). As the other pilots completed Lap 15, Weymann was making up for the time he lost on the first lap and was forging ahead.

Weymann flew wide around the first buoy and kept drifting wide around the second one.

Nieuport Type VI being shown at the Paris Air Show. It is lacking the nose wings that help prevent dig-in of the floats. *S. Hudek*

Monaco harbor during the 1913 contest. Seaplanes are: first row, Henri Farman, De Marcay, Maurice Farman; second row, Donnet-Leveque; third row, Astra, Morane-Saulnier, Leveque; fourth row, Deperdussin, Breguet; fifth row, Deperdussin, Nieuport; sixth row, Deperdussin, Nieuport, Breguet. *Hirsch Collection.* Below, Eugene Gilbert's Morane-Saulnier sitting on the ramp in the harbor. It was not listed as a contestant, and it was unlike Garros' Morane-Saulnier. *S. Hudek*

He was making up for lost time on the straight runs, clearly showing the Nieuport was faster. His fastest lap was 71mph (114km/h).

State-of-the-Art Seaplanes of 1913
Deperdussin

There were two Deperdussin manufacturing companies: the mother company in France and the British Deperdussin Aeroplane Co. Ltd. The British Deperdussin aeroplane was called the Seagull. It is characterized by its strong wing bracing, effected by an understructure of steel tubing attached to the front and rear spars of the wing. This is somewhat similar to a biplane structure but there is no lower wing. The machine had a single-row, 9cyl rotary engine and a more rounded and deeper fuselage of the monocoque type.

The tail float is located about 6ft (2m) ahead of the rudder post. It is of three-ply wood, covered with fabric and boat varnish. Its aerodynamic profile supported its own weight in flight. The British Deperdussin design team felt that the streamlined tube bracing under the wing gave no more air resistance than the usual wire bracing.

Louis Bechereau designed the Deperdussin sport and racing monoplanes. Armand Deperdussin, a French silk broker, financed it, beginning in 1909. The F.1 model won the Gordon Bennett trophy twice in a row, in a runaway contest prior to World War I. It was capable of 130mph (209km/h), a speed not equaled until the last part of the war, four years later.

Maurice Prevost's French Schneider Deperdussin was much like the standard 1912 two-seater. The difference was that it had a 14cyl, 160hp Gnome rotary engine, the same as the one in the Gordon Bennett racer. The struts for the two flat-bottomed floats were heavily supported by wires. This stiffened the float attachment points and held the float true to the flight path. These wires were fastened between the two struts.

Weymann in front of Monte Carlo, banking around the pylons. Note the float wings to prevent nose-over. Below, Leon Levavasseur in his Nieuport with passenger, ready to start up. The engine had to be cranked for start-up from inside. *H. Nowarra*

Weymann in his Nieuport on the course during 1913 Schneider contest at Monaco. That year his engine was a single-row rotary. He had lost about 7min on the water tests, but at the halfway point he was up with Maurice Prevost's Deperdussin. At the three-quarter point he was ahead, but then a burst oil pipe forced him out of the race. *Hirsch Collection*

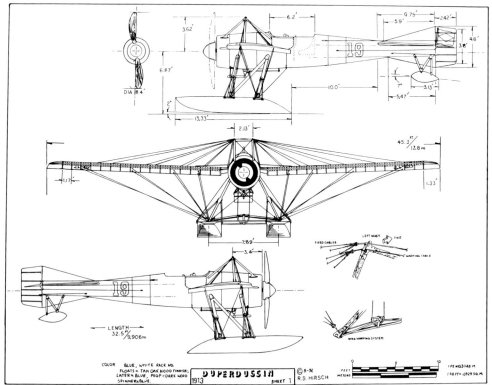

The sport single-seater B.1 model with a 50hp Gnome engine sold for about 24,000 francs. It was built extensively of wood, and was similar to the Monaco machines. Their monocoque construction consisted of three layers of tulip wood veneer about 1/8in thick glued together. An outer surface of linen was glued on and coated the shell to form a smooth surface. The final coating consisted of several coats of varnish sanded smooth.

The Monaco machines were longer in the fuselage than the standard Deperdussins, giving them a better fineness ratio. They had a larger cockpit for quicker escape if an accident was to submerge the craft. The propeller was mahogany, and there was a large round spinner, which left a ring gap open between the cowling inlet. Airplane designers use the same system today on radial engines.

The wing—although similar to the Seagull planform—had a completely different bracing. The machines were like most other monoplanes of French design because the flight and land wires were rigged so they could bend downward the outer rear-wing panels. Thus, like a flap on today's aircraft, lift is increased in that area. The designers did not yet consider upward movement on the opposite side necessary.

The Monaco Deperdussins used two types of floats on the tail. One was a simple, somewhat flat shape that seemed oval from the side and rectangular from the top. The second type had a rectangular planform, with an airfoil shape. Various photos from the era have created some confusion as to which aircraft entered which contest. The Prevost Deperdussin had floats with a wide-chord trailing edge. About two-thirds of the way forward, this edge curved inward to about one-third of the width of the trailing edge. Tubular struts lay diagonally from the sides of the floats to the middle of the principal struts.

Although several Deperdussin monoplane seaplanes were raced at Monaco, Prevost's model received the most alterations of which was that the engine air intake lay beneath the fuselage with its opening facing the propeller blast, which created a ram-air effect.

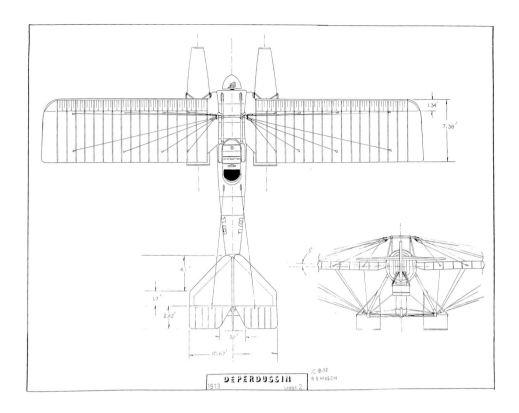

Nieuport

Edouard De Nieuport formed the Nieuport establishment at Issy-les-Moulineaux, Paris, in 1909. Gustave Delage joined the company in January 1914. The company's pre-World War I products were all monoplanes. In the 1910 and 1911 models the pilot was completely enclosed except for his head, by the 27.5ft (8.39m), fully covered fuselage. On May 11, 1911, a Type IIN with a 28hp Nieuport engine obtained a record speed of 74.37mph (119.7km/h). Nieuports were well represented in the Gordon Bennett Aviation Cup race.

The Nieuport monoplane was exhibited in England at the 1911 Aero Show. It proved to be fast with as little as a 30hp engine. With more powerful engines and innovations in its streamlining, it was capable of much greater speeds. However, the tragic deaths of the Nieuport brothers within a short time period proved a great loss to the science of flying. Edouard died in a plane crash on September 6, 1911, and Charles died two years later also in an air accident.

The Nieuport seaplane was first exhibited at the Olympia Aero Show in England. It resembled the land versions, except that the chassis accommodated floats instead of

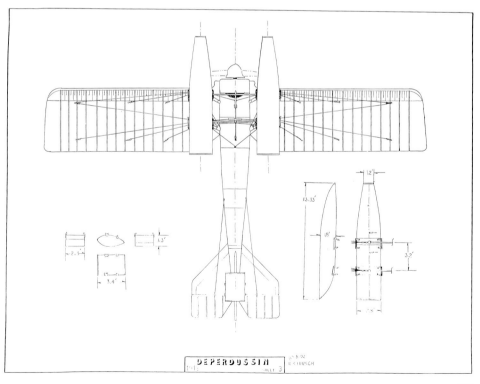

wheels. The craft that appeared at the show had a single-step-type pair of floats; the step was halfway back along their length. They were set widely apart, and were integrated to the fuselage through a structure of stream-lined-section steel tubes. The machines at Monaco had a three-stepped keel about 1ft (0.31m) wide.

At that time it was difficult to state an opinion on the advantage of the Nieuport's triple-step keel float. Nonetheless, it seemed to observers that it fared better when it came to skimming the water, regardless of the wave size. Designers knew about hydroplaning with fast, small boats used in racing long before the seaplane existed. Anyone who has watched or been in a speedboat has seen the force that water can deal against the boat's bottom at high speed. The Nieuport monoplanes were the only machines at Monaco with stepped floats.

On both sides of the rounded nose of each float was a metal airfoil wing about 6–8in

Maurice Prevost on the course in his Deperdussin. Note stringers on the bottom of floats. Right, Gabriel Espanet standing up talking to crew before startup. The Nieuport in back is Weymann's. *H. Nowarra*

(15.24–20.32cm). It was set at a high angle of incidence to keep the water spray away from the propeller and to keep the float from dipping underneath the water in rough waves. The two main floats were built of cypress wood with canvas-covered tops and were doped for sealing. The tail float looked like the Goodyear blimp, and steel tubes connected it to the fuselage.

The Monaco Nieuports had Gnome 100 and 160hp, 14cyl engines driving an 8.5ft (2.59m) diameter propeller. This propeller had brass-covered tips to prevent splitting. Lower down in the cockpit was an engine-cranking handle which allowed the pilot to start the engine without outside help.

The pilot had a bucket-type seat with no back or shoulder straps. The Nieuport control system differed from others because of how it warped the wing tips. The pilot carried out this function by resting his feet on a cross bar that was attached to a rocking shaft.

Warping cables went to the outer rear spar area. When the pilot moved the centrally pivoted hand lever forward and aft, the elevators moved up or down from the stabilizer plane. Movement of the hand lever sideways actuated the rudder.

Morane-Saulnier

The Morane-Saulnier biplanes were mainly the Farman and the Voisin type. The hydromachine at Monaco had an 80hp LeRhone rotary engine. The LeRhone differed from the Gnome by its valve system. It had mechanically operated inlet valves that were fed by an external radial manifold of induction pipes. It also had two floats tied together by cross bracing along the horizontal plane, and by wires attached between the bracing along the horizontal plane and between the bracings at deck level. Sometimes these bracings would become immersed in the sea when the plane bounced or skimmed on the surface.

The Morane-Saulnier seaplane was unique. It had similarities to the Borel, but it was smaller. The design was plain and simple. It had a 7cyl, 50hp Gnome engine and a wooden, two-blade propeller. The engine had a round cowling extending a little over halfway to the bottom, and there was no spinner. The fuselage was a wooden frame of square and rectangular sections culminating into a flat section at the rudder and elevator bars. There was no horizontal or vertical stabilizer. Instead, the elevator and rudder had surfaces in front of the pivot to counterbalance the aerodynamic forces on the control.

The wing was shoulder high and had two main spars and ten ribs. There were three pairs of warping cables running from the inverted vee structure on the top of the fuselage just ahead of the pilot, to the wing tips. The return lines went to a yoke under the fuselage

Below left, Fischer in his Henri Farman seaplane, approaching a landing in the harbor where there are fewer swells. The sea conditions dictated whether takeoffs and landings would be in or out of the harbor. *H. Nowarra*. Below, Henri Farman, Henri Deutsch de la Meurthe, and Charles Voisin. *Hirsch Collection*

Jacques Schneider at Monaco. Far right top, Labouret preparing to taxi out for takeoff on the Canton Unne–powered Astra. Far right bottom, La Coupe d' Aviation Maritime Jacques Schneider— the Schneider Trophy. The trophy shows a nude female winged figure kissing a zephyr recumbent on a wave, which forms into the head of Neptune and two other zephyrs. It is made of bronze and silver and mounted on a base of dark-veined marble. It now resides in the British Air Museum.
Hirsch Collection

below the pilot. Long forward-raked struts ran from the fuselage to the square–cross-section floats. These had short stabilizer struts at the bottom. The tail float consisted of an upside-down airfoil section about 1.5ft (0.49m) wide. The float's main body was slightly forward of the control pivot points. Its maximum speed was 74.6mph (120km/h). Roland Garros put the larger 9cyl, 80hp engine in it for the seaplane contest. This added 88.4lb (40kg) to the mass and upset the plane's center of gravity (C.G.) and float balance, causing it to crash on takeoff.

Borel

The G. Borel & Cie company of Paris was established in 1910. It had built about twenty-five machines by the time the Monaco races took place. The Borel hydro-monoplane was a double-float machine with the floats attached to the fuselage by steel tubes. These tubes had an oval shape to reduce drag as well as cross wires for rigidity. The Monaco machine had its 80hp engine replaced with a 100hp, 9cyl Gnome engine. In this hydro version of the Borel two-seater the fuselage was elongated and the tail float was made integral with the rudder, so that the float turned when the rudder did. It also had new wings installed just for the Monaco races; an unfortunate mishap in the Monaco harbor bent the steel-tube struts, leaving the floats and the fuselage misaligned. However, they were replaced within a day.

Farman

Two types of Farman seaplanes raced at Monaco, the Henri Farman and the Maurice Farman. Both were large-wing biplanes with a double float. The Maurice Farman was slightly larger. Both of the Farmans had springed floats which came from the same basic arrangement as the landplanes had. The Henri Farman had the largest of the Gnome engines, the 14cyl, 160hp model that drove a two-blade, 12.25ft (3.74m) diameter propeller. It used a rather large single roller chain. The engine, pilot, and mechanic were each housed in an independent framework attached to the main spars of the lower wing. The Henri Farman weighed 2,850lb (1,292kg). It had a wing area of 660sq-ft (61.3sq-m). Its relatively light wing loading helped the machine in taking off

from the water and in landing at slower speeds.

The Henri Farman had a canvas top that covered a set of cross bars as well as the float struts up to the fuselage. Another set of bars secured the bottom of the floats. Rubber elastic straps held the bars close to each other inside the float. Every time the water slapped on the bottom of the float this force stretched the rubber, which created a spring effect.

The Maurice Farman biplane resembled the Henri Farmans in many respects, yet it was larger and had longer wings. Both Farmans had two rudders and two tail floats tied to the two tail mainframes. These also held the elevator at the top.

Breguet

For the Monaco contests there were two Breguets, one with a wide single float and one with the standard pair of floats. The float attached to the fuselage of the single-float machine by two struts going forward and two going to the rear. Telescoping struts attached them and fitted them with oleo suspension to the lower wing. The machine also had small floats hanging halfway outward on the lower wing. These floats were sprung at the heel.

The single-float machine had a 200hp, 9cyl Canton-Unne engine. The double-float machine had a 110hp, 9cyl Canton-Unne. Both had a bathtub tail float attached to the empennage by four struts in front of the rudder bar. This rudder bar was attached directly to the end of the empennage. There was no fixed-plane vertical or horizontal stabilizer.

M. R. Moineau gave an impressive performance for the Grand Prix De Monaco flying the single-strut machine. This brought him a 13,000 francs compensation for having the longest flight before the contest was annulled. The two-float machines had two forward pontoon struts going up to the fuselage frame. They were anchored through a sliding spring collar. The single rear strut held to the float by a ball joint also had the upper end spring anchored. Stabilizer bars went to the lower wing, which ran well below the fuselage.

The Canton-Unne engines were water cooled. Two flattened brass-tube radiators on each side of the fuselage secured onto the two inner-plate struts did the job. The front cockpit had a cranking handle so the mechanic could start the engine while still in his seat. The often-photographed landplane had a spinner fastened to the propeller and a cowling wrapped tightly around the engine; the two seaplanes at Monaco did not.

Cables running forward to just behind the pilot's seat kept the rudder and elevator neutral. Coil springs were incorporated in them to keep the tail planes in neutral automatically. All control cables incorporated the coil spring system to relieve the strain on the pilot. They did this by taking up the shock of sudden gusts. The pilot control was a wheel that moved forward and aft to control the elevator. Rotating the wheel left or right moved the rudder. Two pedals and two cables warped the wings.

De Marcay

The De Marcay hydromonoplane had folding wings that were rigged to the two masts just in front of the cockpit and behind the rear spars. The masts sloped backward and obliquely outward. This arrangement allowed the wings to fold back against the fuselage when the machine anchored and rested. Each wing was hinged. Tubular steel masts carried and controlled the positioning of the wing through bracing wires and steel cables. The wings could be rocked forward and aft in flight to effect lateral control. This system differs from the standard warping of the aft section of the wing's outer panels.

Astra

The Cie General Transaerienne was responsible for constructing the tractor-type Astra hydro-biplanes. The Astras entered in the Monaco contests had 110hp Canton-Unne engines. There were other Astras present that had the 12cyl Renault engine, but for one reason or another, did not enter the competitions.

Earlier Astras had wings similar to the Wright Brothers' Model C biplane. However, those at Monaco had new wings with differently shaped rib sections and three sets of wing struts. The long, sleek pontoons were flat bottomed, and six tubular steel struts rigidly attached them to the lower wing planes. The tail float was attached to the lower fuselage ahead of the rudder. This machine had the general shape of the World War I machines to come.

27

Chapter 3

1914 Monaco

The Monaco Meet and the Second Schneider Trophy Contest

Smaller contests were held in several places almost every week in 1914, and even though the Gordon Bennett race was cancelled due to an impending war, it had attracted competitors from all over the world. The years 1912–1914 brought an onslaught of engine designs and development with no less than 112 types. There were vee types with some up to 16cyl. The rotary was developed into a twin-row with 14 and 18cyl, but cooling of rear cylinders was a problem the engineers could not solve so it faded out for military use.

The warning of impending war led the governments of concerned nations to push development of aircraft suitable for military operations, thus moving builders away from racers and sport planes to payload-carrying machines. Looking at the monoplane and biplane from a safety standpoint, more monoplanes were involved in accidents and crashes. There were suspected structural failures. The monoplane had a higher wing loading and therefore higher stalling speeds. In England there evolved a sort of revulsion to the monoplane and as far back as September 1912, the British War Office actually banned monoplanes from the military. Even this was canceled later, but it had affected British design development.

Winston S. Churchill was appointed First Lord of the Admiralty in 1911 and resigned in 1915. He held that office during the period in which the foundations of airpower were laid, and influenced the progress Great Britain was making. From the start, the policies of the Army and Navy were at odds with each other, each wanting to control flying their own way.

The Admiralty was guided by a Captain Sueter and a small staff of officers and engineers; they were backed 100 percent by Churchill. The Department of Military Aeronautics at the War Office believed in standardization and long before flying machines were fit for it they were trying to standardize. The Admiralty started out with the idea of comparing as many different types of aeroplanes as possible, which did not coincide with standardization. As a result, Great Britain ended up in 1914 with some of each.

So this year Great Britain saw a flurry of tractor biplanes all capable of having floats installed. Among them were the Thomas two-seater, Hall trainer, Grahame-White, EAC twin-screw tractor, Blackburn, Aero, Beardmore, and D.E.W.

Two firms that benefited most from the expanding naval airpower were the Short Brothers and Sopwith. Short produced a tractor floatplane with folding wings that was entered in the Circuit-of-Britain air race and became the basic naval standard during the war. Sopwith went with another line. They produced the first fast single-seat scout, which had a top speed of almost three times its landing speed. It was the outcome of Harry Hawker's design influence and the then-current philosophy of the Department of Military Aeronautics. The single-seater was called the Tabloid, and after the Schneider contest it also changed some European philosophies.

E. Burri holding tow rope just prior to beaching the F.B.A. *Hirsch Collection*

Weymann's modified Type VI with 18cyl rotary engine. It was the favorite and expected winner. However, none of the twin-row rotary engines ran as well as the single-row engines. The rear bank of cylinders never cooled right and those with 18cyl were very unreliable. *Hirsch Collection.* **Right, the new 1914 Deperdussin with 18cyl rotary. Crewmen are inspecting the damaged float after Prevost struck an object.** *H. Nowarra*

The organizers of the 1914 Monaco events were either naive or overoptimistic or they would never have organized so many unrealistic contests, particularly after the 1913 fiasco. Apparently they simply chose to ignore it because they organized a far more ambitious program for that year. The 1914 Le Rallye De Monaco included the following events: Rallye Aerien De Monaco April 1–15, 1914; Coupe d'Aviation Maritime Jacques Schneider Eliminatories April 19; Coupe d'Aviation Maritime

Aircraft	Race No.	Motor/Hp	Pilot
Morane-Saulnier	1	LeRhone 90	Gilbert
Albatros biplane	(2) 2 & 3	Benz 120	Hirth
Deperdussin	4	LeRhone 90	Gilbert
Aviatik biplane	5	Benz 120	Stoefler
H. Farman	6	LeRhone 90	Gilbert
Nieuport	7	Gnome 100	Bertin
Nieuport	8	LeRhone 90	Malard
Nieuport	9	Clerget 110	Legagneau
Morane-Saulnier	11	Gnome 80	Garros
Morane-Saulnier	12	Gnome 100	Lord Carbery
Morane-Saulnier	14	Gnome 100	Audenairs
Morane-Saulnier	15	Gnome 100	Bielovucic
Morane-Saulnier	16	Gnome 80	M. Pourpe
H. Farman	17	Renault 170	Renaux
Aviatik biplane	18	Salmson 120	Gaubert
H. Farman	19	Salmson 120	Gaubert
Deperdussin	20	Gnome 100	Adaro
Breguet biplane	21	Salmson 120	Moineau
Breguet biplane	22	Gnome 100	Devorne
Deperdussin	23	Gnome 100	Molla
R.E.P.	24	Salmson 80	Schemmel
Schemmel monoplane	25	Gnome 80	Verrier
Taube-Gotha	(2) 27 & 10	Mercedes 70	Schlegel

Jacques Schneider Finale April 20.

The Schneider Trophy contest was the culmination of an aerial rally that began with the Rallye Arien De Monaco, a race to Monaco that had seven optional starting points, including Milan, Vienna, Madrid, Brussels, Gotha, Paris, and London. All but Milan and Vienna terminated at Marseilles; they terminated at Genoa. Each of the routes was 673mi (1,083km). Then there was 130mi (210km) of overwater flight to Monaco which made an 803mi (1,293km) total. However, since Marseilles and Genoa were not equal distance from Monaco, any difference was to be made up on the established Schneider course.

For the overwater leg of the Rallye Arien De Monaco, the contestants could either convert their landplanes to hydro operations within a 48hr period by installing floats, or use a second seaplane for the overwater stage as long as it was the same manufacture and type as the original landplane. The starting date was to be April 1 and completion date was April 15. The first five contestants actually started on April 3, however, and the others strung out for three more days. The following lists the machines and pilots signed up for the Rallye Arien De Monaco.

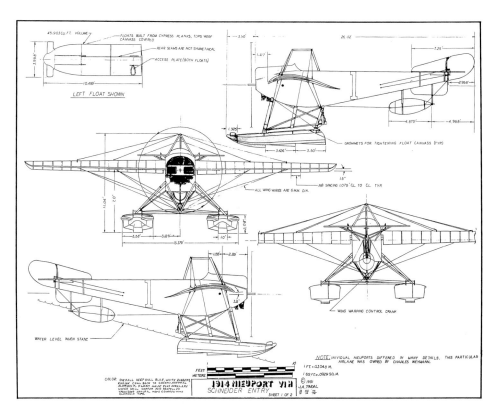

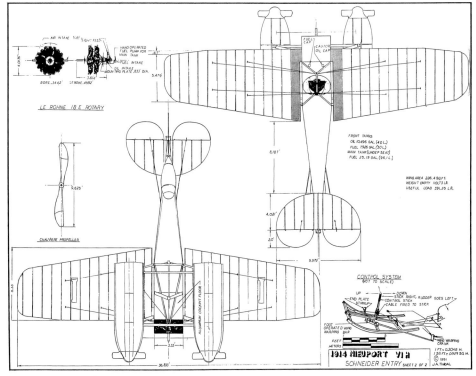

The first to arrive at Monaco was Marcel Brindejonc des Moulinais in a Morane-Saulnier. He departed Madrid and arrived on April 4 with a total flying time of 16hr, 2min, 32sec. He landed on rough water and slightly damaged his machine. Roland Garros on a second attempt made a Brussels–Monaco time of 12hr, 27min, 13sec, which gave him first place.

The Monaco meet of 1914 that included the Schneider contest was held from April 15–20. It was beginning to be realized, even at this early stage, that the Schneider contest was likely to become considerably more important than other club races. This year Great Britain, France, the United States, Switzerland, and Germany all had entries which indicated keen national competition.

Schneider Trophy Elimination Trials

To select its best three competitors, the Aero Club of France held its elimination trials April 15–19. Following is the list of machines and pilots in the elimination trials: Prevost in a Deperdussin, Garros in a Morane-Saulnier, Brindejonc des Moulinais in a Morane-Saulnier, Janoir in a Deperdussin, Espanet in a Nieuport, Lavasseur in a Nieuport, Moineau in a Breguet, and Bertin in a Nieuport.

Sopwith Tabloid, a dark horse from England, being towed to the ramp after its flight test.
H. Nowarra

4. Handling—The machine is brought to the crane (only in the harbor) and attached so that it can be raised and lowered.

5. Towing—The machine must be taken into tow by a rowing or motorboat craft, and be towed over the course first leg.

6. Navigability—Travel without leaving water by aid of the motor over a course of 3.88mi (6.25km).

Of the eight contestants, only Dr. Gabriel Espanet completed the required four laps of the course. His average speed was 99.76km/h (62mph). Roland Garros and Pierre Levasseur both completed two laps each and so joined Espanet in making up the French team. Prevost had a 200hp, 18cyl engine in his Deperdussin but could not get it off the water because of engine problems.

Stoeffler of Germany had entered an Aviatik but it unfortunately crashed during the April 19 trials. On this Sunday the following entries are those that survived the elimination trials:

Aircraft	Country	Motor/Hp	Pilot
Sopwith Tabloid	Great Britain	Gnome 100	Pixton
Morane-Saulnier	Great Britain	LeRhone 80	Lord Carbery
Nieuport	France	Gnome 100	Espanet
Nieuport	France	Gnome 100	Levasseur
Morane-Saulnier	France	LeRhone 80	Garros
F.B.A. (boat)	Switzerland	Gnome 10	Burri
Nieuport	USA	Gnome 100	Weymann
Curtiss pusher	USA	Gnome 100	Thaw
Aviatik	Germany	Benz 120	Stoeffler

Since each country could enter only three contestants in the finale, the elimination trials were France's way of entering their best.

The elimination trials consisted of the following tests.

1. Getting Under Weigh—The seaplane is brought to a standstill on the water and the motor stopped. The pilot must then be able to restart the motor without touching the propeller, using only those resources on board. He then must cover a distance of 328ft (100m) between two lanes of buoys.

2. Altitude—Take off from the water and climb to at least 1,640ft (500m) and return to the water in less than 30min.

3. Volplaning—Take off from the water and climb to 328ft (100m), and then descend without the aid of the motor.

The crated Tabloid seaplane and spare parts arrived at Monaco on April 16, and on that same day, Howard Pixton tested a landplane version in Britain. He then left for Monaco. Victor Mahl had tuned the engine before the machine was crated and had left with the earlier team and Tommy Sopwith. The Tabloid was erected on the seventeenth outside the Herview tent, which Sopwith also rented. Just two days before the elimination trials. Sopwith, Mahl, Syd Burgoine, and Fred Sigrist worked around the clock to ready the plane. New floats were installed, leaving the originals made from the sawed-off halves of the original single float as back-up in case of a flight-test mishap. The engine was still sweating salt and showing signs of rusting. Mahl worked all day on the engine cleaning it and ensuring it would run.

At about 5:00am on the nineteenth the Tabloid was taken out of the tent and at 6:30 it was launched. It set with its tail float submerged enough for the elevator to droop into the water. Pixton started the Gnome Monosoupape (single valve) engine, then taxied out of the harbor and opened up the power. In a very short run the Tabloid was airborne. Within about 8min he came back down, made a smooth landing, and taxied back into the harbor and up to the slipway. The French competition witnessing the flight began to pull out their slide rulers and compute their chances.

The test revealed one problem: the propeller pitch was too flat and, judging by the amount of water sprayed, its diameter was too great. Gnome experts claimed the rpm was too high for the 2hr-plus race. So a propeller of smaller diameter and higher pitch angle was found and installed. Also, for good measure a small 5.5gal (20.88ltr) tank was installed in the cockpit making a total of 29.5gal (111.81ltr). For the additional 47lb (21.15kg) added, heavier stay wires were spliced onto the floats and bottom wings.

Lord Carbery suffered a mishap in his Morane-Saulnier during the April 19 trials and could not compete any further. He borrowed a 160hp Deperdussin and could not get it off the ground either.

Schneider Trophy Contest

Following are the seaplanes and pilots of the April 20 race Coupe D'Aviation Maritime Jacques Schneider finale.

Registered as flying supplemental designs (alternates) were Lawrence Sperry and Lincoln Beachy for the United States, Prevost, Brindejonc, and Janoir all with Deperdussins from France. Sperry and Beachy were a no-show. William Thaw's Curtiss Triad received so many puns, he did not attempt to start the race.

The 1914 Schneider contest had become the main event at Monaco even though it was only the second time the trophy was up for grabs. It was scheduled for April 20, and the four-sided course was the same 6.2mi (10km) laid out just as it was in 1913 between Monaco and Cape Martin. The same twenty-eight laps gave the distance of 173.6mi (280km). Two

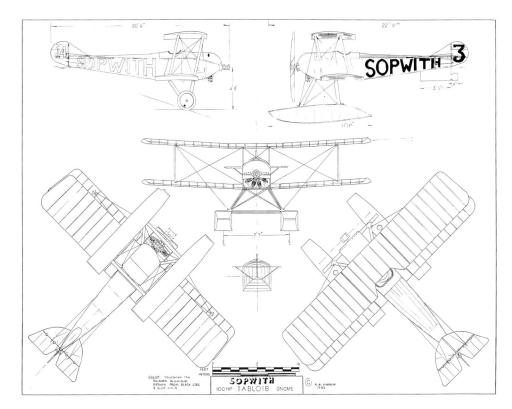

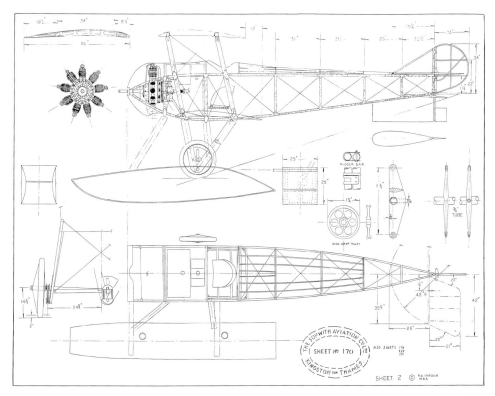

Hydroaeroplane	Country	Motor/Hp	Pilot
Sopwith Tabloid	Great Britain	Gnome 100	Pixton
Curtiss hydroplane	USA	Curtiss 75	Thaw
Nieuport	USA	Gnome 160	Weymann
Nieuport	France	Gnome 100	Espanet
Nieuport	France	Gnome 100	Levasseur
Morane-Saulnier	France	Gnome 150	Garros
F.B.A.	Switzerland	Gnome 100	Burri

touchdowns and water navigation had to be accomplished on the first lap.

It was a difficult course since the turn at Cape Martin was 165deg at about 30–45deg banking. These hydromachines were still much like the 1913 machines that suffered so many mishaps. The Monaco pylons were only 787ft (240m) apart, resulting in almost the same turning as at Cape Martin and producing some exciting flying for the spectators.

Promptly at 8:00am the starting bomb was exploded and Espanet and Levasseur taxied out for the starting line and takeoff. The touchdowns mandatory after Cape Martin were handled easily by Levasseur, but Espanet overran his second mark and lost time going back again. Ernest Burri got off in a series of hops and finally porpoised into the air and hung on. He negotiated the touchdowns by skimming along over the top of the waves losing very little speed and completed his first lap in 9min, 15sec, which put him temporarily in the lead. However, the superior speed of the Nieuports wiped this out after a few more laps.

Pixton in the Tabloid got off 15min behind the two Nieuports and the F.B.A. Weymann and Garros waited to see what was happening

Sopwith Tabloid beached after winning the second Schneider contest. Note oil smears on side of fuselage after long, hard run. *S. Hudek*

Vic Mahl working on the Tabloid propeller change. He had decided that the 1350rpm with the Lang propeller was too high, causing the engine to overheat. A coarser pitch propeller was substituted to bring rpm's down to 1300. *S. Hudek.* Below, Switzerland's F.B.A. being readied for launching prior to the contest. The machine performed better than expected. *Hirsch Collection*

and how the contest was shaping up; there was plenty of time, and they were looking for a more positive outcome. Pixton's first lap was only 4min, 27sec and after that they settled down to about 5sec over the 4min mark. This was 14.88mph (24km/h) faster than the next fastest, Espanet. After ten laps Pixton was almost 10min up on Espanet and 13min up on Levasseur, with the F.B.A. trailing all three.

After fourteen of the twenty-eight laps Espanet and Levasseur both began to notice popping noises from the rear banks of their twin-row rotary engines. This preignition was due to overheating. Espanet set down on the seventeenth lap and Levasseur followed one lap later. by this time both Weymann and Garros decided they couldn't win unless Pixton's engine quit. Neither attempted a takeoff while Pixton was still airborne, so the contest had narrowed down to the Tabloid and the slower F.B.A. Both were biplanes and had a single-row rotary engine. When Pixton crossed the

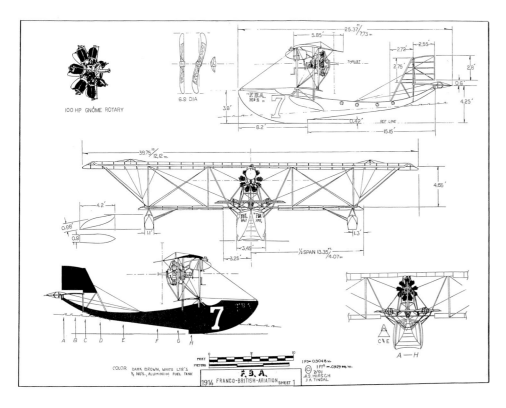

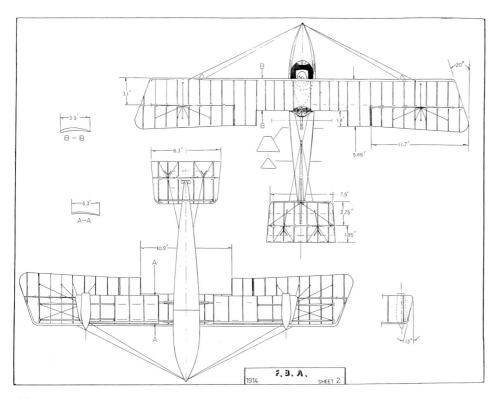

finish line he had an elapsed time of 2hr, 13sec, averaging 86.57mph (139.63km/h), which put the Tabloid 25mph (40.25km/h) faster than last year's Deperdussin. Pixton continued on the course for two more laps to set a 186mi (300km) speed record of 86.6mph (139.34km/h). Pixton made a smooth landing, then shut down and waited for a tow, which came quickly. However, he sustained some elevator damage in the process since the machine sat normally at a pretty high angle of incidence to the water.

Burri ran out of fuel on his twenty-third lap and set down in some rough water. After refueling, he restarted and finally completed the course and was listed in second place. With Garros not competing, Prevost, in his dark brown Deperdussin, decided he would give it a try so he launched his machine and started his engine. However, before he could taxi out of the harbor his engine quit completely and he couldn't get it started again. He got a tow back and gave up. Levasseur borrowed Weymann's Nieuport and tried again to at least gain third place for France, but after nine laps his engine also overheated and he gave up.

The prestige value of the British victory was enormous and came as a blow to French national pride, and to the undisputed leadership of France in aviation. They could no longer view the British entries with contempt and amusement and the biplane as inferior for racing. It was the most important event that happened to British aviation and had a profound effect on the next four years of World War I. Pixton was greeted by Jacques Schneider and invited for a drink. That evening, Pixton and Sopwith dined with Schneider in Hotel De Paris. Harry Delacome and Harold Perrin of the Royal Aero Club (RAeC) were also invited. The Cup was formally presented the next day by Prince Albert I of Monaco.

So France, although hosting the contest, didn't complete the course. With such a large supply of contenders who were considered to be the best, it was a bitter pill. They also changed their thinking about the biplane versus the monoplane, causing a traumatic effect on France's airplane development. The only consolation for the French from the 1914 Schneider was that it was won by a French Gnome engine. Curiously enough, Great Britain paid little attention to their win. There

was a lack of press coverage and few comments in the airplane magazines other than advertisements of equipment and materials.

Pixton's remarkable victory passed almost unnoticed in England. He was entertained at a dinner banquet on his return with the Sopwith and crew. It was the least the RAeC could do since he brought home what seemed to be an increasingly important trophy. But the most prominent daily newspaper, which at that time was championing aviation, gave him only a couple of inches at the bottom of a column on the same page that featured a story of a blind man being flown for 5min as a passenger.

Results of Distance versus Time

The 1914 Schneider contest brought out only two very different designs; they were about as much alike as a cat and a dog. The Sopwith Tabloid was a landplane on floats and the F.B.A. was a flying boat. However, they both had single-row Gnome rotary engine of 100hp.

Sopwith Tabloid

Sir T.O.M. Sopwith, known as Tom Sopwith and often called Tommy Sopwith, turned constructor from pilot. He acquired the closed Kingston Skating Rink on Canterbury Park Road in Kingston-upon-Thames, Surrey, in 1913 with his prize monies earned as pilot. He started the Sopwith Aviation Co. and hired Harry Hawker as pilot and manager of production, and engineer Fred Sigrist, who was already taking care of his yacht. Bill Eyre and Herbert Smith were also part of the ideas group.

The Sopwith Tabloid was at first a side-by-side two-seat, single-bay tractor biplane designed by Tom Sopwith and Fred Sigrist. It was first flown in 1913 by Harry Hawker who

Howard Pixton and gentlemen from the RAeC being congratulated by Jacques Schneider for their victory at Monaco. The cup was presented to the RAeC by Prince Albert of Monaco. Top left, the Tabloid under tow after winning the 1914 Schneider contest. Winning pilot Howard Pixton stands on the float.

Results of Distance versus Time

Place	Pilot	31mi (50km)		62mi (100km)		93mi (150km)			124mi (200km)			173.6mi (280km)			186mi (300km)		
		M	S	M	S	H	M	S	H	M	S	H	M	S	H	M	S
1st	Pixton	20	37	unknown		1	2	31	1	24	4	2	13		2	9	10
2nd	Burri	29	17	57	54	1	27	36	1	57	4	3	24	12			
3rd	Espanet	28	13	51	53	1	16	47									
4th	Levasseur	30	5	54	46	1	22	56									

Note: M = minutes, S = seconds, H = hours.

also influenced the design, and was later made into a single-seat scout to be used for demonstrations and competitions for Royal Flying Corps (RFC) and contracts.

On November 13, 1913, Hawker demonstrated it at Hendon before a crowd of 50,000 in which he achieved 90mph (144.9km) in the landplane configuration. The RFC ordered twelve of them and from one of these, Sopwith built the Schneider machine. What is surprising is that as late as three days before it was due to be shipped to Monte Carlo, it had not yet been flown. Then, on its first flight test, it nosed over on its large, almost square single float and became stuck in the muddy river bottom. It was pulled out the next morning for repair and rework. The single float was cut into two floats and this proved to be the correct configuration since the next flight test was successful.

The Schneider machine had a 100hp Gnome Monosoupape installed instead of the standard 80hp Gnome—the first 100hp Mono engine to come to England. It was supported in the Tabloid by two bearer plates both at the rear end of the crankshaft, which was the standard practice of letting the rotary engine overhang its bearers. But the Tabloid had a third support added between the propeller and engine to carry the long propeller shaft and extend the nose for streamlining. Ball bearings were interposed between the propeller and the support. The Mono engine turned at 1300rpm but a Lang propeller was selected to achieve 1350rpm. This was changed at Monaco, however, to use the 1300rpm that Gnome recommended.

The successful development of the Schneider version of the Tabloid led to the Royal Naval Air Service (RNAS) purchasing some as single-seat seaplane scouts. The main changes were an extra pair of struts to the pontoons and a rudder attached behind the rear float, ailerons (upper and lower) instead of wing warping, and some extra area added to the vertical stabilizer. This development was eventually known as the Baby. During the transition period it was often called the Schneider Baby. Regardless of the differences, they were basically the same dimensions as the Tabloid. Even Fairey and Parnell built the Hamble Baby, but power now was 110hp and 130hp in the Clerget engines.

F.B.A. Boat

The Franco-British Aviation Co. was located at Venon, Eure, in France and was founded in 1913. They built the Donnet-Leveque flying boats which had complete hulls with empennage and integral flight controls. The Schneider machine was developed from the 1912 two-seat patrol bomber, which was serialed No. 18.

The hull was of all-wood construction using spruce for stringers mounted on spruce and ash formers and then covered with a laminated sheeting. The bottom of the hull was concave back to the step, which was about one-third back. The aft section had a flat bottom except where it blended into the upswept tail that transformed into an inverted vee (triangle). The upper wing had large ailerons, fourteen ribs to each side, and a span of 39.4ft (12m). The lower wing had only six ribs and a span of 24.6ft (7.5m).

The gas tank was shaped like the Goodyear blimp and was above the centerline of the engine and fastened to the upper-wing center section. The two outboard floats were similar in shape to the later Italian wing floats and located close to the tip of the lower wing.

The open cockpit was immediately in front of the lower wing which was on struts just above the hull. The rudder and elevator cables entered the top of the hull about halfway forward to the lower wing. The 100hp 7cyl Gnome engine had the best power-to-weight ratio of all the Monaco engines.

The No. 26 on the hull could have meant it was the twenty-sixth serialed flying boat built, or the twenty-sixth of its type. It must have had something to do with production since its assigned race number was 24. Accounts of this F.B.A. do not show how it arrived at Monaco, but since Switzerland is close enough to Monaco one can assume it was flown there.

Rotary Engines

The pre-World War I air-cooled radial engine suffered cooling problems that made them undesirable. Laurent Sequin of Gnome provided a solution of rotating the engine with the propeller around the fixed crankshaft, thus creating the rotary engine. There were several makes such as the Gnome Clerget, LeRhone, Monosoupape with a sleeve valve, Bentley, Oberursel, and Siemens-Halske all with 5, 7, 9, 14, and 18cyl producing 50–200hp. The rotary engine became the primary aircraft powerplant. During 1909–1918, the rotary engine was unmatched in the medium-horsepower class for weight-to-power ratio.

The rotary engine acted as its own flywheel, damping the engine's internal vibration. The flywheel inertia of the rotary engine mass gave a much smoother running engine than any other available type.

This rotating mass had a gyro-torque effect on the airplane, which made maneuverability tricky. If the pilot turned in the direction of rotation, the gyro effect resisted the turn. If the pilot turned opposite, the gyro effect would snap the aircraft into the turn. These effects could be overcome by pilot technique.

Since the fuel-air mixture filled the crankcase along with the engine lubricating oil, they mixed, which reduced the oil's lubrication qualities and diluted the combustion mixture. What wouldn't burn would be passed out the exhaust. Since the only oil that would stand the heat and pressure inside the crankcase was castor oil, it became the standard lubricant.

There was no exhaust manifold on the rotary engine; the hot gases were simply expelled out the revolving cylinders, which resulted in a sort of pinwheel fireworks, which were a danger to flammable, fabric-covered aircraft until cowlings were developed.

The magneto for the rotary engine ignition system was attached to the non-rotating plate for the fixed crankshaft plate and was driven by a pinion on the revolving crank chamber. Mounted on the end plate in back of the driving pinion was a high-tension distributor plate and brass segments. Each segment was connected to a spark plug by brass wires.

The Monosoupape (single valve), although considered at first to be undependable, became a prime choice during World War I. Its operation was by intake ports surrounding each cylinder which would open when the piston reached the bottom of its stroke. The mixture entered the cylinder through these ports and was compressed by the upward stroke of the piston. The exhaust valve operated at the end of the combustion stroke by weights. The piston then pushed exhaust gases out the valve as it rose. At the bottom, the pressure within the cylinder would have dropped to that of the crankcase when the cylinder ports were open. On the intake stroke the pressure drops below the crankcase pressure and fuel mixture and castor oil is pulled in.

The LeRhone had a more conventional induction system. The fuel mixture went into an annuler chamber at the rear of the crankcase and then through polished copper tube to standard intake ports and cam-operated valves in the cylinder heads. Valve operation was by a single rocker arm, which pivoted near the center. Pulled down, it opened the intake valve. Pushed up, it opened the exhaust. This meant the pushrod had to be push-pull. The Clerget valves were actuated by two pushrods per cylinder.

The rotary engines were started in a nearly flooded condition and frequently caught fire from spilled excess fuel. The pilot would then shut off the fuel and let the engine run out the internal excess. Also, they would sometimes move the plane back away from the spilled fuel burning on the ground.

The basic drawback of the rotary engine was the power wasted in turning the mass of the engine. It was estimated that the 9cyl version lost almost 30 percent of its output just to rotate for cooling. The high fuel and oil consumption meant the rotary engine was unsuited for long-range aircraft. Also, materials then available and construction methods of this unusual engine limited it to about 180hp. Performance fell off rapidly as altitude increased, especially for those with automatic-sleeve valves. This was due to the mixture becoming too rich.

Oil consumption varied on the rotary from 20–45 percent of the fuel consumption. Practically all of the lubricant reached the cylinders by centrifugal force and would be either consumed or ejected out the exhaust valves. This made for partly burned oil coming out the exhaust, polluting the air breathed by the pilot. Castor oil is known to be a powerful laxative and often resulted in emergency landings despite a small flask of blackberry brandy carried by many as an antidote.

Although the rotary engine dominated the powerplant scene from prior to World War I through at least half of it, it was only an interim engine. Until better cooling fins were developed during the war, the rotary dominated in powerplant selection.

Chapter 4

1919 Bournemouth

The First Post-War Schneider Trophy Contest

About April the FAI notified Britain's RAeC that the Schneider Contest should be held in 1919. The RAeC then let it be known the date for applications was July 31. Then in the early part of August the RAeC announced that the contest would be held at Bournemouth on September 10. The choice was ideal, as far as spectator viewing was concerned, but it seemed that the organizing committee had almost no concern for the competitors in choosing the central pier as the focal point for the contest. It is strange that the facilities of Poole harbor were not used when you look at its protected waters.

Of course, the four months that were available for competitors to prepare new or modified machines and test them were too short and eventually Belgium, Spain, and the United States withdrew leaving only France and Italy as a threat to the British team. This was Italy's first entry into the contest series. Cowes at the Isle of Wight was selected to accommodate the competing aircraft due to the generous offer by S. E. Saunders Ltd. and their facilities that could be provided. It was reasoned that the distance to Bournemouth was unlikely to cause inconvenience. Actually, the competitors and their aircraft were far better prepared for the contest than were the organizers. The racers flew in to Bournemouth from Cowes on race day.

On Wednesday, one week prior to the contest, *Flight* weekly aviation magazine could not find out from the RAeC what race numbers would be assigned to which aircraft and

what would be the takeoff assignments, or even how the race start would be conducted. Then one week after the contest the magazine made a statement: "It cannot be said that the Schneider Race at Bournemouth on September 10, was a success. In fact, in modern slang, it would be termed a 'wash-out.'"

The general public that gathered on the beaches to promenade, swim, go boating, or to watch the contest were in the tens of thousands. Where this might have been good for the spectators, it was a poor arrangement for the contestants whose aircraft had to be beached. Due to the number of officials involved, proper management in organizing the contest was anything but effective. The omission of such fundamental facilities as launch slips on the beach, roped-off areas of the beach so mechanics could make final preparations to aircraft, or even safety boats to keep the starting areas clear, made the event seem even more disorganized.

Then while the 170 organizers and ranking members ate fancy meals aboard the RAeC yacht *Ombra*, there was no catering facility set up on the beach or pier and the pilots and ground crew went hungry except for the good graces of S. E. Saunders.

British Racers
Sopwith Schneider

Although Britain was further along with capable types like the Nieuport Nighthawk and Nieuhawk and the Avro Spider, they were only capable of producing four types for elimi-

The Avro 539A being towed out to startup and takeoff. *J. Albanese*

The little Avro 539 being readied for pontoon installation after its first mishap. It had hit some floating debris, damaging a float. The Avro 539 was designed to be the smallest possible airframe that could safely hold its 240hp Siddley Puma engine. Bottom right, the Sopwith Hawker Schneider racer (Rainbow on floats) at Cowes being readied for the Bournemouth contest. It was powered by a 450hp Cosmos Jupiter engine. Top far right, Harry Hawker in the Sopwith Schneider taxiing out for takeoff during the elimination trials. In the contest, Hawker started out of position, taking off before signaled to do so by the starter, and was disqualified *J. Albanese*

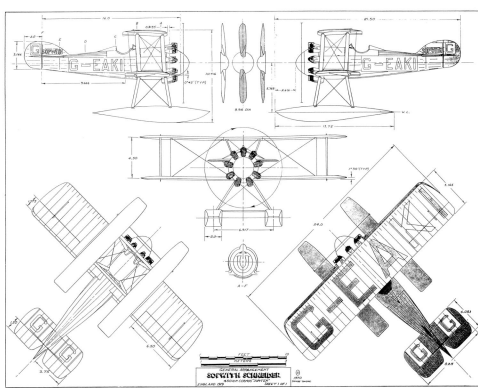

nation trials. Included was the Sopwith Schneider stemming from the Sopwith R.M.I. Snapper. It was actually Harry Hawker's Rainbow racer on floats and was much like the Tabloid in general appearance. It had the 450hp Cosmos Jupiter engine, which was designed by Roy Fedden, and its pilot was Harry Hawker. It was designed by W. George Carter. The craft had ailerons on its upper and lower wing interconnected by a streamlined wire. There was a 2.5in (6.35cm) negative stagger of the upper wing behind the lower. The three fuel tanks were mounted in front of the cockpit and behind the engine bulkhead. It had a large, somewhat flat spinner and wooden two-blade propeller. Aluminum panels enclosed the forward round fuselage back to the cockpit. Registered G-EAKI, it was reengined with an ABC Dragonfly air-cooled radial and flown in the 1920 Aerial Derby. Plans to convert it back to floatplane configuration for the 1922 Schneider contest never materialized and on October 5, 1923, it was heavily damaged in a forced landing and written off.

Fairey N.10

The Fairey seaplane known as N.10 made its first public appearance at the Schneider contest with new civil registration G-EALO. It

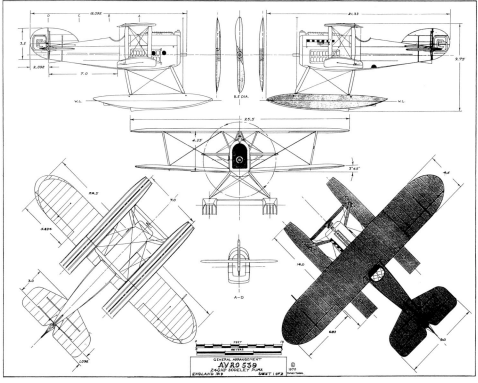

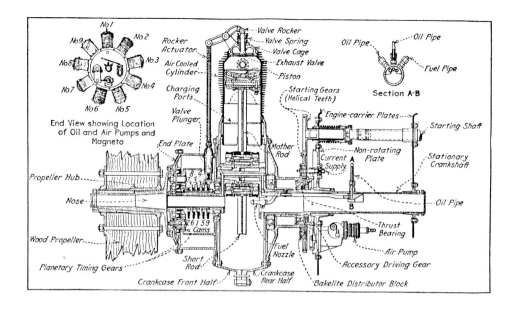

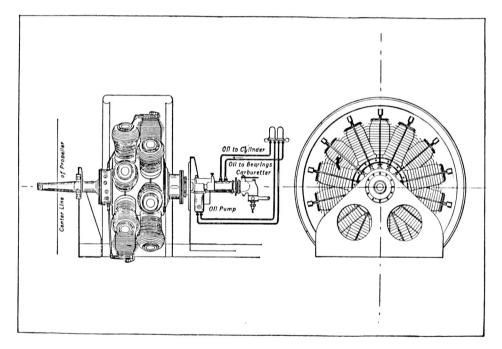

The arrangement of a double-row rotary engine. Top, the inner workings of a single-row rotary engine.

was a modified Type III seaplane, fitted with standard floats. Before the contest it was tested with a newly installed 450hp Napier Lion engine. Prior to the contest it still retained its two bay wings of 36ft (11m) span. The new engine necessitated replacing the standard radiator with two projecting sections on each side of the fuselage.

For the Schneider contest, a set of single-bay wings of 28ft (8.5m) span was installed. Both upper and lower wings had full-span ailerons, but the lower-wing ailerons had a geared variable-chamber capability, allowing them to function simultaneously as flap and aileron. The N.10 was of wood construction, spruce and ash, and covered in fabric. It also had been made into a single-seater with fuel tanks replacing the forward cockpit area. The pilot was Lt. Comdr. Vincent Nicholl. This particular aircraft was scrapped in 1922, but it had won £2,000 in a 1920 competition.

Avro 539

The Avro 539, registered G-EKLG, was rushed through the Hamble works for the 1919 Schneider contest. The 539 was the smallest biplane that could be built around the 240hp Siddeley Puma engine. It first flew on August 29. On September 3, it took off for Cowes to enter into the elimination trials but hit some floating debris, damaging a float. Therefore a separate trial was arranged for September 8.

While the floats were being repaired the rudder received a balancing horn and the vertical stabilizer was extended forward. The aircraft was then known as the 539A. The floats were 14ft (4.27m) long and had a spread of 7ft (2.14m) on center line with three longitudinal runners on the bottom for stability on water. Since it was tested after the others it was assumed that this had something to do with it being placed as back-up and not as one of Britain's three main contestants. The pilot was Capt. H. A. Hamersley.

The 539A was converted back to a landplane at Hendon and entered in the Aerial Derby race in 1920. In 1921 it had a Napier Lion engine installed and was redesignated 539B, G-EAXM, but was damaged beyond repair at Hamble on August 15, 1921.

Supermarine Sea Lion I

The story of Supermarine's notable participation in and contribution to the history of the Schneider Trophy contests starts here with the three racing Sea Lions. The Sea Lion I, registered G-EALP, was a development of the N.1 Baby designed by J. Hargreaves and Reginald J. Mitchell. Its name stems from the Napier Lion engine that replaced the Sunbeam and Hispano-Suiza engines. Wingspan decreased to 30.5ft (9.29m) upper wing and 26ft, 4in (8.02m) lower wing, from 35ft (10.66m) upper wing and 28.25ft (8.61m) lower wing. Also, all control surfaces were aerodynamically counterbalanced.

The engine was on an independent pylon mounting and was partly cowled with an oval automobile-type radiator up front. It had the same T-tail as the Baby, but with increased area. The hull was of Linton-Hope construction.

Sea Lion I was registered G-EALP. It was claimed to be the fastest flying boat in the world at 147mph (236.67km/h). Although the development of this aircraft was to produce a pure racing machine, it was fully equipped with such things as sea anchor, mooring equipment, towing equipment, and a bilge pump. Its first test flight was delayed by a propeller manufacturers strike, but was accomplished late in the day on September 5, 1919, before the trials. A propeller change giving it an extra 5mph (8.05km/h) helped make the final decision to include this machine instead of the Avro 539.

After the Schneider contest the aircraft was dismantled and the hull was loaned to the Science Museum for a 1921 exhibition.

Savoia S.13

The lone entry from Italy in the elimination trials was a Savoia S.13 S from Sesto Calende and the Societa Idrovolanti Alta Italia (SIAI) and was the little brother of the S.12. The Schneider version was a single-seater and smaller in dimensions than the SIAI S.13bis (*bis* indicates an improved or modified variant) which was a two-seater. The S.13 racer was powered by an Isotta-Fraschini V–6 of 265hp; the original S.13bis had the 250hp version.

The hull was of wooden formers and stringers covered with marine plywood. All flight surfaces were fabric covered. Wings were two-spar conventional wood construction with ailerons only on the upper wing.

The engine was mounted above the hull behind the cockpit by two N-struts, and two more N-struts to the top wing. The engine was cowled only in the front and lower surfaces, leaving the upper rear open. Radiators and oil coolant were forward of the engine in an in-

verted U enclosure. The propeller for the Schneider machine was a four-blader where the standard S.13bis used a two-blader. All flight control surfaces were cable operated.

The S.13s was shipped across Italy and France by railroad, then shipped to Cowes where it was assembled and tested by pilot Sgt. Guido Jannello.

French Racers

There were no elimination trials in France since only three entries were sent to England, two Nieuports and one Spad. The Spad-Herbemont was shipped to Cowes and assembled and tested there. The two Nieuports were damaged during flight testing on the Seine and replaced by two modified machines. The delay prompted flying to Cowes on September 7 and 8, barely making it in time for the contest.

Spad S.20

Louis Bechereau, an engineer and graduate of Ecole des Arts et Metiers at Angers with an interest in speed, met a merchant named Armand Deperdussin through a friend Clement Ader and found unlimited success in the Societe De Construction d' Appareils Aeriens, later Societe pour les Appareils Deperdussin (Spad), founded by Ader's nephew. He and Dutch designer Fritz Koolhoven laid out shapes to be used in the Deperdussin racers. Spad shop foreman Papa built the aircraft. Bechereau de-

Avro 539A in tow with Capt. H. A. Hamersley on the floats. It was powered by a Siddeley Puma engine of 240hp.
H. Nowarra

Pilot Guido Jannello sitting up high out of the cockpit of the Savoia S.13, while being towed to beach at Bournemouth. *S. Hudek*

It was built in one piece. The lower wing was straight. They were connected by plywood I interplane struts. The engine was a Hispano-Suiza Model 42 of 260hp and turned a two-blade propeller. The stabilizers were wire braced. Floats were carried on three struts, also of plywood. Race No. 6 was painted on the white rudder.

Nieuport Type 29

Two Type 29 Nieuports were modified and prepared for the Schneider contest. The first, race No. 4, was prepared by Chassraux who was Gustave Delage's assistant. It used the long-span two-bay wing with the standard overlapping ailerons of the Standard Type 29. It also had the dual-stepped short broad floats and a tail float and was designated 29C-1. It was heavily damaged on landing after test flight by pilot Henri Malard when he plowed into a bridge pillar at Artentevil. The second 29C-1, race No. 2, was a clipped single-bay version with long, single-step floats. This also was destroyed during testing by pilot Jean Casale. Both Nieuports were quickly replaced and readied for flight to Cowes. And both had the Hispano-Suiza Model 42 of 275hp.

On Sunday, September 7, just three days before the race, Casale left Paris for Cowes via Brighton. Arriving at Cowes, the rough sea made him set down on the Medina River outlet shelter. As he touched down, the 29C-1 hit a buoy and Casale found himself upended with a sharp hiss with the hot engine and submerged in water. Eventually he was rescued and the aircraft towed ashore. Henri Malard left Paris in the other Nieuport on September 8, but was forced down in mid-channel. He was rescued 24hr later by the British Admiralty search prompted by the RAeC. The 29C-1 was a total loss.

Casale's Nieuport was repaired and a new engine installed, but one of his floats again was damaged and developed a leak. He was the last competitor to arrive at Bournemouth.

signed the World War I Spad fighters, but Andre Herbemont and Louis Bleriot were also part of the company. Herbemont had designed the wings for the famous Deperdussin F.1. When Bechereau left Spad, Herbemont became director and the S.20 inherited the name Spad-Herbemont, although Bechereau was also involved in its design.

The Schneider Spad S.20bis with smaller wings made its first flight with pontoons on August 28 with Joseph Sadi Lecointe as pilot. Early in 1919 Robert Duhamel began to study the pontoon design for the S.20bis. He believed the short main floats and tail float were better at water handling than two long one-step floats, but they created too much drag when airborne. Often the two-float systems seemed to porpoise badly, and post-step and chine shapes hindered takeoff. He came up with two torpedo-like float systems that had no step but had two sets of hydroskis underneath that were to raise the pontoons upward. These were built, but not completed in time, so the standard Spad floats were used. The standard version was a somewhat flat, one-step wooden float about 17.06ft (5.2m) in length. The upper wing had the center area forward of the cockpit, but was sweptback in outer areas.

The Contest

The long sandy beaches at Bournemouth were split in two by the long pier. The RAeC yacht *Ombra* was anchored just a short distance from the end of the pier. About a mile out were two large Royal Navy warships. The morning was quiet with still waters on the bay and patchy fog banks so that specific land-marks outlining the course limits and bay were not visible. The contest organizers aboard the *Ombra* counted on the mist clearing and starting time was set for 2:30pm. After 12:00 noon, the competitors started arriving one by one from Cowes and either docked at a provided slip or beached their hydrocraft. The crowds on the beaches eagerly watched the spectacle and in some cases were in harm's way. The pier was emptied at 1:00pm and then reopened to the public for a special fee. A band was playing and people were dancing.

The starting and completion points were off the end of Bournemouth pier, between it and the *Ombra*. It was a three-leg course with turning points at Swanage Bay just beyond Poole harbor, Sandbanks, and Studland Bay. Then northeast 9mi (14.49km) to Hengistbury Head near Christchurch Bay, then back along the beaches to Bournemouth where the two landing and taxi runs would be made. Each of the contestants would be signaled for their start. The line-up was to be as follows:

Aircraft	Race No.	Pilot
Fairey III	1	Nicholl
Nieuport	2	Casale
Sopwith	3	Hawker
Supermarine	5	Hobbs
Spad	6	Lecointe
SIAI	7	Jannello

The start at Bournemouth was held up until Casale's Nieuport had arrived. The Fairey III had been signaled back to the beach by an official motor launch when Nicholl was taxiing out to start. There was excited interest from those on the pier when Casale tried to take off in his listing Nieuport. When he discovered that one of his floats was taking in water, he gave up and beached the Nieuport. Sadi Lecointe's Spad also developed a leaky float and was beached.

The next delay was due to weather conditions: the mist had thickened and the warships had disappeared on the horizon. This prompted the contest committee to postpone the start until 6:00pm. Then it was moved up to 4:30pm. It proved to be an aggravating afternoon for the flyers, waiting for further word from the committee. The French team was not informed of the latest time change and were

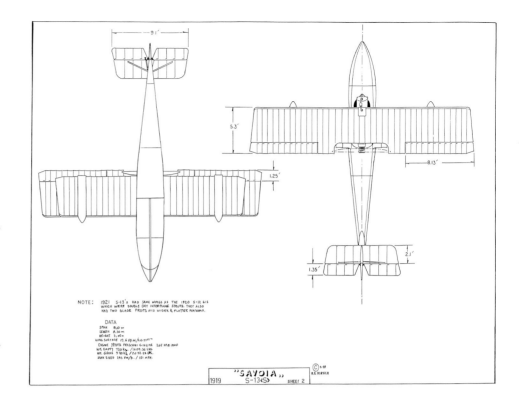

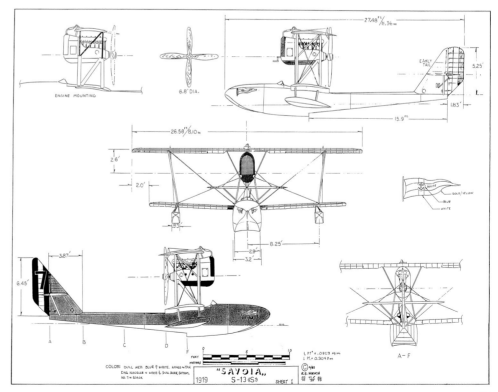

The Supermarine Sea Lion I being towed to position for the start of the contest. The Sea Lion I was a development from the N–1 Baby designed by F. J. Hargraves and R. J. Mitchell. Its name is derived from its Napier Lion engine. *S. Hudek*

busy working on their floats, thinking they had till 6:00pm. No attempt to check out the course had been made, although the little Avro 539 had been circling overhead.

At about 4:30pm the motor launch came around warning contestants the start would be in 15min. This brought a howl of disgust from the French team. Finally the somewhat bungled start was under way, when Nicholl in the Fairey III started up at about 4:50pm, taxied out to position, and set up a clean takeoff, heading south until he disappeared in the mist. Having narrowly escaped a collision with what he thought to be the marker boat, he returned to Bournemouth, landed in a clear stretch, and beached his machine.

To add to the confusion, the next to take off was Basil Hobbs in the Supermarine, since he had started up and was in position. Although he was badly balked by rowboats that strayed onto the course, he finally made a clean take-off.

Since Casale's Nieuport was still on the beach, Hawker started up his Cosmos Jupiter engine and taxied out to the starting position. Since he arrived out of position, the starter was confused as to what to do with his start flag. Hawker did not circle, waiting for the flag

but pushed the throttle to full-open and roared off in a splashing takeoff, disappearing into the mist toward Swanage Bay.

Shortly after, Hawker circled over the pier area and disappeared again, and then suddenly the Sopwith reappeared and landed. Hawker then taxied to the beach. By this time Jannello, in the Savoia, was already airborne after making a correct and smooth takeoff. Now only the Savoia and Supermarine were on the course, with two of the four starting contestants disqualified. There was a heated discussion aboard the *Ombra* with Nicholl and others who wanted to call off the race, but the decision was to let the contest continue.

Hobbs found Swanage Bay in dense fog and getting a glimpse of Nicholl in the Fairey III, flashed past in the opposite direction and set down on the water to get his bearings. After several minutes of taxiing he took off again to climb up above the mist and continue to Christchurch. Just as he was lifting off he felt a sharp jolt and knew he had hit something. He continued to Christchurch, rounded the marker boat, and ran along the beach to Bournemouth and started his required landings. The hull had a large opening ripped in it and sucked in water. The flying boat nosed in and the machine upended, stopping with its tail up. Hobbs was thrown out and was soon rescued, but it was awhile before the machine was salvaged.

Now there was only Jannello left, who would fly over the yacht about every 10min. The plucky Italian was lapping steadily and making it look easy. The course was 20nm (23.02mi, or 37.06km) and so there were only ten laps. All those concerned, except the Italian team, were waiting and hoping he would give up and come back down short of completion. However, he kept flying over the *Ombra* until he completed eleven laps, and then came in for a smooth landing.

Jannello was asked by his team captain Lorenzo Santoni to go back up for one more lap to guarantee the distance. Although Jannello felt he did not have enough fuel left for another lap, he took off anyway and ran out of fuel on the northeast stretch. It was some time before they found him in the fading daylight and heavy mist. The Savoia was towed back to Bournemouth where Jannello was told he had been disqualified for rounding the wrong marker boat. (There was an extra marker boat in reserve anchored alongside the course at Studland Bay. He had been rounding this boat instead of the one at Swanage Bay.) Needless to say, there was an uproar from the Italian team, but the committee had already declared the contest void.

As a result of strong protests from the Aero Club of Italy, on September 22 the RAeC held a meeting and decided to award the trophy to the Italian club and the last of the 25,000 francs to Jannello. However, there must have been some unofficial protesting because when the FAI met in Brussels on October 24, it officially rejected the gesture and ruled the contest void. So as a concession to Italy, the Italian club was asked to organize the 1920 Schneider contest.

At this point in time America had not constructed a Schneider contestant. This would continue for three more years.

Spad-Herbemont S.20 starting the flotation test. It already is listing to starboard. Note sawed-off top wing. *J. Albanese.* Left, Jean Casale transferring from pontoon to boat after tying up the Nieuport 29 for its float test. *S. Hudek*

Chapter 5

1920 Venice

Revival of the Competition Scene

To understand the 1920 and later Schneider contests, we must look at what was going on outside the contests during the same years, since development for any one contest greatly influenced all other competitive events.

France was still concerned with the problem of air drag and was working to produce high-speed aircraft capable of new world records, along with the ability of pilots to land on small aerodromes. New monoplanes with engines up to 600hp were being developed hoping for speeds of 218mph (350km/h) and having landing speeds below 125mph (200km/h). Hard at work were Spad, Hanriot, Nieuport, and Bernard, all hoping their efforts would compel companies from other countries to remain satisfied with previous records.

The United States was also hard at work at the same game with such companies as Curtiss, Dayton-Wright, Navy-Wright, Loening, Thomas-Morse, Verville, and Bee-Line. All these, of course, were landplanes since the United States and France have large land masses. Britain and Italy were mostly interested in seaplane development and only somewhat interested in racing and competition. The excitement of the prewar Monaco contests still lingered in France sufficiently to warrant another try. France's winning of the Gordon Bennett Aviation Cup for the third time and finishing in other contests led to further interest keeping sport flying and aircraft development alive. The United States organized the Pulitzer Trophy race and England hosted the Kings Cup race, plus several others, one of which was for seaplanes.

The International Club of Monaco sponsored a series of seaplane contests from April 13–May 2, 1920 under the rules of Aero Club of France and FAI regulations. The preliminaries were April 13–15, and the contest was April 16–May 2, with prizes as high as 60,000 francs for the Monaco–Tunis contest.

The distance contest was to Corsica, then to Tunis, and finally to return to Monaco via Corsica. The long haul of such a round trip to Tunis was overambitious, requiring intensive competition in technical advancement. To qualify, the contestant had to climb to 6,500ft (2,000m) within 45min, and then to reach 9,800ft (3,000m). There was also an absolute altitude contest in which Jean Casale set a new world record of 21,330ft (6,500m), winning the Prix Garros.

There were also two types of speed contests: one was from Monaco to Cannes, then to Mentone, and finally returning to Monaco; the second was over a 0.61mi (1km) marked course. Items such as the Lamblin lobster-pot radiator—as used on the Nieuport 29—were used to reduce drag. These were accessible, and they weighed much less and could be mounted anywhere.

The Monaco meet was a show between France and Italy. It allowed the public to see new configurations in seaplane development. From France there were three Spads—two Spad 26bis machines, one flown by Bernard De Romanet, and one standard World War I

The Savoia S.17, Nieuport-Tellier, and Savoia standard S.13, with Monaco in background. *A. Coccon*

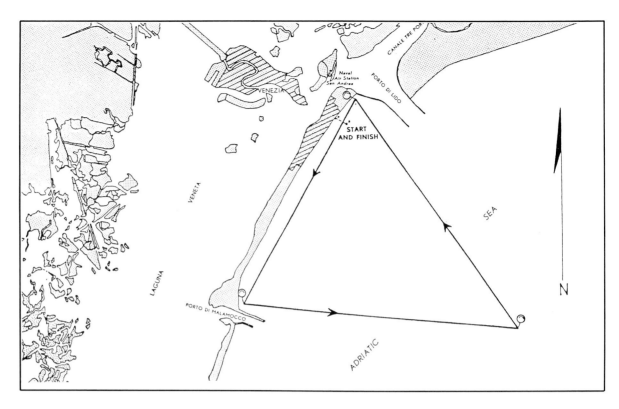

A World War I Spad on floats arriving at Monaco piloted by Ensign Tece. *H. Nowarra*. Right, the 1920 Schneider contest course at Venice, Italy, 1920. Left photo, next page, the Nieuport 29G with the three-float system used on the 1919 Schneider racer. *H. Nowarra*. Top far right, the Savoia S.17 and Sadi Lecointe's Nieuport-Tellier-Sunbeam beached at Monaco during the 1920 contests. The S.17 was the smallest of all the Schneider boat-hull racers. *A. Coccon.* Bottom far right, Jean Casale's Spad-Herbemont S.26b is being lowered into Monaco harbor for the competition. The sweepback of the outer wing panels and the forward position of the center section is noticeable. *A. Coccon*

Spad on floats. There were also two Nieuport 29s, one flown by Sadi Lecointe, who also had a Nieuport-Tellier with a Sunbeam engine for the long flight to Tunis and the return.

There was another Tellier with two Hisso engines in tandem; there were also three French Navy F.B.A. seaplanes with Renault engines. The most modern looking of the French entries was a Caudron with three rotary engines. It was similar to the cabin passenger machine at the Paris air show, but smaller and without a cabin. It had two rectangular section pontoons mounted directly below the outboard engines.

Italy was represented by the Savoia S.12, S.12bis, S.13, and the S.17 racer. There was a race between Jannello and De Romanet over a course of 80.5mi (129km) to Cannes and Mentone. Jannello took 54.05sec longer then Romanet by flying very wide turns, and he was facing the wrong direction at the starting signal. The S.17 was faster on the straightaway. On the day of the final speed contest, Jannello skidded in the S.17 on his takeoff. He skidded sideways and flipped, damaging the racer beyond repair. It was shipped back to Italy.

The speed race entries on the last day were Arturo Zanetti in the Nieuport-Macchi, De Romanet in his Spad-Herbemont, and Morselli in a Nieuport-Macchi. Zanetti was the winner but turned over in the harbor on landing. Bellot arrived at 4:15pm in the F.B.A. No. 41. He was the only pilot to complete the entire round trip to Tunis. Since he represented the Naval Air Service, he received no prize money. Sadi Lecointe placed second, having returned as far as Bizerta. For his efforts, he received 50,000 francs.

The Monaco events were a prelude to the Venice, Italy, Schneider contest. New seaplanes were being tried by both nations. The next big event would be the Schneider Trophy, due in five months. The Aero Club of France and the International Club of Monaco both were anxious to compete at Venice, but the results of the events at Monaco put ice on the various projects.

Venice, 1920

The FAI's decision to allow Italy to organize the 1920 Schneider Trophy contest was accepted, but their refusal to give Italy the Tro-

phy was unpopular and had a bad effect on the remaining series of contests. To foster some interest in the event, the RAeC offered a total of £500, broken down into £250, £150, and £100 for British first, second, and third place, regardless of where in the contest they placed. This failed to attract any entrants.

Early in 1920 the Aero Club of Italy issued its first program notice. They were very precise and intended to run this event properly so that competitors would be certain of what was expected of them. The course was to remain 200nm (230.2mi, or 370.62km). Taking from the Monaco meet, for which several of Italy's machines were present, they established a 660lb (300kg) nonconsumable payload requirement.

The navigability tests were detailed and specific. Each machine would have to navigate on water a course of several nautical miles with full load. The competitors were required to satisfactorily complete the test during the week preceding the contest. The contest requirements were:

Each contestant had to 1) taxi over the starting line; 2) take off and again land at a position marked by a buoy; 3) cover a distance of 984ft (300m) on water to a second marker; and 4) take off and complete the course, then land and taxi across the finish line. The course was marked by balloons attached to a buoy next to the observation marker boat. All machines had to be the same configuration as when they passed pre-race trials.

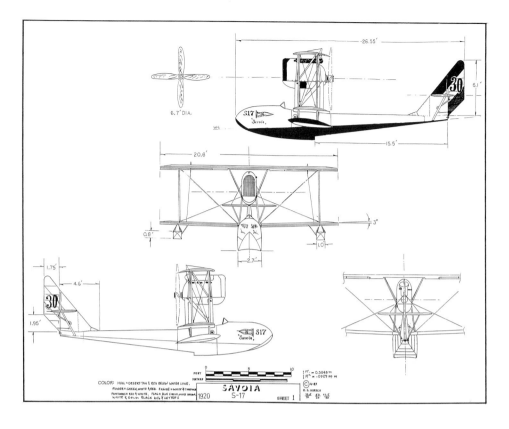

COLOR: HULL ← DESERT TAN & RED BELOW WATER LINE.
RUDDER← GREEN, WHITE & RED. ENGINE ← WHITE & CHROME
PONTOONS← RED & WHITE. FLAG ← BLUE CHECK, NOSE ARROW
WHITE & GOLD. BLACK NO. & LETTER S

SAVOIA
S-17
1920   SHEET 1

1 FT. = 0.3048 m
1 FT. = .0929 sq m

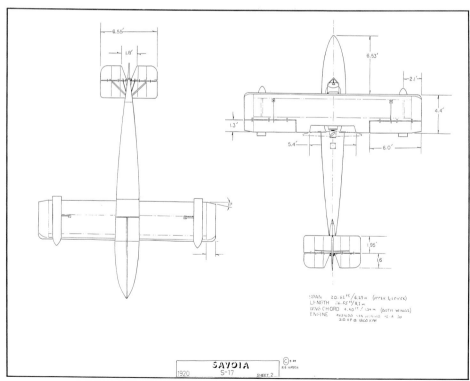

SPAN   20.62 FT / 6.29 m (UPPER & LOWER)
LENGTH 26.55 FT / 8.1 m
WNG CHORD 4.40 FT / 1.34 m (BOTH WINGS)
ENGINE   ANSALDO SAN GIORGIO 4E-14 SIX
         310 HP @ 1860 RPM

SAVOIA
S-17
1920   SHEET 2

By publishing precise instructions the Aero Club of Italy hoped to avoid the confusion that dominated the Bournemouth event. Since the payload requirement seemed to favor the Italian machines, the Italians were confident of a better showing. Although the United States was diligently preparing for the Gordon Bennett race, it showed no interest in the Schneider contest. There was a rumor of an entry from Switzerland, but it failed to materialize. France did forward two entries, a Nieuport 29C and a Spad-Herbemont with pilot Jean Casale. There also was a Borel that was said to have been readied for the contest.

The fourth Schneider Trophy contest was scheduled to be flown on September 20, but stormy weather and heavy seas prevented any attempt to complete the course until the following day. The Savoia S.12bis had completed its trials by September 19, so far the only contestant to qualify. Comdt. Luigi Bologna tried to cover the required 200nm on September 20. He covered five laps (76.4mi or 123km) in 1hr, 15min, 24sec but retired on Lap 6 because a squall limited his visibility. He reflew the entire course on September 21, thus winning the trophy since no other contestant was able to complete the trials before contest start date. Bologna took 2hr, 10min, 35sec, giving an average of 97mph (172.5km/h).

Of the other contestants, the Borel was not ready and withdrew. Britain withdrew the Fairey III with no reason given. Sadi Lecointe and Jean Casale were busy getting ready for the Gordon Bennett race which followed only a week behind the Schneider contest. But France was more interested in a third win of the Bennett race, and the United States was there with some advanced designs.

The Schneider contestants for Italy were:

Savoia (SIAI) S.12bis, serial number 3011, reconnaissance flying boat, reworked for the Schneider contest.

Savoia S.19, 2002, tractor-thrust flying boat built exclusively for the contest.

Societa Anonima Nieuport-Macchi (SANM) M.19, 3098, tractor-type flying boat designed for the payload regulations. A Macchi M.17 was substituted for the M.19 when it was not ready in time. But the M.17 was also withdrawn because it could not be made ready to handle the payload requirement.

SANM M.12, a 1918 reconnaissance flying boat with twin booms.

Savoia S.12

The S.12 appears to be the closest to Jacques Schneider's concepts of what he was striving for than any of the seaplanes entered in the contests up to 1913. Developed from the S.8, the S.12 was introduced by SIAI shortly after the end of World War I and was designed by Raphael Conflenti and proposed to the military in 1917. Its Ansaldo-San Giorgio 4E-28 V-12 engine of 2,014ci (33ltr) developed 480hp at 1650rpm. Its large wood hull had the concave bottom and housed fuel tanks in the middle near the C.G. for long range. Twenty were ordered but the order was never finalized.

The S.12 bis had a wingspan 9.84ft (3m) less than the standard model. Also, it had a 9.5ft (2.9m) tail plane where standard was 16ft (4.8m). Standard fuel capacity was 60gal (270ltr); gross weight was 5,202lb (2,360kg), and empty weight was 3,438lb (1,560kg).

Savoia S.19

Since the S.13 could not be made to haul the payload requirement, SIAI was also preparing the bigger S.19 for a 663lb (300kg) commercial load, and went about tailoring it for entry in the Venice competition. It was larger than the standard S.13 and smaller than the S.12. Power was by a 550hp Ansaldo 4E-29 V-12, driving a special-built four-blade pusher propeller. Ailerons were on the top wing and had aero-balanced horns. The lifting wires were double, and covered by a sheath since there were only outer pairs of interplane struts. It was designated serial number 2002 and had race No. 9 S. The S.19 was to be flown by Guido Jannello, but a transportation labor strike taking place in Italy at that time allowed workers to occupy the factories, including Ansaldo of Turin which was to have supplied the engine, and so the S.19 was withdrawn.

Macchi M.19

The Macchi designer Tonini produced plans for a 52ft (15.85m) span flying boat for the Schneider contest especially to meet the load requirement. It became the M.19, serial number 3098, and was the only two-seater flying boat in the contest. It had a Fiat A-14 V-12 engine of 650hp mounted by a pair of N-struts off the fuselage which acted as the center section of the top wing. This flying boat, unlike other Macchis, had non-swept wings, and it used a four-blade tractor propeller. The M.19 was first flown by Arturo Zanetti in August but was extremely hard to control and had

The standard Savoia S.13 on a ramp near Sesto Calenda on Lake Maggiore. This is the standard two-bay wing. Jannello put on a great aerobatic show in this aircraft. *SIAI Marchetti.* Top left, The Savoia S.17 being prepared for the Monaco contests. *A. Coccon*

The Macchi M.12 was a standard military type before being reworked for Schneider competition. Note Warren-truss wing bracing and twin-boom tail section. *H. Nowarra.* Top right, three-quarter view of a Macchi M.12. This was the only flying boat that did not provide a hull step. Even without the step it handled very well on the water. *Hirsch Collection.* Right, the Savoia S.19 was built especially for the Schneider contest and its 663lb (300kg) load-carrying requirement. Its 650hp Fiat engine produced too much torque, so the hull had to be lengthened. *SIAI Marchetti*

very high torque. It was withdrawn from the 1920 contest, and the fuselage was lengthened for 1921.

Macchi M.17

The M.17 was a small flying boat developed for the Schneider and Monaco contests. During the final speed tests at Monaco, while being piloted by Zanetti, it was destroyed on landing. There were two built. The first, at Monaco, had a large black No. 36 on a forward beige hull, and dull light blue flight surfaces. The number two machine (M.17bis) carried race No. 9 and registration I-BAHG on the

fuselage and I on the white rudder. Like the M.19, the M.17 had its engine mounted on N-struts and had the upper wing counter section, but the wings were slightly sweptback. Both M.17 machines had a two-blade pusher propeller. The M.17 was substituted for the M.19 in the 1920 Schneider contest but also was withdrawn. It did not show up for 1921 but was entered in the 1922 contest.

Macchi M.12

The M.12 was to be flown by Giovanni De Briganti, but was withdrawn. Basically a three-place reconnaissance seaplane built in 1918, it was powered by an Ansaldo-San Giorgio 4E-28 engine of 430hp driving a 9ft, 10in (3m) pusher propeller. The Warren-truss wings were similar to those on the M.17 and M.19. The wide flat-bottomed hull did not extend to the tail but melded into twin booms culminating into the vertical stabilizer and rudders. Wingspan was 55.76ft (17m) and length 35ft, 4in (10.77m). Speed was 118mph (190km/h) so its entry was dependent on its reliability. Although it had a wide flat-bottomed hull with no step, the M.12 handled well on the water, and takeoffs and landings were relatively smooth.

Above, Count Le Marquis Bernard De Romanet talking to Louis Bleriot by his Spad racer. *Hirsch Collection.* Top left, the Macchi M.12, waiting for engine installation in preparation for Schneider contest. *A. W. Yusken.* Left, the Macchi M.18 with military equipment. It is powered by an Isotta-Fraschini (Asso) V–6 of 250hp. The Asso V–6 did not have enough power to make such a large seaplane competitive. *Hirsch Collection*

Chapter 6

1921 Venice

The All-Italian Contest

The Monaco Meet

Again the Monaco meet was to be the practice ground for Venice, and like 1920, it had an effect on what machine was to compete. Typical bad weather for April in Monaco is winds and fast moving storms. The April 13–21 Monaco meet fizzled as compared to the previous year. There was a scarcity of machines, partly owing to crashes and partly to bad weather preventing contestant arrival. It was supposed to start on April 13, but the weather held up the motorboat meet, and they had not completed their races. Also, contestants were not ready to go.

April 14: Four French naval F.B.A. seaplanes arrived, creating some excitement while landing in the middle of the motorboat finale. Late in the afternoon Roget went up in his Renault-powered Breguet 14-A-2 with a passenger from Pathe News Co. to film an exhibition. He crashed by landing on a rough sea. Both men were picked up, but the 25,000 franc movie camera and the Breguet were lost.

April 15: About 6:45pm a Savoia S.12 arrived, piloted by Umberto Maddalena. Also, Sadi Lecointe arrived in his Nieuport 29C, but he did not win any race.

April 16: The four French naval seaplanes withdrew from the competition and departed. There were more warships at anchor than there were seaplanes present. A Caudron three-engine C.39, F-ARBI, piloted by Maicon, arrived. It fueled and took off for Ajaccio in the Monaco–Corsica–Monaco competition. Also, a single-engine Caudron F-AIBL, piloted by Poiret, arrived and entered the Cannes–Cape Martin contest. However, it missed the markers and had to refly the course; however it did win the contest prize.

April 17: Maddalena in the Savoia S.22 tried to enter the contest but could not get one of the Isotta-Fraschini engines started. This huge plane fell into Lake Maggiore on July 28, 1922, during flight test in preparation for the Schneider trophy, killing pilot Gianni Del Maschio. La Louette tried to get his Spad-Herbemont off, but he smashed a float and was towed into the harbor. He then tried unsuccessfully to get off in his Renault-powered Farman G.L.

April 18: Very heavy storms prevented any attempt to fly.

April 19: The Caudron C.39, piloted by Maicon, covered the 176mi (284km) San Ramo–Cannes flight in very high winds. He covered the distance in 2hr, 25min, 41sec to win the prize. He luckily managed a safe landing and taxied into the harbor. Bologna accidentally punctured the hull of his Savoia S.12 on takeoff, and it had to be beached by motorboats.

April 20: After working all night to repair his pontoons, La Louette tried for the altitude contest. He got off with a smooth start and reached 11,480ft. (3,500m), but coming back down he hit the water too hard and cracked both floats on rough seas. He was picked up by motorboat, but the Spad sunk into the water and was destroyed. Maicon had an engine failure and put down his craft in the open sea,

Guido Jannello sitting in cockpit of a Savoia S.21. This was expected to be the top performer and likely winner of the Schneider contest.
A. Coccon

The Macchi M.18 skimming the lake prior to the Venice contest. Two of these were withdrawn from competition. *Hirsch Collection.* Top right, the Savoia S.22 tandem twin-engined flying boat. It had two Asso engines of 250hp each. It crashed on a preparation flight. This was the first of the tandem two-engine competitors. *A. Coccon.* Right, the Savoia S.21 on Lake Maggiore before the contest. Note short top wing and Warren-truss bracing. *A. Coccon*

near d' Autibes. He and his mechanic were picked up, but the C.39 had cracked floats and was destroyed during tow-in. Poiret entered his small Caudron in the 77.7mi (125km) speed competition, covering it in 44min, 46sec to win. He had the only flyable machine left.

April 21: Most of the warships anchored outside the harbor to watch the event left. Poiret's Caudron was the only machine still tied to the buoys, all other contestants had either withdrawn or had destroyed their machines. The meeting was a washout for spectators. Like 1920, this meeting would have an effect on the Venice meet.

1921 Venice

After reviewing the effect that the 663lb (300kg) payload requirement had on the 1920 contest, the Aero Club of Italy felt it was detrimental to the spirit of the contest and dropped the payload stipulation. However, in staying with the spirit of Jacques Schneider, it was countered by a greater set of seaworthy requirements for the 1921 contest. Added to the rules was a 6hr float test qualification to be held after the taxi-navigation tests. The test would remain in effect until the 1931 contest.

The navigation course was 5nm (7.55mi, or 12.16m). There were two stretches of 0.5mi (0.8km) each that had to be taxied over. The navigation qualification allowed two attempts to qualify. Then in the water-tightness tests, water could not be drained off before the speed event. Machines were to move right from their moorings to takeoff point and fly with whatever water leaked in.

An additional rule was put into effect, that of a registration deposit of 5,000 francs (in addition to the entrant's fee). It was to eliminate any nonserious applications. If the entrant showed up to race, the 5,000 francs were returned. Entry registration closing date was May 15, at which time there was only one non-Italian entry. It was Sadi Lecointe and his Nieuport-Delage 29C on floats, the same machine he flew to the earlier Monaco Meet. What modifications, if any, were made is not known.

Britain claimed at the time to have seaplanes second to none, and yet they ignored the invitation to prove it by a nonresponse. Then during the navigation trials on August 6, Sadi Lecointe hit the water too hard and buck-

led his float struts. His engine and propeller dipped into the water, causing damage he could not repair at Venice. He was not hurt but was forced to withdraw, again leaving only Italy to compete. France's De Romanet was killed on September 23 while testing a De Monge racer for the Coupe Deutsch De la Meurthe. Also, Harry Hawker was killed July 12, in a British Nieuport Goshawk when the machine caught fire during a practice flight for the Aerial Derby.

Aircraft technology had advanced to a point where participation was far beyond the individual's pocketbook. Also, flying clubs were not so solvent that they could fully finance a contestant. Speed in the air was requiring a lot more testing of theory, which was becoming much more sophisticated and costly.

Italy allowed a total of sixteen contestants to enter in the trials. The aircraft entered were: five Macchi M.7s, one being an M.7bis; two Macchi M.18s, standard transport types, slightly modified; one Macchi M.19, specially built for the event; six Savoia S.13s, standard machines, not the single-bay strut of Bournemouth; one Savoia S.21, with a 475hp Ansaldo engine; and one Savoia S.22 with

The Macchi M.19 was built specially for the 1921 Schneider contest. The Fiat A-14 engine, Warren-trusses, and up-front propeller make this an interesting contender. It also lacks the typical Macchi wing sweep-back. A. Coccon

Rare in-flight view of the Macchi M.19. The M.19 was built specifically for the Schneider contest. *A. Coccon.* **Top right, Joseph Sadi Lecointe and friend in front of his Nieuport-Delage 1921 sesquiplane.** *Hirsch Collection*

push-pull tandem 260hp Isotta-Fraschini V–6 engines (two 330hp Fiat A-12 engines were planned for the contest).

As the contest time drew near, things started to happen. First, the S.22 tandem two-engine flying boat crashed on its early test flight and was a total loss. This plane was entered in the Monaco seaplane event in April with pilot Umberto Maddalena, and Del Mashie as back-up. It had undergone engine change. Also, during the elimination tests Jannello became sick, and Gaurnieri took over as back-up pilot. However, engine trouble on his familiarization test flight prevented the S.21 from participating. Then, all six S.13s were eliminated during the trials because of various reasons, such as not completing navigation trials or not completing the course because of mechanical or engine problems. The two M.18s were no match for the M.19 and M.21, so they were withdrawn during the trials, before Jannello became sick.

Only two of the Macchi M.7s made it through in flying colors. They were: H. Giovanni De Briganti in the M.7 bis, No. 1, with a 200hp Isotta inline six and smaller wing of 215sq-ft; and No. 14, Piero Corgnolino in the standard M.7 with a 250hp Isotta and 290sq-ft (26.1sq-m) wing area. He averaged 120.87mi (194.95km/h), and De Briganti averaged 119.66mph (193km/h). Finally, the M.19 with

pilot Zanetti and mechanic Pedetti finished an easy first at 131.76mph (212.51km/h) and so the team of three Italian flying boats was qualified for the coming event.

The Venice contest was run on August 7, and for the second time it was a disappointment. Only one was able to complete the contest, thus becoming the winner by default.

All three contestants got off alright but on Lap 12, the M.19's Fiat engine suffered crankshaft failure and caught fire. Both Zanetti and his mechanic Pedetti were rescued with the help of a motor launch. The M.19 sat there in the water and burned itself out. Before the engine fire Zanetti was lapping at an average of 129.82mph (208.92km/h). This left the two Macchi M.7s on the course.

Corgnolino was leading the contest averaging 119.03mph (191.55km/h). Then within just a little over 1.24mi (2km) of the finish line his engine coughed and quit. He had run out of gas and had to set down on the water just short of the Lido Hotel on the home stretch—a very disheartening event for Corgnolino. De Briganti completed the sixteen laps and was declared the winner.

No takeoff time was recorded and made available to the press, but De Briganti completed Lap 5 at 10:38:32am and Lap 16 at 12:11:52.5pm, which created questions about the published total time of 2hr, 4min, 39.8sec, giving a speed of 117.86mph (189.68km/h). The Aero Club of Italy published the speed of

119.63mph (192.52km/h). This was based on the M.7bis covering a full 248mi (400km) in the 2hr, 4min, 39.8sec, which is not true. The 4.16mi (6.7km) beyond the finish line was probably traveled by De Briganti but it would not have been recorded by the timers. This fifth Schneider contest was just about as much of a washout as the previous two.

In retrospect, there were three new aircraft in 1921 that deserve to be mentioned: the Macchi M.19, the Savoia S.21, and the Savoia S.22. All were built for this year's event. The M.19 as described earlier was modified for the event by lengthening the rear hull section to compensate for the high torque of the Fiat A-14 engine and four-blade tractor propeller. The new serial number was 3098.

The Savoia S.21 was a pusher flying boat that used the Warren-truss interplane construction style, although the wing was of very short span. What is so noticeably different was the 25.26ft (7.69m) lower wing and 16.23ft (5.1m) top wing. The slender single-step hull was 22.97ft (7m) long and made of wood with a concave hull bottom. The rudder was horn balanced with the horizontal tail surface about two-thirds up on the tail plane. Flight surfaces were fabric covered. The S.21 was powered by a 475hp Ansalda-San Giorgio 4E-28 V-12 engine housed in a large oval nacelle with a small forward opening for the radiator. It was held high up between the wings by N-struts to clear the four-blade, 7ft (2.13m) propeller. The wings had a pronounced curved airfoil; stress wires were kept to a minimum. Maximum weight was 1,543lb (700kg) and maximum speed has been quoted as 180.19mph (290km/h).

Built in 1920 but not competed until the following year, the Savoia S.22 was a different

approach to the payload requirement of 1920. Its wingspan was 44.25ft (13.5m) with a length of 35.36ft (10.78m). The high-placed engine nacelle housed tandem 260hp Isotta-Fraschini V-6 engines with four-blade propellers. (Note: The Isotta-Fraschini V-6 engine was not of the vee arrangement; it was of inline arrangement and water cooled.) The S.22 was a two-seater, equal-span, two-bay biplane with an all-wooden hull with integral vertical fin and rudder up high, just below the horizontal stabilizer. Ailerons were on the bottom wing only. Wings were fabric covered. This aircraft originally was to have two Fiat A-12 inline 6cyl engines of 300hp, for a maximum speed of about 137mph (275km/h), which was not equivalent to the S.21, but size and water handling were supposed to improve its chances.

Chapter 7

1922 Naples

A Convincing British Victory

Naples, Italy

The sixth Schneider Trophy contest was first scheduled for August 24–26 and then suddenly was moved up to August 10–12. It was flown at Naples, Italy, and was laid out in a triangle of 17.68mi (28.52km) to be flown thirteen times to total 229.87mi (370.77km).

After three years of misfortune through accidents and aero club bungling, impatience and anticipation mounted in Italy. Engineer Alessandro Marchetti had joined Savoia and was busy with a new Schneider design designated S.51. He also took an old 1918 design, the S.50, dusted off all the drawings, and readied it for water flying and the Schneider contest. Despite misfortunes, the Savoia company was still Italy's main hope for keeping the trophy permanently.

CAMS 36

For three years, France had only halfheartedly coveted the Schneider Trophy, mainly through efforts of Sadi Lecointe and his Nieuport. This year Raphael Conflenti, who was chief engineer for Savoia, moved to France and joined D. Lorenzo Santoni, who left Savoia in 1920 to establish a new firm at St. Denis called Chantiers Aero-Maritime De la Seine (CAMS). Flying boat construction began in 1921, but when Conflenti arrived he set about designing a racer based on work he had done at Savoia. It was known as the CAMS 36, but was design Model 42 and was based on the CAMS 31. It had the familiar Savoia concave hull bottom opposite of the normally accepted vee bottom. Otherwise, its hull was generally oval. Two examples were built: F-ESFB with race No. 11, and F-ESFA with No. 12. They were barely finished with flight testing when the contest date change dictated crating and shipping. Flight tests showed a speed of 155mph (250km/h). All this was of little consequence, however, since while en route the crated aircraft was halted by rail strikers in Italy, eliminating any competition from France.

Supermarine Sea Lion II

Between November 1918 and 1923, starting with the N.1B Baby, Supermarine built twelve new types of experimental flying boats, eight of them at their own expense, in search of contracts. Hubert Scott-Paine was appointed works manager of Supermarine by Noel P. Billing and in 1916, managing director of the new Supermarine Aviation Works Limited. As company head he hired the self-taught engineer Reginald J. Mitchell.

On November 8, 1921, the racing committee of Britain's RAeC met with the Society of British Aircraft Constructors to consider proposed race programs to be held in 1922. The Schneider Trophy contest was shelved in the discussion.

In June 1922, Supermarine decided to ready a new challenger. Since this was a private venture with no government subsidies, there was no fanfare or outside entities monitoring its development. The basic airframe came from the second production, the Sea King II, and the competition machine was named Sea Lion II, G-EBAH. H. T. Vane of

The Supermarine Sea Lion II undergoing tests prior to being shipped to Naples for the Schneider Trophy contest. The Sea Lion II's airframe was based on the production Sea King, but the Sea Lion was given a powerful Napier Lion engine. In the capable hands of Henri Biard, the Sea Lion II won the 1922 Schneider Trophy.

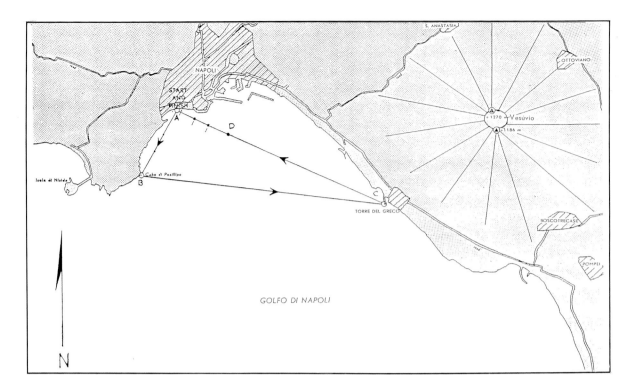

The 1922 Schneider contest course at Naples, Italy. Bottom right, the first CAMS 36 at completion and before flight testing in 1922. This is the early design and different from the 1923 CAMS 36. *A. Coccon*

Napier was instrumental in providing a 450hp Lion and engine specialists. Shell Oil Co. provided fuel and octane boosters and Wakefield Oil Co. provided engine oil. Another firm loaned a four-blade, high-speed propeller. The General Steam Navigation Company provided transport on the SS *Philomel*, and the services of its Captain Field and crew. Regardless of all the contributed help, Scott-Paine spent over £6,000 before the race was over. The Napier Lion alone would have cost £3,000. Even the insurance company reduced its premium by 50 percent for the venture.

The Sea Lion II bore very little resemblance to a racer. It was built originally with strength as a prime requirement. The Linton-Hope principal hull of mahogany planking attached to rock elm frames by nonferric fittings, and riveting was covered with fabric and doped. It was capable of being dropped (in landings) from 30ft (9.15m) onto the water without damage. The Sea Lion II was agile enough to be rolled, looped, and spun like a fighter. After the contest it was assigned serial number N-159 when it was purchased by the Air Ministry.

The greater torque of the larger engine required enlarging the original Sea King II vertical fin and rudder areas. Propellers were four wooden blades 8.5ft (2.59m) in narrow-chord wing with a 1.5ft (0.46m) span increase. The engine was mounted high between the wings producing a high thrust line and an upward pitching movement, so the horizontal tail surfaces had a reverse camber. Fuel was pumped to the engine by a high-pressure air system. The engine nacelle contained the oil tank cooler and water radiator in front of the engine.

Moving the contest date forward two weeks meant less time for final checks and flight testing. Pilot Henri Biard took the Sea Lion II up on the first test hop and while climbing out only a few hundred feet above the Southampton docks, the engine suddenly quit. Biard put it down between ships and was towed back to the Wooston slipway, where it was worked on all night. The problem was in the fuel system causing starvation and was easily corrected. After thoroughly checking the machine, just before sunset the following day Biard took off again and the tests were successful. He got his airspeed indicator up to 150mph (241.5km/h)

before backing off. Then he landed and taxied back to the slipway before dark. After a few more flights and adjustments, the machine was crated up and hauled aboard the SS *Philomel*.

Biard had acquired his flying skills at the Grahame-White school at Hendon in 1912 and services in the RNAS through the war. He had served as Supermarine test pilot since 1920. His experience included all the test work required for the Sea King II. Biard had some doubts that this racer would be fast enough to win, but it was clear to him that Mitchell and Scott-Paine believed it could. Considering what was known about the S.51, it seemed that the whole endeavor depended on good judgment and well-planned effort.

At Naples, the team from Great Britain which included Mitchell, Scott-Paine, and Napier company engineers assembled the Sea Lion II. It was then placed on its light pneumatic-wheeled undercarriage and the holder sockets were snapped into placed. Then the craft was wheeled to the slipway and into the water where it began testing under temperatures and humidity typical of the Mediterranean.

The Supermarine team launched their own cloak-and-dagger operation to assess the Italian team, the same as they were being assessed. Whenever Biard flew, the experts and onlookers watched every move he made. He was careful not to open the machine up too much, and he flew around the pylons widely. The Italian opposition watched and timed the Sea Lion II and publicly stated its inferiority to their S.51 and M.17.

Savoia S.51

The S.51 with its graceful lines looked like a sure winner. This small, elegant flying boat was at first advertised as a fighter by SIAI. Its sesquiplane configuration provided just enough lower wing to provide lateral stability from the outrigger floats while on water. The struts to the large upper wing formed a rigid Warren-truss and were totally free of bracing wires.

The S.51 upper wing was 32.81ft (10m) and lower wing 13.12ft (4m). It had a 300hp Hispano-Suiza engine driving a two-blade propeller and mounted flush with the top wing and underwing exhaust. The machine was

The Savoia S.51 at Naples after placing second in the Schneider contest. With a new propeller and strengthened engine, it set a speed record, proving to be faster than it was in the contest. *A. Coccon*

registered I-BAIU and had the concave, one-step hull bottom typical of Savoia. Its fuselage was very narrow and tapered into a thin tail. The S.51 sustained some minor hull damage during the navigability trials and took on water during the 6hr mooring test and capsized. It was quickly hauled in and repaired for the contest by the next day. The British team did not object to letting the S.51 continue.

The Contest

August 12, the day of the contest, dawned clear with a vivid blue sky and calm waters on the Gulf of Napoli. The contest was to start by 1:00pm, but the heat of the sun prompted the race committee to move it to 4:00pm when it would be cooler. Biard drew first-off position, to be followed by Piero Corgnolino in the M.7bis, then Arturo Zanetti in the M.17bis, and Alessandro Passaleva in the S.51.

Biard climbed into the cockpit in trousers and shirtsleeves, cranked up, and taxied out to the starting point with the Italian trio moving in behind him. At 4:06 the start signal was given and Biard taxied across the start line, pushed the throttle open, made a clean take-off, and climbed out on course. He found himself at Cabo di Posillipo for his first turn almost before he was ready to level off.

His first lap was his fastest, 7min, 10sec, or 148.043mph (238.779km/h). By the time he was on his second lap, Passaleva in the S.51 was taxiing into takeoff position, and he was airborne when Biard straightened out on the backstretch. Corgnolino in the M.7bis had been airborne 45sec after Biard, with a first lap of 8min, 39.2sec. Zanetti took off 4.5min behind Biard in his M.17bis and his first lap was 8min, 2.6sec. This put the four machines strung out on the course. They would soon bunch up, however.

With all four machines on the course, for the first time since 1914 the Schneider contest looked like a race. It was apparent from the first lap that the Macchis were no match for the Sea Lion II, so they set up their game plan of bunching up and holding Biard back so Passaleva's S.51 could catch up from behind. But the S.51 had its own problems. The wooden propeller, having had a dunking during the capsizing, started delaminating at the tip, and at high rpm created vibration that startled Passaleva. He throttled back and the vibration became tolerable so kept flying at reduced rpm. He kept easing the throttle open, but the vibration became so violent he had to throttle back.

Biard, having caught up to the two Macchis, couldn't go around or under them so he just opened the throttle wide and climbed above them. The two Macchis could not climb without losing speed and dropping back. Biard leveled off above them and passed overhead on Lap 5 in the backstretch with a 26mph (41.86km/h) advantage. He could see the pilots' goggles looking up at him as he slipped by, and then he lowered the nose and left them behind. His indicated speed was up to 165mph (265.5km/h). Biard could see that he was far enough ahead, so by the ninth lap he could throttle back and save the engine to be sure to finish.

About Lap 9, the S.51 was picking up lap speeds from the concentrated efforts of Passaleva and by Lap 11 he was flying faster than Biard. By the end of Lap 13, the S.51 was up to 145.738mph (235.062km/h) and Biard had slowed down to 141.715mph (228.573km/h). But it was too late, even though the spectators were on their toes cheering Passaleva on. The S.51 averaged 143.334mph (229.571km/h), completing the course in 1hr, 36min, 54.2sec.

The Sea Lion II averaged 145.434mph (234.571km/h), completing the course in 1hr, 34min, 51.6sec, thus winning the contest. The M.17 averaged 132.465mph (213.653km/h) and the M.7bis averaged 123.756mph (199.607km/h). This was the first Schneider contest in which all starters finished.

There was still general agreement, however, that the Italians would come back after the trophy in 1923 and probably win it. On December 22, over Lake Maggiore, the S.51 set a world speed record for seaplanes of 174.08mph (280.1km/h) over a measured straight course. It was clear that the S.51 was faster than the Sea Lion II. If a country gains three wins in a five-year period it would be an outright win and the trophy would remain there. It would then end the competition much the same as for the Gordon Bennett racers. Italy still had a chance!

In Europe, the Aerial Derby was won at a speed of 176.4mph (283.83km/h), so some high speeds were expected for the 1923 Schneider contest. The 145.434mph (234.15km/h) win of 1922 was projected to be beat by at least 30mph (48.3km/h). What was not known within the European circles though, was that there were some startling surprises on the horizon.

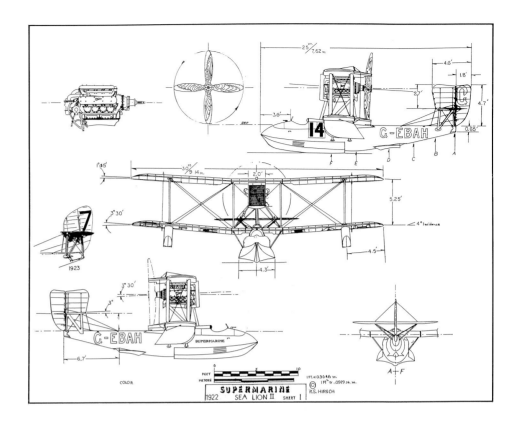

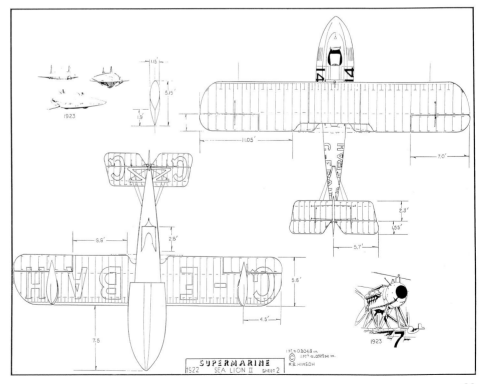

Chapter 8

1923 Cowes

The American Invasion

A Change of Pace

Up to 1921, international airplane racing had been conducted in a gentlemanly fashion but organized in an amateurish manner. Races were usually organized by various aero clubs, with funds mostly from publishing organizations that would gain directly from it (Pulitzer, for example). By this time, governments began letting military pilots compete on a regular basis and military observers always attended. And for the first time, manufacturers received financial backing for developing fast airplanes. From 1920 on, there were at least four major contests for speed, the Schneider Trophy contest being one of them.

While it is generally difficult to trace ancestry of aircraft designed for military service, there is no doubt that the famous Curtiss Hawk series originated from early designs of the Navy Curtiss CR-1 and CR-2 of 1921 and the R-6 of 1922. The CR-1 and CR-2 were to be flown in the 1921 Pulitzer, but the Navy decided not to enter. Curtiss then requested permission to enter the CR-1. It was piloted by Bert Acosta who flew it to victory at 176.9mph (284.63km/h) at Omaha, Nebraska, on November 3, 1921. Of six aircraft that took off at 3min intervals and raced against time, Acosta was first away and with close, steeply banked pylon turns covered the course in 52min, 45sec.

Up to 1922, no airplane in America had achieved a level flight speed of 200mph (322km/h). The Curtiss engineers removed the lobster-pot Lamblin radiators and built wing-skin radiators of paper-thin brass sheets on the CR-1 and installed a Reed metal propeller. New gross weight was 2,165lb (974.25kg). The plane's speed was 190mph (305.9km/h) maximum and 75mph (120.75km/h) on landing. Actually, none of these airplanes built in response to Mitchell's request could ever have served as fighting machines.

On May 27, 1922, Curtiss Aeroplane and Motor Co. signed a contract with the US Army and proceeded to build the R-6. On September 27, 1922, the first was flown at Mineola, Long Island, New York, over a measured 0.62mi (1km) course, which was then the official FAI speed course, at 211.4mph (340.143km/h) and became the first American aircraft to exceed 200mph (322km/h). The second was flown October 2, 1922, and attained a speed of 219.4mph (353.02km/h). Then on October 18, Gen. Billy Mitchell set a new world record of 222.97mph (358.765km/h).

On September 13, 1922, Lt. H. J. Brown, US Navy, attained an officially recorded speed of 244.15mph (393.08km/h) over a 0.62mi (1km) course at Mineola, Long Island, in a Curtiss R2C-1. This was the newer breed of racer that was to fly at St. Louis on October 3. It was also a preview of things to come.

In 1923 the Navy Bureau of Aeronautics commissioned Curtiss to build two new racers. The R2C-1 was designed with an entirely new Navy model system with considerable refinement in detail. Its new D-12A engine delivered 597hp, and it had a maximum level flight speed of 266.59mph (428.94km/h). It could

The Naval Aircraft Factory TR-3A being built up for 1923 Curtiss Marine Trophy race and as a Schneider back-up. The TR-3A was developed from the Curtiss TS-1, the US Navy's first postwar seaplane fighter. *S. Hudek*

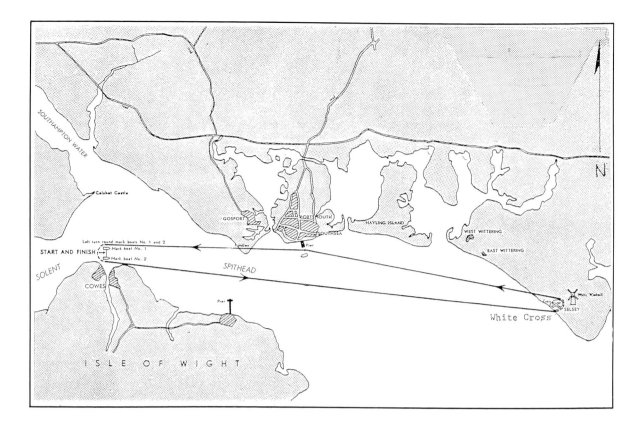

The 1923 Schneider contest course. Bottom right, the Curtiss 18-T-1 at the Navy depot for 1922 Curtiss Marine Trophy race. Although this seaplane was not flown in the Schneider contests, it was a preview of things to come. *Hirsch Collection*

climb to 5,000ft (1,524.4m) in 1.6min and had a service ceiling of 31,800ft. The two aircraft placed first and second at 243.68mph (392.3km/h) and 241.77mph (389.25km/h) in the Pulitzer contest at St. Louis, Missouri. The two Curtiss CRs were third and fourth.

The 1923 Schneider Contest

By 1923 the racing fever was well established, both in the United States and in Europe. It was also the first year in which the high cost of racing became evident. The Curtiss CR-1 and CR-2 were well known to the American racing public but not to the European air-minded public, who were busy familiarizing themselves with their own aircraft such as the Spads, Nieuports, De Monge 5-1, Borel, Sopwith Rainbow, Martinsyde racers, Bristol Bullet, 72 and 77 racers, the Ansaldos, and the huge-engine Fiat 700.

The 1923 Schneider Trophy contest was held at Cowes, on the Isle of Wight, off England's southern coast. The RAeC once again organized it, and entries had to be received by

Gallaudet D-4 at the launch ramp for the Curtiss Marine Trophy race. Note propeller location. Left, the Naval Aircraft Factory (NAF) TS-1 with a Lawrence J-1 engine. This engine was developed into the J-4 and Wright Whirlwind J-5. *Hirsch Collection*

The NAF TS-2 just after new race wings were installed. Machine was redesignated TR-2. *Hirsch Collection.* **Below, a frontal view of TR-3A showing the pontoons and lower wing struts. Note the peculiar method of wing and fuselage attachment.** *S. Hudek*

March 1, accompanied by a £10 entrance fee and a "good-intent" deposit of 5,000 francs. All competing aircraft were to be at the S. E. Saunders works by September 20 and ready for competition by September 26, when the good-intent money would be returned. On September 27, contest navigation and water-tightness tests would start, and September 28 would be the contest day. Competitors from each country were started together, with an interval of 15min between each country.

Rules remained basically the same as in Naples, differing only in that taxiing tests would be at a minimum speed of 14.4mph (22.2km/h). Also, no repairs beyond propeller change during the test phase were allowed (water spray damage to wooden propellers was prevalent). The start line was to be crossed on the water and the finish line in flight. This year, for the first time, there was an excellent entry list for the contest with Great Britain, France, Italy, and the United States being represented.

The Schneider Trophy competition committee of the RAeC held a meeting on Wednesday, September 5, chaired by Maj. Gen. Sir W. S.

Brancker, and it decided upon the course turning points and race headquarters for officials. Some of those named were: Col. M. O. Darby, clerk of the course; Lt. Col. C.P.B. Ogilvie for the United States; Capt. R. J. Goodman Crouch for France; D. C. MacLachlan for Italy; and Capt. L.T.G. Mansell for Great Britain. Brig. Gen. D.F.L. Festing was press steward.

The choice for a suitable course was debated among the British and French aero clubs and the press for some time. Some wanted it to be on both British and French coastlines so that both nations could view the contest. But this was found to be impractical and it was eventually laid out at Cowes, England, with less total distance than in previous contests. It was 186nm (214.09mi, or 344.47km) in five laps with start and finish line at Cowes. Turning points were at Selsey Bill, and a marker boat was anchored off the South Sea pier. The five-lap course was unique. It not only provided the longest lap of any of the contests, but also the longest leg (37.2 nautical miles, 42.82mi, or 68.47km). Original Schneider rules stated the course was not to be less than

Three-quarter rear view of the TR-3A, showing details of empennage stress wires. *S. Hudek.* Left, a CR-1 frontal view showing the lobster-pot radiators, landing gear, and wire bracing of fuselage to upper wing. Note its wooden propeller. The photo was taken November 19, 1921. *L.A. Historical Branch AIAA*

Bert Acosta and the CR-1 after winning the Pulitzer race in 1921. *J. Albanese.* **Top right, the Curtiss CR-2 as of September 1922. Note strut replacing rear wire bracing.** *L.A. Historical Branch AIAA*

172.36mi (278km) in either a straight line, a broken line, or in a closed circuit.

It was inevitable that some of those within the RAeC would retain memories of the fogbound course and the brain-fogged race committee that caused so much bitterness during the 1919 contest. Also, there was little concept of who were to be the defenders. An editorial in the British magazine *Flight* argued the urgency for Great Britain to make determined efforts to keep the trophy. Eventually, the British came up with three entries.

Entries for the 1923 Schneider Contest were as follows:

Aircraft/Motor	Country	Owner	Pilot
Sopwith Hawker, G-EAKI, 400hp Jupiter	Great Britain	H. G. Hawker Engineering Co. Ltd.	Longton
Supermarine Sea Lion, G-EBAH, 450hp Napier Lion	Great Britain	Supermarine Aviation Works Ltd.	Biard
Blackburn Pellet, G-EBHF, Napier Lion	Great Britain	Blackburn Aeroplane and Motor Co. Ltd.	Kenworthy
Curtiss CR-3A, A-6080, 465hp CD-12	United States	US Navy	Rittenhouse
Curtiss CR-3A, 465hp CD-12	United States	US Navy	Irvine
Wright NW-2, A-6544, 700hp Wright T-2	United States	US Navy	Gorton
NAF TR-3A, A-6447, 290hp Wright-Hispano E-4A	United States	US Navy	Wead
Latham No. 1, F-ESEJ, two 400hp Lorraine tandem	France	Societe Industrielle de Caudebec-en-Caux (SICC)	Duhame
Latham No. 2, F-ESEK, two 400hp Lorraine tandem	France	SICC	Benoist
CAMS 36a, F-ESFC, 360hp Hispano	France	CAMS	Pelletier d'Oisy
CAMS 38, F-ESFD, 360hp Hispano-Suiza	France	CAMS	Hurel
Blanchard, F-ESEH, 400hp Gnome Jupiter	France	Blanchard/Blériot	Teste

The Curtiss CR-3 during testing in the United States before leaving for England for the Schneider contest. *J. D. Canary.* Below, front view of the CR-3 showing its small frontal area and the struts fore and aft to the wing. *Hirsch Collection*

Curtiss CR-3

The Curtiss CR-1 and CR-2 sporting the newly developed wing radiators were readied for the October 14, 1922, Pulitzer race due to Lt. Al Williams' continued insistence and Adm. William A. Moffett's approval. CR-1 A-6080 had been pulled into the shops and given the same treatment that A-6081 had been given earlier, emerging just a few days before the race. An oil-cooling duct was fitted at the head of the wing pylon that extended beyond the wing trailing edge. A-6080 had its lift wire replaced by a set of struts connecting wing to fuselage, as did A-6081, for handling the additional load on the wings. Lt. H. J. Brown in the CR-2, race No. 40, placed third in the Pulitzer. Lt. Williams placed fourth in the CR-1, race No. 9. First and second place were taken by 1st Lt. Russell Maughan and 1st Lt. Lester Maitland, both flying the Army Curtiss R-6 racers. Also, in the hands of Gen. Billy

Navy-Wright NW-2 seaplane A-6544. Then there was team captain Lt. A. W. Gorton in the TR-3A, which was reworked from the winner of the 1922 Curtiss Marine Trophy race. This also had the wing radiator treatment, shortened wings, and Wright-built Hispano engine. The American Schneider team and their machine arrived at Southampton on August 24 on the US liner *Leviathan*. They were met by Hubert Scott-Paine and Capt. H. C. Biard of Supermarine Aviation Works Ltd. This group was to become the center of a raging controversy, which still existed after World War II because the aircraft were for the first time in Schneider history not products of private sporting groups but of a national government.

The CR-3's twin pontoons were integral to the undercarriage struts. The four streamlined wooden struts and spreader bars extended into the pontoons and became part of the pontoon structure before covering. The long, narrow pontoons, nearly 18ft (5.5m) long, had shallow 155deg vee bottoms with a single step directly below the C.G. Each contained an 8gal (30.32ltr) auxiliary tank for fuel. Front and rear struts were braced by interconnecting streamlined wires. The D-12 engines were tuned to put out 465hp on a 50 percent benzol mixture. The cowlings were recontoured to a more streamlined shape, and the vertical fin area was increased and all control surface gaps had been reduced to bare minimum. Fuel tank and access doors were patched over with linen and doped to a smooth finish. Stalling speed was now 76.2 mph (122.36km/h).

Wright NW-2

An especially interesting entry for this year's competition was the Navy-Wright racer. It was designated NW-2 and was developed as a hydro-biplane from the sesquiplane NW-1, a Pulitzer racer. It had a Wright T-2 high-compression 12cyl race-type engine weighing 1,150lb (517.5kg) and providing 700hp, which made it the highest powered single-engine seaplane. On its first flight it averaged 180mph (289.8km/h) over a 2.5mi (4.03km) course.

Wingspan for the NW-2 was 28.375ft (8.651m). It had cellular-constructed, plywood-covered wings with wing radiators like the Curtiss racers on both sides of the top wing

CR-3 No. 2 with Lieutenant Irvine in the cockpit prior to a test flight. When the Navy decided to go for the Schneider Trophy, they went all out. *J. D. Canary.* **Top far right, the Navy-Wright NW-1 Mystery racer at Mitchel Field, New York, Pulitzer race in 1921.** *US Navy.* **Bottom far right, the NW-2, rebuilt from the NW-1, being prepared for flight testing in early 1923. The NW-2 was a modification of the NW-1 that was not damaged in the Pulitzer contest.** *Hirsch Collection*

Mitchell, the R-6 did 222.98mph (359km/h). After the October 14 race, the Navy, smarting from having been beaten by later and faster designs, considered the two CRs obsolete and placed them in storage. No one could foresee the destiny that still awaited them.

In February 1923 the two CRs were taken out of storage, cleaned up, and fitted with floats. Since the CR-1 had already been modified to remove the lobster-pot Lamblin radiators, it and the CR-2 were treated alike. They were fitted with new CD-12 engines and new all-metal Reed propellers and were redesignated CR-3, maintaining the same serial numbers. The US Navy then, through the recently formed National Aeronautic Association (NAA), sent the proper paperwork to England to enter the Schneider contest. Ten years after the first Schneider contest had been staged at Monaco, the United States entered the contest for the first time. They didn't just *enter* it, they *invaded* it, and inaugurated a whole new phase of seaplane racing. For the first time, Europeans saw pure racing aircraft in the Schneider contests.

The US team consisted of Lt. David Rittenhouse in CR-3 A-6081 and Lt. Rutledge Irvine in CR-3 A-6080. Lt. Frank Wead piloted the

and on the top side of the bottom wing. The radiators were deeply corrugated to provide maximum cooling surface to the slipstream per square inch of wing, but did not detract from the speed and lift characteristics of the airfoil. The oil temperature control was unique in that it used the hot water from engine-to-wing radiators to warm the oil. Then when the oil was up to proper temperature, the water flow was reversed and came from the cooled water returning to the engine, thus cooling the oil. The fuselage and tail surfaces were attached to welded tubular-steel framework. The propeller, made of duralumin, was of a three-blade design and screwed into a forged steel hub.

Navy TR-3A

The Navy TR-3A was developed from the Navy TS-1, which was the Navy's first postwar seaplane fighter, and built by Curtiss. It was developed under Comdr. Jerome C. Hunsaker using the new 200hp Lawrence J-1 radial engine. Development of a good radial engine for Navy fighters was the desire of Adm. William A. Moffett and his engine-section chief Bruce G. Leighton. For racing, however, the Wright E-4 Hispano engine was used, and the aircraft were designated TS-2 or TR-2. The designations related to the wings, TR meaning racing wings and TS meaning scout. Dash numbers denoted specific airframe developments, including engine.

During the Curtiss Marine Trophy contest two TR-3As were equipped with racing wings and raced with Wright-Hispano E-4 and Lawrence J-1 engines. The E-4 engine had been tested at wide-open throttle for 573hr at Anacostia. The TR-3A had race No. 5 assigned and painted on the sides. Both Irvine and Rittenhouse used the TR-3A to fly over the triangular 48.26mi (77.7km) Curtiss Marine Trophy course to familiarize themselves with the layout, turning points, and markers. The TR-3A was brought to Cowes as a reserve racer.

The state of the art, as related to the Schneider contest, came to a complete halt in Italy. This was mostly due to the transportation labor strikes and the volcanic profile of the population. Also, Savoia could not obtain an engine powerful enough to install in the S.51 and be competitive. They were also watching developments in the United States

much more closely than those in France and England. Macchi was not ready with any competitive design, but was busy filling military orders for the M.18, M.24, and the Macchi-Nieuport 29C-1.

CAMS 36bis and 38

The CAMS 36bis, F-ESEC and CAMS 38, F-ESFD were brought to Cowes from France in a French naval vessel. The 36bis was a refinement of the 1922 flying boat that did not make the Naples contest. The 38, almost identical in structure, was a pusher and weighed slightly more. The 36bis had a wing surface of 222sq-ft (20sq-m), while the 38 had a wing area of 209sq-ft (18.8sq-m). However, the 38 was 12mph (20km/h) faster than the 36bis. Oil coolers were repositioned from the front to the back of the mounting posts on the 38, reducing drag. The 36bis had a four-blade propeller up front enclosed in a large-diameter spinner, and the 38 had a two-blade pusher propeller and a large, blunt, round enclosure up front of the engine.

All CAMS flying boats sat low in the water leaving very little freeboard on the sides, so pilots preferred the calm water of lakes. But the waters of The Solent, a channel separating the Isle of Wight from England, were not calm. The 36bis pilot sat behind the lower wing rear spar while the 38 pilot sat up front with a clear view over the nose. Raphael Conflenti was not entirely satisfied with the 1922 tractor-propelled 36bis, so he laid out a pusher version to test which one was faster. The CAMS 36bis attained a speed of 162mph (260km/h), and the CAMS 38 attained a speed of 168mph (270km/h). Both machines had the same power, so the engine installation —which affected the C. G.—propeller efficiency, and slipstream over the engine area made the difference. He made both racers as similar as possible in order to make a good comparison. After the contest the 38 was returned to the CAMS testing site at St. Raphael, France, and used for various flight hardware testing projects.

Latham No. 1 and No. 2

The strategists of the Aero Club of France felt that its entries should include a flying boat that could complete the tests and competition in rough weather. They contacted a young relative of Hubert Latham and owner of the new SICC-Latham & Co., and ordered two large flying boats (Latham No. 1 and No. 2). Each had two 400hp Lorraine-Dietrich Model 13 V–12 engines installed in tandem. They were placed back-to-back producing a push-pull thrust, and the propellers rotated in opposite directions. The two-blade propellers were of wood construction with metal tip covers. Cooling was by new-style Lamblin radiators with 78sq-ft (7sq-m) of radiating surface, and mounted to the engine cabane struts. Oil coolers were placed under each engine on the cabane nacelle at the bottom. The hull was conventionally constructed of wooden formers with wooden strips laid over and veneered. The hull had a deep vee bottom swept forward to a sharp nose. The Latham-patented laminated streamlined wires were used for all external bracing. The horizontal stabilizer was placed on top of the vertical fin and was integral to it.

The Latham's cockpit was between and just aft of the engine mount struts. It had a metal air deflector rather than a transparent windshield since it was close to the front propeller. Looking at the machine from the side, it appears the whole engine assembly could have been moved about 1ft (0.3m) aft and the cockpit moved forward, ahead of the propeller. This would have given the pilot much better visibility. The wings had a single-bay bracing with the usual two spars of spruce with plywood ribs. The wings were fabric covered with long-span ailerons on both upper and lower wings.

Blanchard

The Blanchard-Bleriot C.1 flying boat, registered F-ESEH, was designed by a former French naval officer Blanchard, and built by Blanchard-Bleriot Aeronautique. It had a French-built 320hp Bristol Jupiter radial engine STAe 9Aabis, which was not supercharged and directly drove a two-blade, fixed-pitch, wooden propeller. Blanchard previously designed aircraft for the Farman brothers and some for George Levy.

The Blanchard was a parasol-wing monoplane. Its wing was constructed of two wooden spars with plywood leading edges. It spanned 40ft (12.2m). The wing passed through the en-

gine nacelle slightly below the engine thrust line with the outer panels braced by two parallel, streamlined struts attached to the lower end of the hull side panels. The engine nacelle was a streamlined aluminum design enclosure with cylinders protruding for cooling and was supported by two huge center-section struts. The wing and engine nacelle were integral.

All flight surfaces were fabric covered and of wood construction. The unusual vertical stabilizer was two-finned, one being dorsal. The balancer floats were mounted on each side of the hull by struts since there was no lower wing. The fuselage measured 31ft (9.7m) long and 9ft, 10in (3m) high. The cockpit was well aft, about one-third back, between the engine nacelle mounting struts and the empennage.

Maximum speed was about 150mph (241km/h), not fast enough to be competitive. There was a second machine constructed with a more powerful engine, registered F-ESEH. However, it lagged and during its flight testing crashed after a midair collision. This ended the Blanchard hopes for a good Schneider contest showing since there was no time to rebuild and test a second machine. So Blanchard withdrew.

The CAMS 36 at its mooring during the Schneider contest. *S. Hudek.* Top far right, the CAMS 38 during testing in France. The new-type Lamblin radiators are fitted to the front engine nacelle struts. *H. Nowarra.* Center far right, the Blackburn Pellet taxiing out for navigation trials. *S. Hudek.* Bottom far right, the Supermarine Sea Lion III.

Sopwith Hawker

The Sopwith Schneider Trophy racer was designed in 1919 under the direction of Wilfred G. Carter with input from engineer and pilot Harry Hawker. Originally it had a number of characteristics typical of a Sopwith. It was designed especially to use the brand-new Bristol 450hp Jupiter radial engine, about four times as powerful as the 1914 Tabloids.

The Sopwith Hawker Rainbow was developed from the Schneider Trophy racer into a landplane racer by installing the ABC Dragonfly engine and reducing the wingspan 3ft (0.9m). Landing gear installation was a simple vee-strut arrangement. The engine was neatly cowled with cylinders protruding into the slipstream. The wings had a 2.5in (6.5cm) negative stagger.

The Jupiter engine had 25 percent greater displacement than the ABC Dragonfly. It was at first prefixed by the company name Cosmos instead of Bristol. The designers were Roy Fedden and L.F.G. Butler of Cosmos Engineering Co., which liquidated in 1920.

At the 1923 Aerial Derby held at Croydon, England, in August on Bank Holiday, G-EAKI appeared with "Sopwith Hawker" painted on the tail fin. It had the Jupiter engine with installed streamlining "hats" on the cylinders. Piloted by Flt. Lt. Walter Longton, it finished second at 64.02mph (103.07km/h) behind Larry Carter in the Gloster I. It was planned to be refitted with floats for the upcoming Schneider contest. However, while still in its

land configuration and on a test flight, the spinner broke and tangled in the propeller causing it to break and setting up vibration. Longton had to shut down completely and make a forced landing near the Brooklands Burgh Hill Golf Course. He lost the undercarriage on the butt of an oak in a hedge; the machine landed on its fuselage and rolled over. Longton escaped injury by crawling out, but G-EAKI was a complete loss . . . And then there were two.

Blackburn Pellet

The Blackburn N.56 airframe called N.1B, which had been in storage at Brough since 1918, was the hull for the Schneider Pellet. It was built by the Blackburn Aeroplane and Motor Co. Ltd. An interesting feature of the airframe was the two-step hull designed by Lieutenant Linton-Hope of the Royal Navy. The circular hull section had a forward single-step-planing bottom structure built into it. The second small step was a tiny skeg aft of it and was positioned aft of the waterline when moored. The hull was built up by circular formers of wood and stringers planked diagonally. Narrow mahogany strips of two laminations crossing at right angles covered the strips, forming the outer skin.

The N.1B had a 200hp Hispano-Suiza engine and two-blade, fabric-laminated mahogany propeller with the tip almost too close to the hull and cockpit. The Napier Lion installed in the Pellet was the same engine that came out of the Gloster Bamel, which won the Aerial Derby earlier in the year.

The high costs involved in building and flying a one-of-a-kind seaplane in a contest with no rewards other than prestige for the winner kept Blackburn from entering any earlier contests, particularly when the contests were overseas. However, with Great Britain as host and because not as many companies were involved as there were in 1919, Blackburn decided to build the Pellet. The board of directors was faced with either building the Pellet or paying a dividend to shareholders. Since there was no negative reaction of shareholders recorded, the competitive spirit must have predominated.

Work began at once on constructing wings suitable for racing and the Pellet emerged with a very narrow gap semi-sesquiplane wing setup. The small lower wing was set directly on top of the hull, and the 450hp Napier engine sat on top of the upper wing and was held by a pair of N-struts. The single-bay outer struts also were streamlined N section. The biplane had dihedral upper wing only, which carried relatively wide-span ailerons—10.4ft (3.2m) long and 1.35ft (0.42m) wide—that were operated by pushrods. Upper span was 34ft (10.4m) with a 4.83ft (1.47m) chord and the lower span was 29.4ft (9.0m) with a 3.5ft (1.1m) chord. The wings were wire braced, and the tail unit was a heavy, wire-braced strut mounted halfway up the vertical fin, which was also fabric covered. Elevators and rudder were cable operated. The windshield was hinged to move forward for easier cockpit ingress and egress. The headrest fairing was small and short because of the propeller proximity. A wind-driven generator provided power for the instruments. The large, wooden-tip floats were from the N.1B and came out of storage with the hull. They were attached directly below the outer bracing struts.

Pilot Reginald W. Kenworthy wanted the Pellet to be available for practice flying by August in order to clear up any teething problems and to become familiar with the mechanics of the machine. So on July 23 it was allocated civil registration G-EBHF and given race No. 6. It was not until the first week in September, after initial engine run-ups, that the Pellet was launched.

With only three weeks until race time, the first of the Pellet's bad luck struck. Shortly after it slid down the slipway at Brough and during taxiing and attempted takeoff, it was caught sideways in the Hamble River tide. The starboard under-wing float dipped deep into the water, burying the wing tip. The force of the water kept pushing down on the wing until the Pellet slowly turned over on its side, allowing Kenworthy time to scramble out and into the water.

The seaplane was quickly salvaged and taken back to the Blackburn Co. sheds at Brough-on-the-Humber where the engine was dismantled, cleaned, and dried out, as was the rest of the machine. The crews worked night and day to put it back together. There was not enough time for flight testing, so it was shipped by rail to Southampton and reassembled at the Fairey Aviation Co. Ltd. works at

Hamble. Early in the morning on September 25, the Pellet, with race No. 6 on the rudder, was eased down the Fairey slipway and launched into the Hamble River.

After some routine preflight checks, Kenworthy started up the engine, began taxiing tests, and took off for the first time. The machine produced a heavy water spray before getting up on the step to lift off, and it proved to be extremely nose heavy in flight. Also, the cooling water came to a boil and started blowing steam. Kenworthy put it down on The Solent off Calshot Spit and sat there for about an hour before a tow launch reached him. The Pellet was towed back to the S. E. Saunders Co. works at East Cowes. Working all night, the Blackburn and Saunders crews installed a large Lamblin radiator onto the center-section strut, bypassing the underwing radiators. The Pellet was in the water ready with engine running the next day with only minutes to spare before the deadline for navigability and watertightness tests.

Supermarine Sea Lion III

The Supermarine works on the River Itchen at Woolston, Southampton, next to the Billing Yacht basin was busy building flying boats, the Sea Eagle, and working on modifications for other companies' seaplanes such as Avro, Bristol, and Sopwith. The company was not, at first, going to furnish an entrant for the 1923 Schneider contest until Hubert Scott-Paine realized there would be only two British competitors. Also, it became known in Britain that the United States was entering four aircraft that were rumored to be fast, and France had six entries. Scott-Paine acquired the Sea Lion II on loan from the Air Ministry, and designer Reginald Mitchell and his drawing staff of seven rapidly produced designs for a general modification program aimed at a cleanup to increase the fineness ratio wherever it could be done.

The hull was lengthened by 2ft, 9in (0.83m), a new planing bottom was integrated, and the nose section was refined. An estimated 400lb (180kg) increase in weight was also accompanied by a wingspan reduction from 32ft (9.76m) to 28ft (8.54m). The Napier Lion was boosted from 450 to 525hp and so the fin and rudder received increased area and were supported by an eight-wire-and-strut brace. The tail skid from amphibian operations was left on. The engine nacelle was fully enclosed with a long, round cowling for the radiators, thus providing better streamlining.

The floats were more oval, semi-flat, and self-lifting to reduce drag. They had a small pair of hydrovanes near the nose somewhat like the 1913 Nieuport's. A small glass windshield was installed in front of the cockpit, and it swung forward to ease ingress and egress. The propeller was still a four-blade but with slightly wider blades to allow for greater pitch at higher speeds. Fuel lines were routed to the engine from the hull tank inside a streamlined radiator support strut. The engine crank handle was attached permanently, on the port side of the engine nacelle. The hull was blue and wings and tail surfaces were silver. The "No. 7" "G-EBAH" markings were black on white, with the face of a sea lion painted on the nose of the hull and each pontoon.

Henri Biard was selected as pilot. He predicted that it was going to be unpredictable on takeoffs, and he was right. It wanted to lift off the water before it was ready to fly, which of course is how porpoising gets started. To achieve better control, Biard would run all-out at takeoff and then hold the nose down as it tried to bump up; then at the right speed he'd pull up and climb out. The Sea Lion handled well in the air, and he could record 160mph (258km/h) on the air speed indicator. Following the contest, Biard made a few more test flights and then the Sea Lion III was taken to the Royal Air Force (RAF) at Felixstowe, given back to the Air Ministry, and assigned serial number N-170.

The Contest Begins

At Cowes, England, on Thursday, September 27, the Schneider International Maritime Aviation Trophy contest began with the navigation tests. Prior to this, the two Italian Savoias had been withdrawn, the Sopwith Hawker had eliminated itself near Brooklands, the Navy-Wright had decapitated a float with a lost propeller blade, the Latham No. 2 flying boat was eliminated because it was nearly torn apart by would-be helpers after a forced landing, and the two Blanchards never left France. Left to compete were the Sea Lion III, the Blackburn Pellet, two Curtiss CR-3s, a Navy-Wright TR-3A, a Latham No. 1, and the CAMS 36 and 38.

Although the French team had suffered some misfortunes, the three remaining contenders looked very impressive in their navigability tests. It looked as though they were easy to handle on water even though the CAMS 36 bounced into the air early on, and fell back, hitting the water hard. This brought about some wagering by the crew on damage to the hull. It repeated the same bouncing a few more times before becoming airborne to stay. The Supermarine Sea Lion III followed, with Biard performing all maneuvers smoothly, and then was towed to the Saunders works at the mooring area.

The Blackburn Pellet piloted by Kenworthy taxied out in great style and as it passed the pier, Kenworthy waved affably to the observers. As he then accelerated to get up on the step for takeoff, the Pellet started porpoising. The Pellet porpoised several times before tilting to one side because of engine torque and high engine position and came down on its lower wing tip, pontoon, and nose, stuck its nose into the water, and turned over in a beautiful somersault. When it came to a stop, it was upside down and sank immediately. There was apprehension for his safety as the

The Curtiss CR-3 and the Sea Lion on the ramp in front of the Saunders hangar. *Hirsch Collection.* Top far left, the Sea Lion III was flown on its first test flights by Henri Biard. *Hirsch Collection.* Center far left, the Sea Lion III on the step for takeoff during the Schneider contest. Bottom far left, the CR-3 beached prior to the speed contest. *S. Hudek.*

The Sea Lion III on course during the speed contest. Biard flew low for most of the course, banking steeply around the turns. Biard flew well and obtained maximum performance from the Sea Lion III, but it was not nearly enough. US Navy Lts. David Rittenhouse and Rutledge Irvine came in first and second, lapping as much as 20mph (32.2km/h) faster. *S. Hudek*

rescue boats sped to the scene. Kenworthy had been trapped in the cockpit upside down, which created an air lock within the hull. Once he got his legs through the cockpit opening, he was able to push himself downward and egress completely and bob up to the surface, where motor launches were approaching. All this took 61sec by the timekeeper's watch. The British press was quick to rename the machine the Plummet. This was Kenworthy's second bath in the aircraft.

The Pellet wreck was brought ashore during the night by George Newman and his Saunders crew and taken back to the Saunders hangar. Kenworthy stated that he had had to swerve to avoid a couple of boats, but onlookers thought if he had been in less of a hurry, he might have gotten off OK. The racing committee was blamed by the press for entering an unproven machine with an unproved seaplane pilot. So now Britain had only one machine left.

On September 28, the day of the speed tests, the morning was calm with no clouds or haze. But by noon the wind was just enough to ruffle the water and assist the takeoffs and, being from the west, help speed the times on the first lap. Before the flying started there was a general meeting held by the British aircraft industry at the Saunders seaplane sheds where the competing machines were housed. It was generally agreed that the main hope for Britain, with the Sea Lion III as its only contestant, would be the breakdown of the two Curtiss CR-3s. Some of those at Supermarine were not too sure the Americans would run away with the contest and refused to believe the rumors of speeds in excess of 175mph (281.75km/h). Just before the tests were to begin, the warship USS *Pittsburgh* dropped anchor off Cowes. Some of those onshore said that it promptly trained its guns on the committee and town just to ensure fair play and no 1919 nonsense. Others commented that if their aim was no better than the British fleet's, it would not matter much anyway!

The American preparations were faultless. Lt. Frank Wead and Wright representative George Mead had reason to be proud of their team. Everything, down to their steerable pontoon landing trolleys and the handlers' rubber hip waders, were exactly right for the job. The French were also well organized and displayed

the characteristic French enthusiasm. D. Lorenzo Santoni, formerly from the British Deperdussin Co. and later from Italy, was the moving spirit. But he and designer Raphael Conflenti admitted that their aircraft was not fast enough because of its 360hp Hispano-Suiza engine.

Long before race time thousands of spectators lined every vantage point on the shores. The crowd was predominantly British and was there to watch their favorites perform. The Americans drew the first-off position. About 10:56am, American Navy lieutenants Rutledge Irvine and David Rittenhouse taxied out from the sheds to a point about a mile behind the starting line. As the 1min cone was hoisted on the starter's barge they stepped up their speed slightly, judging their pace. As the cone was dropped for the start, they were only about 600ft (183m) from the start line. Their engines both let out a roar and the two little CR-3s leaped for the start line and moved up on the step. The American pilots held their machines down on the water so as to make no mistakes about being on the water while crossing the line.

Irvine crossed the line about 1.5sec before Rittenhouse. Then both pilots sat their machines on the heels of the floats and leaped into the air. Then they split, with Irvine to the left over Cowes and Rittenhouse to the right over the Royal Yacht Squadron boat. On completion of the 180deg chandelle, the two CR-3s bore down on Selsey.

Several yachts were at Selsey, their occupants socializing and watching the contest. The weather was clear and Castle Point at Cowes could be seen through binoculars. An RAF D.H.9A was hovering around the turn points well above the course. At 11:05am the two CR-3s could be distinguished near Horse Sand Fort. They quickly grew larger and before the onlookers on the yachts could comprehend their speed, they roared around the turning point. Rittenhouse in No. 4 was leading slightly. They made wide turns appearing to lose mileage but not speed, which was astonishing to those watching, who were looking for steep-bank tight turns. After Lap 2 they were turning closer.

Fifteen minutes after the Americans took off, the Sea Lion III taxied out neatly between a crowd of boats moored on the south side of the reserved area. The taxi area was well controlled by the RAF motor launches and the Cowes harbor master. Hubert Scott-Paine in his comic motorboat made from a World War I flying hull and named *Tiddleywinks* led Biard to his choice spot. When the cone was dropped the Supermarine started to accelerate, and Rittenhouse banked around the marker boats.

By this time, the ripples on the water were a little larger and Biard was trying to get his machine steady on the water and quell the bouncing inherent in this machine. As he reached the start line, the machine was bouncing on and off the water but was not actually flying. As Irvine rounded the boats, the Supermarine became airborne and continued on. This, however, raised an argument among committee members. The argument grew quite fierce, with some claiming that it didn't matter anyway because it would not affect the outcome. The ultimate decision was that unless the machine could remain in the air, it was not airborne.

In another 15min, the French team started. First, Maurice Hurel on the CAMS 38 took off, circled around, and landed. He then made an excellent start by holding down on the water and lifting off slowly and smoothly after crossing the start line. The CAMS 36bis came out next and somehow bumped into a moored steam yacht. Damage was light but sufficient to put Georges Pelletier d'Oisy and the 36 out of the contest. The Latham No. 1 never came out because one of the Lorraine-Dietrich engines backfired on start, shearing off the magneto dog, and thus was unable to run. Hurel made his turns very flat and seemed to be pretty fast, but after the first lap his engine seemed to be running rough. The CAMS 38 came down on its second lap with a blown cylinder head. Race officials failed to report Hurel's absence to the other marker boats and finally, in an hour or so, sent a casual inquiry if they had seen him. Soon after, Hurel was seen about 5mi (8km) out being towed toward Cowes by a Selsey lifeboat.

Since the French challenge had collapsed, there were only three contestants remaining out of eleven. After each remaining contestant had completed a full lap the conclusion was evident. Rittenhouse was rounding each lap very close to even with 14min, 22.2sec versus 14min, 24.8sec on two of the laps and within 0.2sec on two others. The first lap was 44sec slower due to takeoff and climbout. Irvine was 20sec per lap slower. Since Irvine was faster on acceleration and slower on the speed course, it appears that the pitch of the two Reed propellers was not exactly the same. George Mead told the British press that it was because CR-3 No. 3 had stouter struts to its pontoons than did No. 4.

Biard came in third after flying an excellent circuit, but his time was almost 2min per lap slower. He flew low and racked his machine over into steep, sharp turns, especially at Selsey, which made the engine sputter due to carburetor fluid level drop. At the finish he pulled up into a high chandelle after crossing the line and then spiraled down to land close to where the Americans were stopped.

Rittenhouse averaged 177.374mph (285.475km/h). Irvine averaged 173.35mph (278.97km/h). Biard averaged 157.17mph (252.93km/h). Although the Sea Lion III was 12mph (19.32km/h) faster than the 1922 machine, it wasn't nearly fast enough.

The quantities of liquor found aboard the USS *Pittsburgh* for the victory celebration amazed everyone—especially since the United States was in the fourth year of Prohibition—and the American air crews were thoroughly lionized. Then on October 9, the jubilant team reembarked on the *Leviathan* for the five-day voyage home with the magnificent silver trophy as the centerpiece of the ship's cavernous main salon.

So the Schneider Trophy came to the United States and the NAA, for the first time, would have to host the next contest. There were many in Europe who, after witnessing the American invasion of the contest and reasoning that Americans would not let grass grow under their feet, believed the trophy would stay in the United States permanently. The winning CR-3 (A-6080) was the same machine that had won the Pulitzer Trophy in 1921 as a landplane and finished fourth in the 1922 Pulitzer behind the newer and faster designed Curtiss R-6 racers. For 1924, designing and building a seaplane that could fly well above 300mph (483km/h) were the problems facing any competitors. They would have to start from scratch. Or was it already too late?

Chapter 9

1924 Baltimore

Preparation for Nothing

The United States raised the world speed record to 266.58mph (429.19km/h) on November 4, 1923, with Lt. Al Williams piloting a Curtiss R2C-1. In 1923, American landplane racing aircraft were required to be capable of landing no faster than 75mph (120.75km/h). The NAA organizing committee merely accepted the word of aerodynamic experts that any machine of weight, wing area, wing curves, and lift-change hardware that was calculated to land at less than 75mph would be acceptable. Britain was trying through the RAeC's racing committee to get it down to 50mph (80.5km/h). All this, of course, would not affect seaplanes.

The FAI held a conference January 2-5, 1924. Countries represented were Belgium, France, Great Britain, Holland, Italy, Japan, Romania, Switzerland, and the United States. It was decided the Schneider Trophy contest would be run under the same regulations as was the 1923 contest. Closing date for entries was fixed at April 1, 1924.

In early February the NAA informed the European aero clubs that the 1924 Schneider contest would be held at Chesapeake Bay, Baltimore, Maryland, on October 24 and 25. The Navy Bureau of Aeronautics announced it would not participate in the Pulitzer or Curtiss Trophy races for that year due to funding cuts by Congress. On February 20, the RAeC met and sanctioned recommendations of the race committee. The Schneider Trophy contest was not mentioned.

Preparations

The British magazine *The Aeroplane* published information on the Italian efforts toward the Schneider contest. They named four firms that were preparing for the race: Piaggio had designed a single-seater scout with 300hp Hispano-Suiza engine which did 181.25mph (291.81km/h) in military tests; Macchi was designing a monoplane flying boat with a Curtiss D-12 engine; Dornier (a German company with design and manufacturing facilities in Italy) was designing a monoplane seaplane; and Cantieri Navale di Monfalcone was working on a design. They all had models in the government experimental department. There was a rumor of a possible monoplane entry from France's Bernard company, but it never materialized enough for a French entry declaration.

British publications and aero organizations were after any and all technical data available from NACA (National Advisory Committee for Aeronautics). They were told by the Office of Technical Assistance to NACA in Europe, that inquiries for copies of technical publications should be addressed to NACA, Washington, D.C., and not Paris.

On February 23, 1924, Charles R. Fairey, of Fairey Ltd. and chairman of the Society of British Aircraft Constructors, returned to England from the United States with a Curtiss D-12 engine and manufacturing rights to Curtiss designs. His argument in response to criticism was, "If we are to beat the Americans and regain our international prestige, the best

Lt. Christian F. Schilt on the pontoon of the R2C-2 at the Long Island, New York, Curtiss test site.
J. Albanese

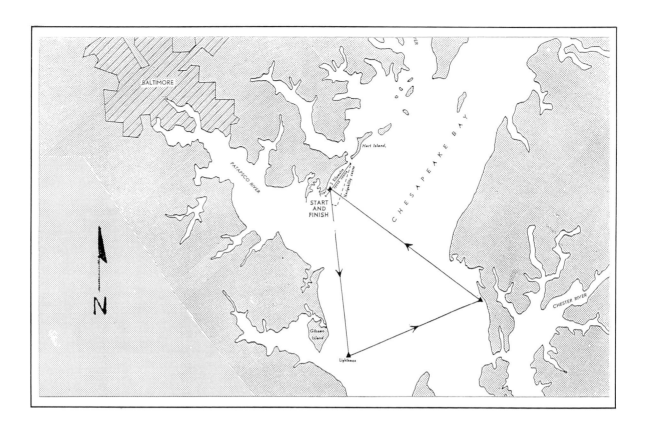

The course for the 1924 and 1925 Schneider contests.

way is to use American brains as well as our own. So let us follow the American practice and combine it with our own experience."

Based on their Bamel Mars I landplane's racing success, Gloucestershire Aircraft Company (GAC, later Gloster) was invited by the Air Ministry through specification number 37/23 to build two special racers for the Schneider Trophy contest and attempts at world speed records. One was to be a floatplane, J-7504, and one was to be a landplane, J-7505 (G-EBJZ), later named Bluebird. They were to be powered by Napier Lion Vs of over 600hp, which were already bench tested.

In April, the RAeC announced a floatplane design by Gloster, and a flying boat by Supermarine with a Rolls-Royce Condor engine. The Gloster Bamel-type racer J-7504, called Gloster II, was being assembled and readied for testing. There was a little decision making as to whether Squadron Leader Rea or Capt. Hubert Broad would make the first flight. Since Broad was smaller and lighter than Rea, he was selected. Broad took off Friday evening on a rather short run with a small amount of

porpoising. He made several circuits of the area with the machine responding well, but it seemed a little tail heavy. With less than full throttle it was doing just under 200mph (322km/h). It could easily have done the 220mph (354.2km/h) expected of it when properly trimmed and detailed.

Weather conditions were ideal and the sea almost calm. Broad came in at about 85mph (138.85km/h) and made perfect contact. All observers breathed a sigh of relief. Then it happened: the little floatplane began to porpoise, the undercarriage buckled, and the machine settled into the water and began to sink. The first thought was that Broad was hurt or killed, but he was soon seen climbing up on the tail of the little Gloster II, which was the only part left out of the water. An RAF motorboat arrived a few minutes before the machine went under and snatched Broad from the tail in a remarkable rescue. It was believed that the step on the floats was unusually far behind the C.G., causing the porpoising. There was no time to repair the machine and prepare it for the contest.

The landplane met its end on June 11, 1925, when Larry Carter was making his fourth flight in the Bluebird over a measured course at Cranwell, Lincs. This ship had a metal propeller, wing radiators, and was hoped to be entered in the 1925 Pulitzer race. As the little machine screeched down the course at something over 250mi (403km/h) about 40ft (12m) over the ground, tail flutter started. Carter chopped back on the throttle but the plane was pitching down violently and plowed along the ground for about 150yd (137m), sliding on its bent back propeller which prevented its nosing over. The plane was demolished, but Carter was gently lifted out of the cockpit after being unstrapped and rushed to an RAF hospital. He had sustained a skull fracture, broken leg, and some internal injuries. Carter was never in good health after being released from the hospital, however, and on September 27, 1926, he died from meningitis at the age of twenty-eight.

In June, Sadi Lecointe was testing a Nieuport sesquiplane racer with a 12cyl, 450hp Hispano-Suiza engine in preparation for a world speed record.

On August 3 at Sesto Calende, Italy, Alessandro Passaleva set a world speed record for seaplanes over a 1.86mi (3km) course four times, twice in each direction, at 189.6mph (303.37km/h). He was flying a Savoia-Marchetti S.51 flying boat with a 300hp Hispano-Suiza engine using Lamblin radiators.

Also in August, the US Navy officers were chosen for the Schneider contest. They were: Lt. Frank W. Wead, team captain, Lt. D. R. Henhouse, Lt. Adolphus W. Gorton, Lt. George T. Cuddihy, and Lt. Ralph A. Ofstie. Lt. L. D. Hundt and Boatswain E. E. Reber were back-up pilots. The Pulitzer Curtiss R2C-1 racers were to be fitted with floats and the two CR-3s would be back-up, but all would enter eliminating trials together.

Schneider Contest Canceled

In September the RAeC cabled the NAA, formally withdrawing the British entry from the Schneider Trophy contest. No entry was made by France, and Italy finally followed England in withdrawing. The United States was left to fly the contest by itself as had Italy in 1920 and 1921. Sadi Lecointe's Nieuport sesquiplane racer could have been put on

floats, and might have been a contender, but by this time Sadi Lecointe was satisfied with being a contender in the French landplane contests.

The NAA notified the FAI that due to withdrawal of England and Italy, the United States would not compete against itself; the Schneider Trophy contest for 1924 would be canceled. This sporting cancellation of the race by the NAA was unparalleled and the only time it was done in the Schneider contests. The RAeC cabled back its appreciation of this action and hoped they would be fully ready next year. Italy had the same comment in its response.

It was unlikely the United States would build any new machines for 1925. They had the new Curtiss and Navy-Wright racers, both capable of over 240mph (386.4km/h), which would be in storage until 1925 and then thoroughly overhauled and cleaned up.

Navy-Wright F2W-2

A third type built for the 1924 contest was the Navy-Wright F2W-2 developed from the 1923 Pulitzer racers. It used the N-9 airfoil, a thinner modification of the Gottingen 398 airfoil, which was low drag but too thick. It had

The NW-2 on its launch dolly. Note the size of its floats relative to airframe size. *Hirsch Collection*

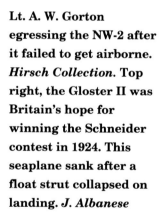

Lt. A. W. Gorton egressing the NW-2 after it failed to get airborne. *Hirsch Collection.* Top right, the Gloster II was Britain's hope for winning the Schneider contest in 1924. This seaplane sank after a float strut collapsed on landing. *J. Albanese*

the T-3 engine, which was developed from the T-2 and was rated at 675hp at 2000rpm for service aircraft, but was rated at 750-775hp at 2200rpm for racing. It had run for 50hr on a test stand. The F2W-2 was a newer, cleaner design using a three-blade propeller and wing lowered onto the fuselage. The hump on top was the water expansion tank connecting the engine to the redesigned wing radiators. Dimensions had been altered slightly from the F2W landplane racers.

Lt. Adolphus W. Gorton was selected as pilot by Lt. Comdr. Marc A. Mitscher. The completed machine was shipped to the Naval Aircraft Factory in Philadelphia and began its testing on the Delaware River. Gorton was briefed by the engineers to land at 110mph (177.1km/h) since the F2W-2 was calculated to stall at 90mph (144.9km/h). The F2W-2 was expected to top 255mph (410.6km/h).

For the F2W-2 first flight, Gorton lined up in the river and eased the throttle open. The three-blade propeller churning the pontoon spray made a larger spray which engulfed the engine as the machine gathered speed. With the stick fully back and full-right rudder, Gorton waited for the machine to ease up on the step. The rudder, however, was insufficient to counter the torque, so the machine just slid somewhat sideways into a circle to the left and

Gorton discovered he was 90deg from his start position. He cut back on the throttle and lined up again. The little pontoon racer never got up on the step or gained directional control. Also, the fine spray got into the engine compartment, causing it to misfire. Gorton tried twice more, then returned to the slope area to be towed in. He told Team Captain Wead and Navy project engineer Lt. Edward W. Rounds that there was not enough rudder to hold it straight against the engine's torque.

Gorton tried again for three days but was unable to get the F2W-2 up on the step. It just plowed through the water, fouling the engine and turning uncontrollably to the left. Gorton asked to be relieved from the project but Wead said he would try himself. He did, and with the same poor results. That convinced Rounds, who finally had a slightly wider rudder made and put on the machine.

On October 11, 1924, Gorton taxied out to the center of the river, lined up, and checked that he was clear. He eased the throttle open to 1200rpm and let the racer pick up speed. Finally he was able to keep the machine straight, and gently got it up on the step with floats skimming over the water, leaving thin white streams behind. The airspeed indicator showed 100mph (161km/h) and so he opened the throttle and pulled back on the control stick. The F2W-2 leaped into the air and climbed out at a steep angle. Before Gorton looked out from inside the cockpit, he was almost 5,000ft (1,524m) over New Jersey.

He noticed he was turning only 1495rpm at 180mph (289.8km/h)—Wow! This is going to be fast! Gorton thought. Gorton then pushed the throttle wide open and found that even with opposite rudder and aileron, the little racer rolled over on its back. He cut back on the throttle and rolled it back upright and decided to take it back in. The gauges now indicated 140mph (225.4km/h) slowing to 130mph (209.3km/h) as he descended toward the Hog Island shipyard; he maintained power enough to control rate of descent. He could tell the machine was tailheavy, as the 1923 NW-2 had been.

Gorton planned to touch down on the Jersey side of the river and, although he was pleased with his 140mph (225.4km/h) approach, he

CR-3 on the bay near Bay Shore Park, Baltimore, for the 1924 speed runs. *S. Hudek.* Left, the Curtiss R2C-2 being launched into Chesapeake Bay, Baltimore, for a Navy air show. *Hirsch Collection*

The R2C-2 being prepared for a speed run. These R2C–2 models had the C–12A engine of 500hp. *Hirsch Collection*

was displeased with the machine. What he didn't know was that some crewman installed the overwing surge tank vent facing backward. As he cut the throttle to settle in, a surge of scalding water filled the water expansion tank and a blast of hot steam hit him in the face just as the floats touched the water. The machine bounded into the air and started to settle back, wobbling onto the surface. By sheer instinct, Gorton ducked his head back into the cockpit, saw 100mph (161km/h) on the airspeed gauge, and shoved the throttle open. The little racer flipped over on its back again and Gorton came back on the throttle and settled in upside down. When he broke clear and bobbed to the surface he had only sustained a bruised ankle.

A tugboat was close enough to be there in minutes and a deckhand threw him a ring life preserver and then hauled him aboard. He was upset over the whole affair but was calmed down with whiskey until they got him ashore. The F2W-2 followed the fate of the other three Navy-Wright racers and would not

compete in a Schneider contest. Thus, the Wright company's efforts in air racing came to an end. Unable to match Curtiss in developing high-output engines, their T-series production also came to a halt. Charles Lawrence became president of the company in 1925, and the radial engine became their focus.

Baltimore Naval Seaplane Races

When it was learned that the Schneider Trophy contest would be postponed, the Bureau of Aeronautics decided to put on a show the public would remember. This show was the Baltimore Naval Seaplane Race, held October 25, with a seaworthiness test on the twenty-fourth. There were to be no less than a dozen events, some with cash and trophies. One was sponsored by the *Baltimore Sun* newspaper. The sponsors of the Baltimore Naval Seaplane Race Committee were R. W. Alexander, president of the Baltimore Flying Club, and Maj. William D. Tipton, secretary of the club. It was through their efforts with the Naval Air Committee of the Bureau of Aeronautics and the Navy that the organizational planning was accomplished.

The United Railways and Electric Company provided use of their amusement resort at Bay Shore Park, which bordered Chesapeake Bay about 14mi (23km) from Baltimore, to the flying club for the month of October. The long pier extending out into the bay made a perfect grandstand for all the events. The shoreline was crowded with private seaplanes; the owners were given the whole 10mi (16km) of Chesapeake Bay to display their machines. The Navy prepared a stupendous air pageant with sixty planes. The city of Baltimore, through the support of Mayor Howard W. Jackson, provided transportation and accommodations for an expected crowd of 30,000 people and 10,000 cars. It also provided some financial assistance. The state of Maryland spent $16,000 on preparing Logan Field, erecting two new steel hangars for the National Guard Air Unit.

On October 24 there was a handicap race for the *Baltimore Sun* trophy for civilian seaplanes and flying boats. There was also a race for torpedo military aircraft of the US Navy scouting fleet; as well as navigability and seaworthiness tests for those to compete or fly on the twenty-fifth.

On October 25 there were demonstrations of all types. To give the public an idea of the speed capabilities of the seaplane racers, the two CR-3s were brought out at Chesapeake Bay and flown over the Schneider Trophy course. The plane flown by Lt. Ralph A. Ofstie set a record speed over 62mi (100km) at 175.8mph (282.86km/h). He went on to 310mi (500km) averaging 161.138mph (259.27km/h), having throttled back to 150mph (241.5km/h) in order to stretch his fuel to complete the final three laps. Lt. George T. Cuddihy dropped out after covering 124mi (200km), then did four runs up and down the speed

course averaging 188.129mph (302.765km/h). On October 26 a straightaway speed contest was held over a 1.86mi (3km) course at Bay Shore Park. A total of thirteen world records were broken at the event.

The two CRs had been pushed to their limit and were retired from service. They were dusted off briefly in 1925, however, for use as crew trainers for that year's Schneider team and then transferred to the Naval Aircraft Factory at Philadelphia. They were stripped of wings and floats and then destroyed in the course of static airframe stress tests.

Previously, on September 27, a Curtiss R2C-2, A-6692, with a 500hp D-12A engine and flown by Lt. David R. Rittenhouse averaged 227.5mph (366.28km/h) over a 4.26mi (6.86km) course at Port Washington, Long Island, between Stepping Stone Light and Execution Light. It was in test configuration with all kinds of items projecting like oil and fuel pipes, socket joints, filler caps not covered, or any detailed streamlining before racing. Fuel tanks were added to the pontoons and control surfaces were increased over the land version of the R2C-1. On the downwind passes he did 242mph (389.6km/h). This machine was held back and put into storage for the 1925 contest.

In mid-November the RAeC of Britain's race committee met and drafted a racing program for 1925. The program included: Easter Meet at Hendon King's Cup race, Aerial Derby, Grosvenor Challenge Cup, Air League Challenge Cup, and an international speed contest. No mention was made of the Schneider Trophy contest.

For America's military racers, 1924 was not a good year. Pilot Burt Skeel was killed in the R-6 when it tore apart while diving for the start of the Pulitzer race at Dayton, Ohio. Then Alex Pearson died when the former Navy R2C-1, redesignated R-8, lost a wing in a dive.

Chapter 10

1925 Baltimore

Doolittle Becomes the New National Hero

Seaplanes are of two general types: flying boats in which a boat hull and aircraft fuselage are combined, and pontoon seaplanes where floats are separately attached similar to the landing gear. The early hydroaeroplanes with small, flat-bottomed floats used a third float on the tail and were flown much like an aircraft with tailskid. Actually, float design for high-speed racing planes is an intricate, complex task almost as difficult as the racer design itself. In either case, the step integrated into the design increased the drag about 10 percent.

Flying-boat hulls have generally adhered closely to hull designs of naval architecture. The boat-hull design was not the best aerodynamically speaking, however, and after much frustration for the Schneider races through 1923, the boat integrated hull began to give way to the pontoon system. This year saw the last of the boat-hull racers for Schneider contests in the Macchi M.33.

Float models in the NACA 20ft (6.1m) wind tunnel showed the drag coefficient (Cd) on maximum cross-section area to be 0.092 to 0.130 for those with rounded top decks and 0.119 to 0.158 on flat-deck floats. The round-deck floats were of lower drag. Because pontoons produce more area up front close to the aircraft nose, larger vertical stabilizers were needed for ample directional control. The added fin below the fuselage or added area on top was not for torque compensation, but for air stability. Early floats were constructed of wood; the shift to metal was gradual. In the

Curtiss shops for the Schneider preparation, two pairs of floats were constructed. They were identical except one pair was primarily wood and the other was metal. The wood floats failed at a pressure of 17,500lb (5,335kg) and the metal floats failed at 27,700lb (8,445kg). Thus the American Schneider aircraft went to England with metal floats.

Torque was also a problem to contend with, and various methods were devised to overcome it such as carrying all fuel in the top float, offset wing designs with one span longer than the other, or one pontoon was larger and set farther forward than the other.

The polar moment of inertia, or static balance, is not the only concern in propeller function; what is called dynamic balance is what matters when the body is rotating. Both blades must be identical in every respect and they must track properly. On a stand, both propeller tips must pass the same point when rotating. As for methods of offsetting torque, the most usual method is to build in "washout," or a decrease in angle of incidence toward the wing tips, which creates relative lower lift and turning moment. The washout may also be accompanied by a "wash-in" on the opposite wing. However, these are drag-creating features and so for high-speed racers, unequal weight distribution about the longitudinal axis of the machine was preferred. Whichever method may have been used, there would have been an upset of balance when the engine was throttled back and torque diminished.

Jimmy Doolittle in the Army's R3C-2. This was the only time the Army entered in seaplane racing. Doolittle won every race he entered except the 1931 Thompson Trophy contest, when his engine gave out. *USAF*

Lt. George T. Cuddihy on the pontoon of the R3C-1. This racer was used for public relations pictures with all the US team pilots. The R3C-1 used the new Curtiss V-1400 of 619hp and a Reed drop-forged aluminum propeller. Flying R3C-2 A7054, Lt. James H. Doolittle averaged 229.982mph (370.271km/h) while winning the 1925 Schneider contest. His teammates, Ralph Ofstie and George Cuddihy, were running second and third in the other two R3C-2s before mechanical failures forced them to quit the contest. *C. Mandrake*

Another aspect of development is the powerplant. The hardest years for the aircraft engine industry were between 1919 and 1925. Military requirements were small and despite a great deal of enthusiastic pioneer work, civil aviation had not yet produced much business for engine manufacturers. At the end of the war, the unfavorable commercial outlook resulting from war surplus and general desire for disarmament left the few surviving engine manufacturers struggling to keep going. The hardest hit were engine manufacturers in Great Britain and the United States; those in France and Italy were able to continue developing newer engines. The greatest catalyst to the technical development of the water-cooled inline engines, especially in Britain and Italy, was the Schneider Trophy contest. In the United States it was first the Pulitzer and second the Schneider contest. Other than for racing, the air-cooled radial became dominant.

The early internal-combustion engineers were not fuel conscious. Petrol, as the Europeans called fuel, was specified merely by its specific gravity and brand name. The anti-knock values varied between 50 and 60 oc-

tane. The reason for lack of fuel development was the wide use of the rotary engine up to the end of the war. Many mechanical improvements upped the power, like the Bentley BR.2 double-valve 9cyl of 240hp, used from 1917–1918. The whole future of the piston engine depended on the quality of fuels and lubricating oils available. Air racing was the testing ground and contributed much to the progress.

It is of interest that the world's speed record of 278mph was set by the Bernard Ferbois racer on December 11, 1925, with a 450hp Hispano-Suiza engine using pure benzol for fuel and castor oil for lubrication. Benzol is a slower burning fuel and so its anti-knock value is much higher. It also must be noted that burning benzol deposits a fine hard soot similar to emery dust. If this dust gets past the piston rings and into the oil system, it grinds away the bearings at a remarkable rate. A race engine burning benzol would need new rings, valves, and all lubed surfaces almost after every big race.

Early in 1925, the Hawker Engineering Co. at Kingston-on-Thames was founded after liquidation of Sopwith. Tom Sopwith and Fred Sigrist were the managing directors in the new firm. Also, in early February, the NAA notified all concerned aero clubs that the 1925 Schneider Trophy contest was due to take place at Chesapeake Bay, Maryland, the same venue as that of the previous year. The date would be finalized and announced by March 1.

The British Effort

The RAeC announced that British entries had to be registered with them by Monday, March 23, accompanied by an entry fee of £10 and deposit of £100. On March 27, the RAeC cabled Washington entering their challenge for the Schneider Trophy at Baltimore the next October. Earlier, in mid-February, the RAeC canceled their Easter air racing meet, but the committee sanctioned the King's Cup race for July 3 and 4. As usual, the RAeC entered only two machines in the Schneider contest and didn't try to recruit a third company to build. With such wealthy members and a little prodding, there might have been a third new design.

Gloster III

In February, the Air Ministry placed orders with Gloucestershire worth £16,000 covering the design and production of two aircraft. They were to use the 700hp Napier Lion VII engine, and they were to be the smallest aircraft for its power ever built in Great Britain. By mid-March the two new Gloster racers were being built. One was to be for the Schneider contest and one for the Pulitzer race. They were serial numbered N-194 and N-195. The sister ship to the ill-fated Gloster II of 1924 was being tested by Larry Carter at Marlesham. It was intended to go to America as a practice and back-up machine, as was the slower Gloster I.

Supermarine S.4

Also in February, the Air Ministry placed an order with the Supermarine works at Southampton to develop and build a Schneider machine to be the second challenger. Since the concept of this machine was new, and being under the Air Ministry, it was placed on the "Secret List." The instructions to go ahead with construction, after detail design review, were given on March 18, and flight testing was scheduled for August 25. Work began on

March 25. It was a real achievement to turn out a machine of entirely new design, with several novel features, and get it into the air in just five months. This machine was designated S.4, serial number N-197, and licensed G-EBLP, and was the product of Reginald J. Mitchell. The press and the public did not see the racer until its flight testing.

The S.4 was a full-cantilever, mid-wing monoplane with the fuselage built in three sections: the engine bay mounting structure, the center section with integral wing, and the rear monocoque section. The vertical and horizontal stabilizers were integral with the fuselage. The rear monocoque shell was of spruce skin laid diagonally over light-plywood formers. The wooden center-section formers joined two A-frames that attached to the forward and aft sections. Covering was with duralumin sheets, as was used for the engine cowling. The small cockpit was well aft of the wing.

The wing was a single piece with two spars, covered with plywood and attached to the two A-frames. It contained ailerons and flaps that could be operated together or separately. Wing loading was in the neighborhood of 23lb/sq-ft (112.9kg/sq-m), although some later wing loads topped 40lb/sq-ft (200.18kg/sq-m). The S.4 was the only Schneider racer equipped with flaps. The symmetrical RAF-30 wing section had been developed in collaboration with the Royal Aircraft Establishment at Farnborough where a sample had been tested to destruction. There were two troughs running spanwise to about half span on the forward bottom sides of the wing. These were for housing the two Lamblin-type radiators. The wing passed through and was secured to the two A-frames.

Lieutenant Cuddihy in the cockpit prior to the contest navigability tests. *S. Hudek*

The Army's R3C-2 preparing for a speed contest. Lt. James H. Doolittle is third from right. This and the Pulitzer contest were Doolittle's baptism in air racing. *J. H. Doolittle*

The single-step floats were of all wood construction with a deep, concave vee bottom. The steel-tube struts to the fuselage had aluminum streamlined glove with large fairings at the fuselage joint. They were welded to the two A-frames and had a center cross bar for rigidity.

The S.4 was powered by a Napier Lion VII direct-drive engine of 680–700 hp. The propeller was the Fairey-built Curtiss-Reed two-blade propeller with a small pointed spinner to form the bullet nose. The oil cooler was on the underside of the fuselage with only the fins exposed to the slipstream.

The Supermarine-Napier S.4 piloted by Capt. Henri Biard broke the world speed record for seaplanes on September 13 by flying four times, twice in each direction, over a 1.86mi (3km) straightaway at Calshot, England. Its average speed was 226.752mph (364.844km/h) with one passage at 231.406mph (372.564km/h). This was the first time in British history that they held a top speed record.

The Italian Effort

Both Macchi and Piaggio firms were building Schneider Trophy machines to compete in this year's contest. There were two types of Macchi machines that would evolve into a pos-

sible contender. One was the M.33 monoplane flying boat fitted with a 450hp Curtiss D-12 engine. The wing was in three sections with the center section integral with the hull. The engine was mounted above the center section by steel tubes. Radiators were of a new type, and the pilot cockpit was just aft of the engine mounting. This machine had an estimated speed of 186.3mph (300km/h).

The second Macchi was the M.27, a sesquiplane with a thick lower wing of very small span which was built into the lower part of the hull. It acted as a balance float while on the water. The upper wing was braced from the hull by diagonal rigid struts and a central cabane that also carried the engine nacelle. The engine was positioned mostly above the wing, somewhat like the M.17. The M.27 was to use either the Fiat 450hp engine or a Curtiss D-12 and was to have a maximum speed of 205mph (344km/h). Wing area was 179sq-ft (16.7sq-m). The M.27 was never completed for the contest. The Italian government limited its support finally to the Macchi company in the form of lending it the two D-12 engines bought in 1924, and so Macchi organized and financed Italy's entry to a large degree.

The Piaggio P.c.3/P.43 was a low-wing, full-cantilever monoplane on twin floats. It also was to have either a Fiat or Curtiss engine and had an estimated speed of 184mph (294km/h). As it turned out, the Piaggio machine was not completed in time so the two Italian challengers left Genoa on September 26 on the steamship *Conte Verde*. Both machines were Macchi M.33s. Giovanni De Briganti and Riccardo Morselli were the pilots.

The American Effort

The US Army Air Service newsletter on April 20 reflected that the Army Air Service, Navy Department, and Bureau of Aeronautics were cooperating in the procurement of suitable high-speed planes to defend the Pulitzer and Schneider trophies. It stated that continued international racing both recognized engineering talent and served as a valuable school for development, and provided a stimulus to public interest in aviation in general. Butting heads in the past three years of racing, while it shot up the speed marks rather rapidly, had proven both expensive and embarrassing. So in 1925 the Army and Navy shelved their rivalry and agreed to work together.

They were looking to jointly procure three planes: one plane for each service, and one to be held in reserve for whomever would need it. A fourth plane would be partially built for destruction testing and safety features. The racers were to be delivered in early September, in time for the Pulitzer race and for the Schneider contest which was to be held the latter part of October.

Never one to tamper with success, Curtiss stayed with the same construction techniques as for earlier record-setters. They included plywood skin over wooden internal structure, flush-brass wing radiators, and an upgraded Curtiss engine. The new airfoil was a Curtiss C-80 with a 6 percent thickness-to-chord ratio, giving maximum lift and minimum drag at the expected speed-range attitude.

The proven D-12A engine was replaced by the V-1400, which had increased bore and stroke of 1/4in (6.35mm) each. External dimensions were the same, but the engine was 30lb (13.6kg) lighter and engine speed was raised to 2525rpm, developing 619hp. The new machines were designated R3C-1 in the land version and redesignated R3C-2 with pontoons. Since parachutes had become mandatory, there were knock-out sections built around the cockpit for emergency escape. They were operated by the pilot pulling wire pins from a single handle.

The Reed propeller was drop-forged from duralumin rather than machined from a slab twisted to the right pitch. The pontoons had the Curtiss philosophy of ruggedness, probably at some small cost in speed. The apparent difference was their vee bottom. The CR-3's pontoons were mounted at an included angle of 155deg and were rather poor shock absorbers on landing. The R3C-2's had a deeper vee angle of 120deg and provided a little smoother sink-in on landing.

On September 11, the first of the racers was moved out of the Curtiss factory for flight testing. It was to be tested by both Army and Navy pilots. Lts. Al Williams of the Navy and James Doolittle of the Army flipped a coin to see who would be the first to take it aloft. Williams won the toss and made the first flight on ship number A-6978. This and A-6979, which was delivered on October 7, went to the Navy. The Army got A-7054. Foul weather forced a two-day postponement of the Pulitzer from October 10 to 12. This delay gave Curtiss a break, allowing A-6979 and A-7054 to be readied barely in time. Williams also won the toss with Capt. Cy Bettis for first flight on the Army machine.

The R3C-1 weighed 100lb (45kg) more than the R2C and had some bugs to be worked out on the first flights. Williams on his first time up lost a wheel cover in flight and the other on landing. After repairs, Doolittle took it up. He noticed the stick kept pushing to one side, and looking out at the ailerons he saw one wing tip pulling up outside the radiators. He quickly cut power, slowed down to approach speed, and brought the little racer back to the factory airport. It was repaired again and in the course of wringing it out, Doolittle and Williams reached some very high speeds. On September 22, while Bettis was running some tests, the propeller spinner broke into pieces tearing a hole in two sections of the wing radiators. This time when it was returned to the factory for repairs it was also mounted on floats in preparation for the upcoming contest. It was on this machine that most of the pictures were taken with the pilots standing on the floats.

Pulitzer Races

October 12 was a dark, cold, windy day. Williams was in the Navy's blue and gold racer with a white "40" painted on the sides. Bettis was in the Army's black and orange racer with "43" painted on its sides. The two were the only contestants in Heat 1 of the Pulitzer. Williams took off first and Bettis followed 2min later. Then Williams barreled by Bettis just after his takeoff and as he settled down on the course, Williams flying full out and Bettis getting his engine warmed up to the task before pushing his machine for all it was worth. Bettis picked up speed on each lap while Williams' speed fell off. Williams was banking steeply and pulled the racer in around the pylons, gaining a little altitude in each turn. Bettis made turns wider and in a slight dive, losing about 50–60ft (15–18m) in each turn. Bettis won the heat with a speed of 248.975mph (400.6km/h). Williams averaged 241.695 mph (388.89km/h). The engines had barely cooled before work began to ready both

machines for the Schneider Trophy contest, which was scheduled for October 24. Heat 2 was flown by Curtiss PW-8s and a Curtiss P-1.

If no greater speed could be extracted from the R3C-1 by Bettis and Williams in the Pulitzer, then American hopes for a Schneider win were anything but sure. Bettis put up a speed just 5mph (8km/h) faster than the R2C-1 in the 1923 Pulitzer race. Williams was the pilot of that win, but this year he was 2mph (3km/h) slower and in a newer, more powerful racer. However, the weather conditions were bad with gusty winds, and the engines were not up to top condition. Also, maximum power was not available because of the short preparation time.

The Schneider Contest

The site for the contest was Chesapeake Bay and an inlet to the Susquehanna River at Bay Shore Park where base operations were established facing the bay. The course was triangular over the Patapsco River inlet to a lighthouse southeast of Gibson Island, then east by northeast to shoreline and back northwest to Bay Shore. The triangle was 31mi (50km) in length and was to be flown seven times, which meant there would be twenty pylon turns.

The British team and their aircraft arrived on October 7. They were the first team to arrive, allowing time for sufficient preparation and practice flights. They soon discovered the site was not ready, however, the contractors had not completed the essential launch facilities nor erected the tents that served as hangars and workshops, so it was impossible to start. The Baltimore Flying Club had built the site from scratch. The gradual slope of the beach dictated shallow water for quite a distance out. The river bottom was dredged, and a slipway was built so machines could be towed on cradles in and out of the water. Wooden floors for the tents with work benches were erected. Six days later, Hubert Broad was able to practice taxiing on the bay in the Gloster III. After his first flight, the machine's vertical stabilizer was made larger, and it was redesignated Gloster IIIA.

Henri Biard managed some flights on the sixteenth in the S.4. Then on October 17, an autumn gale swept over the area with gusts up to 60mph (97km/h), collapsing the tents

ALT
NO LOSS

SPEED
LOSS
5-6MPH

PYLON

SPEED LOSS
2-2.5 MPH
ALT LOSS
50-60 FT.

1000 FT

DOOLITTLE'S
PATH

OTHERS

COURSE HEADING

erected only a few days earlier. A heavy tent pole fell and struck the tail unit of the S.4, damaging it and causing the Supermarine team some sleepless nights to get it ready for the Friday, October 23 navigability trials. The storm also created a faulty ignition system on Macchi M.33 registered MM-48, which eventually prevented Riccardo Morselli from starting on the twenty-third. On October 22, the first day of allowed trials, Biard took the S.4 out to undergo the navigability test and seaworthy trials.

Weather was ideal with calm sea and almost no wind. After becoming airborne, Biard made several sharp turns banking onto the vertical and back opposite while circling the tent area. He seemed to be checking out the tail repairs before heading for the judges' cutter. Then Biard thought he felt a slight shiver of the wings being transferred to the airframe, but it was so slight he didn't give it a second thought. (He was just recovering from a case of influenza.)

Coming back over the pier area in a sharp bank at about 800ft (244m), the S.4 seemed to develop wing flutter and spectators realized the machine was in difficulty and not under control. Within seconds Biard, half in control, brought the racer down, managing a somewhat horizontal attitude in a falling leaf descent until it hit the water. The impact smashed the float struts and the S.4 turned over and came to rest upside down in shallow water. Biard rose feebly to the surface and paddled away from the wreckage. Hubert Broad saw the splash and hurriedly taxied the Gloster IIIA over to the scene. He was the first to arrive, but was of little help. Biard, slightly dazed, was picked up by a launch within minutes and brought ashore.

The weather allowed the navigability trials to be held on October 23. The second Gloster IIIA was finally assembled and at 5:00pm Herbert Hinkler took it up for tests but a wing-bracing wire snapped, forcing him to come back in and try to get repairs in time to complete tests the same day. However, owing to darkness setting in team leader, Capt. Charles B. Wilson ordered the tests to end for that day.

The Schneider Trophy contest was to take place on Saturday, October 24, with the Naval Air Pageant starting at 12:30pm and the speed contest to start at 2:30pm. From a unanimous appeal made by the rest of the competing pilots, the judges and Ericson, the referee, allowed Hinkler to make another attempt at navigability. He was up early and taxied out for the start. But 0.5mi (800m) offshore the water surface was too rough and spray fouled the engine. Hinkler was towed back to Bay Shore Park and beached.

It was apparent that the weather was becoming worse, with high east winds, gusts up to 60mph (97km/h), and heavy rain. Everything onshore was being lashed down, but seven out of seventeen Glenn Martin built SC-1s (torpedo seaplanes that came to be part of the pageant) were torn from their moorings and wrecked beyond repair. So the contest committee wisely postponed the events until Monday, October 26. The judges and stake boats clearly were doing everything possible to help the contestants compete. This meant being at Bay Shore Park early for a third morning. Some supporters had to leave Baltimore at 3:00am to make it in time.

On the twenty-sixth the weather was moderate and Hinkler was up early. At daybreak he again took out the little Gloster IIIA in an attempt to qualify. He got off clean without any difficulty, circled twice, and headed for the beginning of the course where he had to land and complete the compulsory taxi tests. He de-

Lieutenant Cuddihy in the R3C-3 preparing to launch for a familiarization test. *US Navy*. Bottom, a diagram of Doolittle's race-winning technique. Doolittle flew a wider course and cut closer to the pylons, losing less speed in the corners.

Aircraft	Race No.	Country	Motor	Pilot
R3C-2, A-6978	1	USA	Curtiss V-1400	Ofstie
R3-C2, A-6979	2	USA	Curtiss V-1400	Cuddihy
R3C-2, A7054	3	USA	Curtiss V-1400	Doolittle
Supermarine S.4, N-194	4	Great Britain	Napier Lion VII	Biard
Gloster IIIA, N-194	4	Great Britain	Napier Lion VII	Hinkler
Gloster IIIA, N-195	5	Great Britain	Napier Lion VII	Broad
Macchi M.33, MM-48	6	Italy	Curtiss D-12A	Morselli
Macchi M.33, MM-49	7	Italy	Curtiss D-12A	De Briganti

Note: The Gloster I, J-7234, Bamel on floats was not erected in time to qualify.

The Macchi M.33 in construction at the factory near Milan, Italy. Several modifications were made on this aircraft before it left Italy. The M.33 was a monoplane flying boat with a 450hp Curtiss D-12 engine. Two M.33s were entered in the contest, but only De Briganti's MM-49 started. MM-49 was reliable enough to finish the contest, earning De Briganti third place. *Hirsch Collection*

scended for the first 0.5mi (800m) taxi test. The surface out on the bay was still rough with waves 2–3 ft (0.6–0.9m) high from the previous storm. The machine landed safely, but the waves pounding the pontoons bent the steel float struts and the machine settled in the water, with the turning propeller cutting holes in the floats. Hinkler was towed and beached at Bay Shore Park. Thus, the second contender from Britain was eliminated. Now there was only Broad to represent England and De Briganti to represent Italy against the three Americans.

Later in the day the weather actually became ideal for the contest. The water surface at Bay Shore was still a little choppy, but not rough. By noon the wind had died down, and was coming from the right direction, the water became smoother, and the early morning haze had burned off. Since 10:00am the contestants had been testing their motors and preparing their machines for the afternoon contest. However, it was quickly noticed that one of the Macchi engines was not functioning properly. Since the rules prohibited any repairs or adjustments, Riccardo Morselli, the pilot, just walked over to the hangar and cried.

What was left of the Naval Air Pageant started promptly at 12:30pm. A squadron of Navy planes flew in formation over the spectators and Lt. Frank H. Conant thrilled the thousands of spectators with some fancy maneuvering. The torpedo bomber group show was withdrawn due to the losses from the storm. A TC-5 US Army airship from Aberdeen Proving Ground soared overhead like a huge, majestic silver fish. It finally took up a position and hovered motionless over the starting line just before the contest start.

The five remaining machines were put into the water just before 2:00pm. The sun shone

brightly and glistened on the shiny racers. Cy Bettis roamed through the crowd in full flying clothes ready as a back-up for Doolittle. Promptly at 2:30pm, Doolittle left the hangar ramp and taxied to the starting position. As he reached the rougher water, a good-sized spray pounded his aircraft. Doolittle was allotted 5min—2:35–2:40pm—to taxi across the start line. Promptly at 2:38 he taxied across the starting line; then, giving it full throttle, the roar of the Curtiss engine signaled his takeoff to judges and observers. After a short run on the step he hauled back on the stick, making a perfect takeoff, and into a steep climb until about 300ft (91.5m). He then set course for his first turn, intending to keep outside by about 1,000ft (305m).

The other contestants followed at about 5min intervals, with none of the contenders having any trouble becoming airborne. Hubert Broad's Gloster IIIA followed at 2:41pm, just as Doolittle was completing his first lap. Lts. George Cuddihy and Ralph Ofstie were at 3min intervals. The low monoplane wings of Giovanni De Briganti's M.33 were only a couple feet over the water, and the aircraft gave the spectators a thrill with its long run and smooth lift-off. Now with the Macchi airborne there were five contestants on the course, and it was beginning to look like a real contest. From the beginning, it was apparent that Doolittle would be a runaway winner. He was cutting so close to the pylons, the judges could feel a little breeze of air just after he passed.

For the first time in a Schneider Trophy contest, the vast crowds at the various vantage points along the Bay Shore Park were kept informed of the contest's progress. Announcements and commentaries by the local flying clubs were being given through a newly installed public-address system. They informed spectators within a minute or two of the lap completions for each competitor, including the average speeds. These details were also posted on several bulletin boards as the information arrived. This, the roar of the engines, and the high-pitch whine of the propellers proved to be a feature that made the contest exciting for the spectators.

Hubert Broad was trying hard to cut his lap times to a minimum, but found himself slipping outward on each turn, consuming extra seconds. He was below 200mph (322km/h) on each lap, and since Doolittle passed him once he knew his only chance to win was for the Americans to drop out. De Briganti was flying the graceful M.33 beautifully on the turns, but the tired D-12 engine was not developing its maximum power. He was taking the longest times on each lap while producing the slowest speed. The flying boat looked like a commercial aircraft instead of a racer.

Cuddihy was turning the second fastest laps, and Ofstie about 4mph (6.4km/h) slower in third position on the scoreboards. The contest was beginning to look like another interservice rivalry instead of international competition. Then halfway through the sixth lap a magneto shaft broke, forcing Ofstie down on the course 5mi (8.1km) west of Huntingfield Point. Beginning the seventh lap, Cuddihy's oil temperature started rising. He hung on hoping to complete the lap, but the gauge showed a rapid climb in temperature. Finally, with the oil supply depleted, the engine first started smoking and then froze up. With the propeller still forcing the engine to turn, Cuddihy had to cut the throttle back to stop fuel flow and grab the fire extinguisher. He was fairly busy until he got the machine on the water. This put Broad in second place and De Briganti in third. As Doolittle crossed the finish line he zoomed up a couple of thousand feet, circled back in a spiral, and leveled off, setting down in a perfect landing. He then waited to be towed in.

When De Briganti crossed the finish line he continued on course instead of landing. The judges thought at first he didn't know he had finished, that he had misunderstood the signals. Actually, he had seen that Cuddihy and Ofstie were down out on the 31mi (49.91km) course, and he flew out there to give assistance. However, both had been taken in tow and moved toward Bay Shore Park. De Briganti, in searching for them, ran out of fuel and had to set down almost where Ofstie had been. He was soon towed back to Bay Shore Park and for his good sportsmanship received an ovation in Baltimore.

Doolittle pushed the winner's speed up about 54mph (86.89km/h) over the previous contest. Broad's speed was about 20mph (32.18km/h) over the 1923 contest. Even De Briganti had beaten all previous flying-boat records.

The next day, October 27, over a 1.86mi (3km) straight course in front of Bay Shore Park, Doolittle set a new speed record for seaplanes at 245.71mph (395.35km/h). He wrote a report, NACA Report No. 203, which was a detailed account of how to get the most speed out of a machine in pylon racing. It was widely read and the data was used by the whole racing community.

This was the first and last time the Army entered a seaplane speed contest. Had the Army not won, Biard would have taken the trophy back to England. The Napier Lion engine was exceptionally reliable and that was borne out in the contest. Britain came to America with high hopes and prospects of a win. Now, one fact they had to accept was that they were simply outclassed. This was a bitter pill to swallow. But on their return home to

Contest Lap Speeds

Pilot	Machine	Lap 1	Lap 2	Lap 3	Lap 4	Lap 5	Lap 6	Lap 7	Average Results
Doolittle	R3C-2	223.157mph (359.283km/h)	228.75mph (368.288km/h)	230.239mph (370.685km/h)	231.28mph (372.361km/h)	231.705mph (373.045km/h)	232.168mph (373.790km/h)	232.572mph (374.441km/h)	229.982mph (370.271km/h) —first place
Broad	Gloster IIIA	194.275mph (312.783km/h)	196.432mph (316.256km/h)	198.104mph (318.948km/h)	198.921mph 320.263km/h)	199.091mph (320.537km/h)	199.183mph (320.685km/h)	199.169mph (320.662km/h)	197.882mph (318.590km/h) —second place
Cuddihy	R3C-2	211.53mph (340.563km/h)	216.254mph (348.169km/h)	218.206mph (351.312km/h)	219.404mph (353.240km/h)	220.031mph (354.250km/h)	220.452mph (354.928km/h)	out	217.68mph (350.465km/h)
Ofstie	R3C-2	207.959mph (334.814km/h)	213.453mph (343.659km/h)	215.264mph (346.575km/h)	217.155mph (349.620km/h)	218.307mph (351.474km/h)	out	—	214.43mph (345.232km/h)
De Briganti	M.33	166.813mph (268.659km/h)	161.113mph (259.392km/h)	165.148mph (265.888km/h)	166.962mph (268.809km/h)	167.773mph (270.115km/h)	167.93mph (270.367km/h)	168.444mph (721.195km/h)	166.312mph (267.762km/h)

London on the SS *Minnewaska* the team began expressing their sentiments and views and began to explore ways to narrow the margin and build their capability for winning the trophy back. While foreign buyers admitted British workmanship was among the best, workmanship is nothing without performance. And the most visible signs of performance are winning the great air race trophies and holding world records. At that point, England held none of these.

The British press was adamant that if Britain expected to compete and win, the British teams would have to come out of the military and they would need more training. The companies would need to conduct more testing, and the RAeC would need to become more involved. The Americans had been flying fast seaplanes for a year before the contest. Neither Biard nor Broad had 2hr in their machines before the contest, and Hinkler had entered the contest with only two short flights on his machine. Also, the temporary tent hangars were leaky and rickety and late being erected, so the accommodations slowed up assembly and test and caused the reserve machines not to be assembled. The danger of damage due to weather kept them crated until the last minute. There also was a shortage of crewmen for all machines, so attention was given to the machines that needed it most.

The Italians also took defeat bitterly. But through defeat came many lessons. The use of obsolete American engines, half worn out from test-stand research by Fiat, and expecting their reliability simply was not good planning. Although the M.33 was the first full-cantilever-wing monoplane to compete successfully in the Schneider, the flying boat was not the best configuration for a racer. This was the last boat type to be entered in the Schneider contests. The Italians knew full well from their observations that next year the racer would have to be on floats. They also arrived at a conviction that the next racer would have to be a monoplane. During their trip home, sketches were being drawn up even before the team reached Italy.

The economic implications of this year's contest inevitably led the aero clubs to exchange views and considerations for changing the rules and pattern of future Schneider contests. Many aviation industrial experts be-

lieved it was essential to maintain such spectacles, while others doubted they offered an ideal testing ground. However, all agreed that the contests stimulated some great strides in technical and scientific progress. Both the British and Italian governments were being urged to get involved immediately or America would accomplish a third win and keep the trophy in the United States.

There was much discussion in England over what had transpired and what was to happen next. Some of the discussions came out during the second half of the tenth meeting at the sixty-first session of the Royal Aeronautical Society which met in London on January 21, 1926. Air Vice-Marshal Sir W. S. Brancker introduced Maj. J. S. Buchanan who was their representative for the contest in America. Buchanan then presented a paper on the Schneider Trophy race of 1925.

The summary pointed out that the speeds had increased from 45.4mph (73.1km/h) in 1913 to 234mph (376.8km/h) in 1925. That is, in a span of twelve years speed had increased fivefold. From 1913 to 1914 speed nearly doubled. From 1921 to 1925 it doubled again. There were two contributing factors to such progress, the sport and spectacular viewpoint, and the technical and scientific progress, part of which could only be attributed to racing. The spirit of rivalry in racing can be relied on to increase the rate of progress.

The paper also noted that in England little had been done to design real racing machines as was done in the United States. The development of high-speed aircraft was an essential part of the experimental work of the Air Ministry and this just so happens to coincide with existing rules for the Schneider Trophy contests. After the Gloster II failure, it was realized that the experience to be gained justified the allocation of monies for work of this nature.

Obviously, one of the most important tasks is to train the pilots for the contests. It is of little importance for the designers to cut down resistance to gain 5–10mph (8–16km/h) and lose the same through lack of pilot training. It appeared that Doolittle did not exceed a 4g acceleration during the race and on that basis a calculated load factor of 8 appears adequate. This was countered by discussion from builders: as engine and aerodynamic improve-

ments drive speeds upward there comes the question, how much acceleration forces can a pilot stand? It seems unwise for the Schneider contest to develop into a test of pilots' capabilities and not of the seaplanes'. There is little doubt that load factors of 10–12 will someday be required. It may be that a five- or six-sided course will be needed in the future. A pilot cannot look straight down on the pylon in a turn, but must look down at some angle. If he doesn't stay low, he creates a larger turn radius and will lose time in keeping the mark point in view during the turn.

Major Buchanan stated that weight reduction will accrue very little in speed; body drag must be reduced by both airframe size and increased efficiency in wing radiators and propellers. Industry designers stated: A reduction in engine weight brings a further reduction of structure weight of above 40 percent of that amount. This means that wing and tail areas and cubic capacity of floats can all be reduced in proportions, thus reducing air drag. If the designer is not careful how the wings are attached, resistance can easily be doubled by the turbulence. The same applies to all other attachments to the fuselage. It is important to improve the form of the fuselage and reduce its frontal area, a principle concern for the engine designer. You cannot divorce the design of the machine from the design of the engine. Also, it is easy to lose 5mph in just the choice of an airfoil.

Buchanan also noted that the US Navy used benzol and gasoline at a 50:50 ratio. The Army has not, even to the Navy, let it be known what they used. But both Navy machines had their engines break down. Also, the American Reed R-type propeller blades were much stiffer at the tips and were less susceptible to distortion due to air loads, and so a higher efficiency was expected. This propeller was first flown on September 8, 1925, and so it was impossible for Blackburn to furnish the British teams in time.

Another point was that races of this nature required ample facilities, and suggested that it was the duty of the trophy holder to see that such facilities were available. The trophy holders should not delegate such responsibilities to any other body, and the FAI should not permit such delegation. This pertained to the tent facilities at Bay Shore Park and the devastating storms. The NAA representative attending pointed out that the American teams endured the same hardships and therefore the facilities did not have that much influence on the final outcome.

The M.33 up close, with De Briganti in the cockpit taxiing out for tests. The Curtiss D–12 engine and side radiators show clearly here. Top left, the Macchi M.33 sitting on shaped blocks after a storm. Notice the board launch ramp. *Hirsch Collection*

35509

Chapter 11

1926 Hampton Roads

American Swan Song

Advances in speed from 250mph (402.5km/h) were much harder to achieve and required larger increases in power and thrust than those below that speed. This is because drag increases geometrically with speed while engine power was being increased arithmetically.

In a race, seconds may be lost without thought, but they are precious. For instance, the 8sec between first and second place in the 1923 Pulitzer race translated into a linear distance of an amazing 2,800ft (854m) separation and 1.89mph (3.04km/h) speed difference. The pilot of a high-speed plane didn't have to think much faster than when he was in a slow machine, but he did have to plan and look ahead more. He had to move his operations forward mentally and raise his line of vision to compensate for the rate at which he was eating up distance. The small air eddies near earth caused bumps that slammed the machine around with a force and suddenness that made the pilot wonder how the machine stayed together. If he tried to correct for each jolt with the controls, he would have a miserable time. These small, light racers required gentle guidance and would generally fly themselves. After flying at high speed for any length of time, some pilots would circle the area a few times at low speed, about 100mph (161km/h), to get accustomed to handling the ship at slow speed before landing. Most of them had very little time aloft in the racer they were flying. Instruments were kept to only the essentials. They included tachometer, water temperature gauge, oil temperature gauge, cronometer, airspeed pressure gauge, fuel pressure gauge, fuel level indicator, and oil pressure gauge (on later racers).

Compass or turn-and-bank indicators were not needed. The pilot went around the course as many times as was necessary to spot and memorize where each small land or sea marker was located.

During winter 1925–26, it was decided that 1926 would see the last of the service-sponsored international contests. The Bureau of Aeronautics and Adm. William Moffett for the Navy, under pressure, criticism, and threat to cut funding from members of Congress, prompted the decision. The Army had no intention of trying to repeat its past performance. The US government was backing out of competition about the same time European governments were getting involved. On September 12, 1925, President Calvin Coolidge announced the appointment of a President's Aircraft Board. Then the Air Commerce Act of May 1926 left the military with no competition funding. The Morrow Board findings were designed to gratify Coolidge and fostered the 1926 five-year plan for aviation.

The Schneider contest had become the premier sporting event of the aeronautical world. The best designers of Europe and America were producing seaplanes that would be faster than each previous year, and world speed records were being established annually. It is not surprising, then, that many commentators were becoming cynical about the annual

The R3C-3 while at the Naval Aircraft Factory undergoing an engine run-in test. The 700hp geared Packard engine allowed smooth contours of the engine cowling, reducing drag. This aircraft flew in the 1925 contest as R3C-2 A-6978. After the 2A-1500 Packard engine replaced the Curtiss V-1400, the plane was given the R3C-3 designation. *US Navy*

The 1926 Schneider contest course. Bottom right, the R3C-4 showing its pontoon keel runners and stress wires. This airplane was a modification of R3C-2 A-6979, which flew in the 1925 Schneider contest. The aircraft had been overhauled and fitted with a Curtiss V-1550 engine. This engine had high-compression pistons and was timed for fuel that was at least 80 percent benzol. When Lt. Carleton Champion tried to fly the plane with a 40 percent gasoline, 60 percent benzol mixture, the engine destroyed itself through detonation and overheating before lifting off the water. *Curtiss Motor Co.*

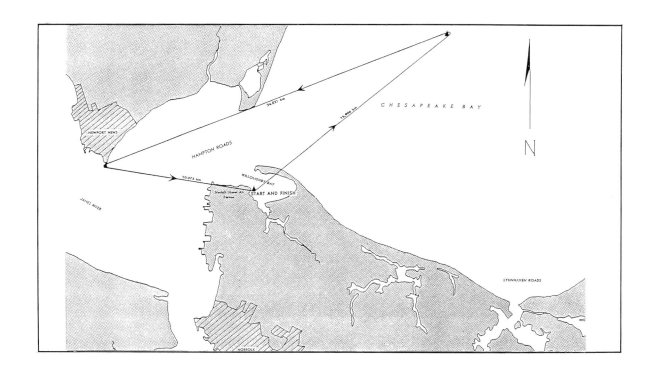

event. Those countries that lost had nothing but sour grapes to read in their newspaper reports. However, those that criticized had missed the deeper significance than that of establishing speed records and winning trophies, which in themselves would hardly be worth spending the money on.

The Curtiss PW-8 was the fastest pursuit plane in the world. It was a direct descendant of the R-6 and was further developed into the P-1 series. The R-6 was a direct descendant of the CR-series. Lt. Rex Stoner averaged a speed of 167.92mph (270.35km/h) in a PW-8 on the 128mi (206.08km/h) Pulitzer course in 1924 at Dayton, Ohio. Top speed was 180mph (289.8km/h) with a high-compression engine and 171mph (275.31km/h) with a low-compression engine. The Curtiss D-12, V-1400, V-1550, and Conqueror engines were considered the best in the world, and the Reed propeller was sold to and built by companies all over Europe. This was all due to intensive development of racing aircraft by the Navy and Army in the previous five years.

In retrospect, it was obvious that in the decade following World War I even the so-called operational groups in the services were merely service-test units. At that time it was rare that a pilot was not a pioneer in some way. It was also rare when a production aircraft was not at least temporarily modified for some new equipment test. Trailblazing flights and competition contests were as enlightening to the services as they were spectacular to the public.

For the American defense of the Schneider Trophy for 1926, the three racers to be selected would be the same machines: the R3C-2s that flew the 1925 contest. The Army turned theirs over to the Navy. This year, however, each racer would have a different engine. The R3C-2 (A-7054) that Doolittle had flown retained its V-1400 engine. A high-compression Packard 2A-1500 was installed in A-6978, and it was redesignated R3C-3. The third machine, A-6979, received the Curtiss V-1550 and was redesignated R3C-4. For get-ready, the R3C-2 had been flown in by Lt. George Cuddihy from the Naval Aircraft Factory at Philadelphia, where it had been overhauled. It was joined by two reserve F6C-3s, A-7147 and A-7128. These were used by the American Schneider team as practice machines and for course familiariza-

tion. Cuddihy returned to the team flying with Frank H. Conant and Marine 1st Lt. Harmon J. Norton.

The pontoon design of the Macchi racers was somewhat different than that of the US Navy racers. The bottoms of the American pontoons formed more of a straight vee, that is, they had flat surfaces, or sides. The Italian pontoons were designed with a sharp, concave-sided vee bottom, which had the effect of reducing spray in takeoffs and landings. It was already noticeable that the Italian machines rode smoothly, whereas the Curtiss racers tended to pitch somewhat, giving the impression of porpoising.

Wright field engineers realized that a substitute for water in aircraft cooling systems would be very advantageous. Using fluid with a higher boiling point could provide a much greater temperature drop and provide more effective cooling. The greater temperature difference between the high heat generated by the engine and the coolant fluid carried out through the radiators would provide greater cooling efficiency. This would be a boon to high-altitude operations. Radiators in service aircraft created as much as 20 percent of the parasitic drag. By substituting ethylene glycol at a 2:1 mix ratio with water, higher operating temperatures could be used and coolant quantity could be reduced from 18 to 4gal (68.22 to 15.16ltr). This reduces the radiator core in size

The R3C–4 at Long Island prior to delivery to Hampton Roads, Virginia.

and weight, reducing drag. The P-1B was first tested with this coolant and the P-6s in 1929 used it as well. But it wasn't until the P-6E that its use became widespread on service-type aircraft.

In England, Air Vice-Marshal W.G.H. Salmond stated Britain was close enough to the Americans in design and performance to rebuild and be competitive. But all that would be for naught if the RAF didn't provide and train pilots for the next team. Then Sir Hugh Montague Trenchard, the Chief of Air Staff, restated his belief that the RAF service pilots should not be entered in private races. He did, however, back the go-ahead with production of high-speed seaplanes.

The RAeC, stating there was not sufficient time to design and build again for the 1926 competition, asked the NAA to postpone the next contest until at least spring of 1927. The problem was that the preparation time regulation of the FAI was not already drawn up for the next contest, and couldn't be until the FAI met in Paris in 1926. Then the rule could only be applied to the 1927 contest; the 1926 contest was still the obligation of the NAA.

The Italian and French aero clubs, although differing somewhat, requested once again a cargo-carrying requirement. France wanted 552.5lb (250kg) and Italy wanted 884lb (400kg) and a minimum control speed of 70mph (113km/h). When it met in January 1926, the FAI turned down both requests and the Schneider was to remain a pure and simple speed contest.

There had been questions within the NAA and the Bureau of Aeronautics as to whether the Italians would be ready in time to compete in the contest. However, the progress of construction in both airframe and engines was such that the Aero Club of Italy did confirm to the Americans in mid-August that they would be ready and able to compete on the scheduled date.

On September 13, Lt. Harmon Norton went out for a practice test flight and was killed when his CR-3 (A6081) stalled and spun into the Potomac River near Anacostia. He was replaced by Marine 1st Lt. Christian F. Schilt. As the October 24 race day approached, Italy requested additional time. Although their aircraft were ready, they needed some extra time to organize. The delay was granted, and November 11 was set as the new race date. This also gave Curtiss more time to work on their R3C-4. The next two and a half weeks were well spent, with both nations honing their skills and capabilities while getting their machines into top shape and watching each others' practice flights.

Frank Conant had been making practice flights over Long Island Sound. On October 30, he was flying from Long Island to Norfolk in an F6C-3 floatplane. He was on the last leg of his trip, headed for Cape Charles, and had dropped down to just a few feet above the water. As he was skimming just above the small wave swells he barely could see Norfolk on the horizon. He was offshore at Winter Harbor near Mathews, Virginia, about 12–13min out of Breezy Point, when suddenly a tremendous unexpected jolt occurred and the F6C-3 plowed into the water, end-over-end. Conant was thrown out of the plane and he died instantly. The plane disintegrated. When all motion stopped, some F6C-3 remains floated on top of the water. The cause for the accident was never identified. A few days earlier, Conant had set an unofficial speed record for seaplanes at 215.5mph (347km/h) in an R3C-4. Also, on May 14, he had won the Curtiss Marine Trophy race at Washington, D.C., and was alternate pilot for the R2C-2 in the 1925 Schneider contest.

On November 11, a sudden change in the weather caused conditions that involved serious risk to pilots and machines during navigability tests. After a joint meeting on November 10 with pilots of both teams, the contest committee decided to move the speed contest to Saturday, November 13. Qualifications resumed late Thursday afternoon, when the high winds finally subsided, and continued into Friday.

The R3C-3 as a racer was even more involved than its description indicated. It was the fastest of the three machines. It had made 258mph (415.12km/h) over a 0.87mi (1,400m) marked course. It had a cleaner, completely redesigned engine cowling with the thrust centerline on the airframe centerline and the 700hp Packard engine turning up 2800rpm. It also had more streamlined pontoons installed. But it wasn't without its pitfalls. The engine was geared and so it turned the propeller counterclockwise, opposite the Curtiss engines

in the other machines. This turned a spirited but manageable racer into a monster, causing the pilots a host of headaches every time they strapped themselves in for flight.

On Thursday, November 11, Lt. George Cuddihy took the R3C-3 out for a test flight. The propeller had been straightened after being bent the day before from heavy water spray on a rough sea. To avoid damaging the propeller again, he cut his engine just prior to landing. Spectators on the beach thought he was experiencing engine trouble, but he managed a smooth landing. While Cuddihy was aloft, Schilt, detailed to fly the R3C-2, No. 6 (A-7054), took it out for elimination trials and completed the tests. He was then moved out for the water-tightness test; he left the mooring tie-up at 4:45pm. Three minutes later Lt. Adriano Bacula started his trials. Watching the American and Italian machines in the sunset presented a striking spectacle. Both machines were beached after their moorings at about 11:00pm.

Late Thursday afternoon, Maj. Mario De Bernardi was carrying out his trials. He was

The R3C-3 being launched for its ill-fated test trial. *US Navy.* **Top far right, the R3C-3 at the Curtiss plant. This was the only R3C series aircraft that did not have a Curtiss engine. Instead, it was powered by a 700hp Packard engine.** *Hirsch Collection.* **Bottom far right, a Navy crew holding the R3C-3 during engine run-up prior to launching.** *US Navy*

not up long because it was growing dark and came in to land. A naval launch went out to meet him and tow him to his mooring spot in front of the Italian hangar situated at one end of the beach at the air station. However, the motor launch, in getting a tow line on the Macchi racer, ran into its starboard pontoon, puncturing it just above the waterline. The racer was towed ashore and repaired. Since the Americans had caused the accident the NAA contest committee waived the flotation rules and the repaired machine was placed back in the contest. Actually, the pontoon was replaced with a spare, and the M.39 was launched back into the water the next morning while the damaged pontoon was being repaired.

About 5:15pm, when it was nearly dark, Lt. Arturo Ferrarin started his trials, anxious to get his mooring done that night in the calmer water. He sped out across Little Bay in his M.39 and satisfactorily completed his first flight and taxi test. Then he went out for the second flight, but failed to return. A Navy motor launch headed out in the direction of Chesapeake Bay, followed by one HS2-L flying boat piloted by Patrick J. Bryne. Bryne soon spotted Ferrarin floating around among the ships anchored at Hampton Roads, with a dead engine. By this time it was almost dark and neither pilot could understand the other. Fearing the little crimson racer might get run down by a ship, Bryne proceeded to taxi circles around the racer for over 2.5hr.

Since neither seaplane had any lights and it was by then very dark, Bryne set his carburetor mixture lean so his engine spat flames out its exhaust ports whenever a vessel came into sight. This proved to be effective until motor launch arrived and took the M.39 in tow and back to the air station. This concluded Thursday's flying activities. The M.39 was beached, and the crews worked all night to get the machines' engines ready for Friday's trials.

At 4:15pm Friday, November 12, the M.39 with De Bernardi set out across Little Bay from the naval base and rose gracefully for its navigation trials. His test consisted of a short flight, a landing, and taxiing over a 0.5mi (800m) stretch at over 10mph (16km/h). It was successfully repeated. Since there was no established time for being airborne in the trials, pilots took advantage of this being their last flight before the speed contest and gave their planes a brief full-throttle test. The machines were then put out for the 6hr mooring float test. Earlier in the afternoon Ferrarin took his M.39 up for his trials and finished satisfactorily. The Italians, overall, were very impressive in the air and on the water.

On Thursday, November 11, the only uncertainty in the Navy camp was who would fly the R3C-4. It still was the machine the Navy camp felt had the best chance because of the V-1550 engine. To compensate for the greater engine displacement and the higher compression pistons, the R3C-4 had additional radiators wrapped around the float struts. But during the test flights these proved to be unnecessary and they were removed before the contest. There were three alternate pilots from the team to choose from: Lt. Carleton C. Champion, Lt. W. G. Tomlinson, and Lieutenant Henderson.

Although it had been announced that Champion would fly the contest in R3C-4, the official position within the camp Thursday evening was that by 9:00am Friday the team captain would announce who was to fly the R3C-4. On Friday morning George Cuddihy seated himself in the cockpit of the R3C-4, and Tomlinson climbed into the R3C-3 for official press photos.

Since Tomlinson was the unlucky pilot to be assigned to the R3C-3, he took it up for his first flight. He was eased down the ramp into the water while riding on the beaching wheel dolly handled by sailors on hard lines. The wind was blowing almost due east and Tomlinson, leaving the slipway, started off well, into the wind. He was barely able to cope with the torque stability problems since the torque effect swung the nose to the right, opposite the direction on all the other machines. In taking off he wallowed and bounced and almost overturned, but he did get it up on the step and airborne. From there he seemed to have everything under control. He logged only a half hour, but may have flown a bit longer feeling the plane out. Then he came in to land and, when he was just over the field edge, a civil service plane operating from the station got in his way.

Tomlinson went around and lined up again for another try. This time he came in well, ac-

cording to spectators on the beach. However, this time he cut his power while still too high and tried to land about 15–20ft (4.58–6.1m) above the water. The R3C-3 dropped in too hard, tearing some skin off the starboard pontoon, and bounced back into the air with a large hole in the bottom of the pontoon. When it came back down and touched the water the starboard pontoon scooped in water and dipped further in. Still doing 50–60mph (81–97km/h) Tomlinson attempted to raise his wing tip as it was dropping. The machine then appeared to do a side somersault to the left and turned completely over. Tomlinson climbed out before the machine settled down with only the floats showing. Within seconds he was on top of one of the pontoons waving to shore. He was only about 900ft (300m) offshore in Little Bay. An HS2-L flying boat happened to be in one of the slips with engine running, and it immediately took off to rescue him. Tomlinson suffered only a cold drenching and a deflated ego. The R3C-3 was quickly salvaged, and hauled aboard a naval ship. It was later scrapped. Tomlinson went straight back out for the tests in an F6C-3 and qualified it for Saturday's contest.

Champion was assigned to take the late Frank Conant's place. Champion had flown the Wright Apache F3W-1 Navy fighter with a Pratt & Whitney Wasp engine and the Wright-Bellanca at the National Air Races. Champion proved to be a headstrong egocentric, which led to the Navy's undoing. The V-1550 race engine had high-compression pistons and was timed for pure benzol, or at least 80:20 while not racing.

When Champion arrived for his first flight he objected to using pure benzol because it was thought to cause carburetor icing. However, anything less for the high-compression V-1550 would cause detonation. This caused a heated argument between Champion and Bill Wait, a civilian specialist. Wait refused to fuel the R3C-4 with the 40 percent benzol, 60 percent gasoline mixture that Champion wanted to use, so Champion ordered the military enlisted crew to do the job. Bill Irwin of Curtiss also tried to reason with Champion. A telephone conversation with Arthur Nutt in Buffalo assured the two civilian engineers that the mixture would quickly ruin the engine. But it was too late: Champion was moving

Lt. Arturo Ferrarin standing on the float with a tow rope getting ready to beach his M.39. *A. Coccon*

down the slipway with the engine already detonating from the 40:60 mixture. As he taxied into Little Bay the engine was heating and clatter could be heard all the way to shore. Then, pointing the racer into the wind Champion opened the throttle for takeoff. The little racer lurched forward and then an agonizing metal scrapping sound was heard on the beach. The racer balked like a wounded duck and clouds of smoke and steam shot upward into a geyser.

The R3C-4 was quickly hauled ashore for inspection. Radiator headers were bulging and several sections along the wing surface were ballooning from steam pressure. Engine pistons were burned clear through from the detonation and the propeller could be freewheeled. Frank Russell was flown to Garden City, New York, by Charles S. "Casey" Jones in his Curtiss Oriole racer. Arthur Nutt had already obtained another engine and drove all night with a new V-1550 from Buffalo to Garden City. But this new engine was lacking the special high-compression pistons and delivered about 50hp less. The tough .005in brass of the ballooned radiators was carefully pounded back to contour. The new engine turned a higher rpm than it should for the race so Champion was removed from the team by Admiral Moffett.

The Contest

On Saturday, November 13, the weather was almost perfect at Hampton Roads, Vir-

ginia, and a crowd estimated at 30,000 gathered to watch the Schneider contest.

The high state of readiness and precision in American teamwork that was so noticeable in the previous three years was lacking and apparent to any observer. Even though the Italians had less time on the course than did the Americans, they appeared confident and ready, much like the US team did in the 1923 contest.

Shortly before 2:30pm the Naval HS2-L flying boat set out to patrol the center of the course to render assistance whenever it might become necessary. This flying boat remained out during the entire contest circling in the center of the triangular course and above the racers.

The starting line was established between the home pylon mounted to the barge and a timer's stand on the extreme northeast corner of the flying field. The starting line-up was decided by drawing lots and was posted as follows:

Aircraft	Race No.	Pilot	Country	Time (pm)
M.39	1	Lt. Adriano Bacula	Italy	2:30-2:35
F6C-3	2	Lt. W.G. Tomlinson	USA	2:35-2:40
M.39	3	Capt. Arturo Ferrarin	Italy	2:40-2:45
R3C-4	4	Lt. G.T. Cuddihy	USA	2:45-2:50
M.39	5	Maj. Mario De Bernardi	Italy	2:50-2:55
R3C-2	6	Lt. C.F. Schilt	USA	2:55-3:00

Capt. G. Guasconi of Italy was a reserve pilot. All were experienced pilots and members of the Regia Aeronautica.

Bacula began warming up the Fiat engine of his Macchi racer at about 2:28pm and was let down the slipway at approximately 2:35pm. He taxied rapidly across the starting line and quickly climbed out onto the course. He took from 20–30sec on the takeoff, which was about the same for all three Macchis. Tomlinson then crossed the starting line in the Curtiss Hawk at 2:38pm. Shortly after, Bacula's machine came into sight out on the horizon speeding along the 14.9mi (24.021km) leg toward the Newport News pylon.

The next machine scheduled to leave was Ferrarin's No. 3 Macchi racer, but he was having some trouble with engine warm-up, causing a delay, so Cuddihy taxied out across the starting line and took off in the R3C-4 after the drop of the starter's red flag in the mark boat.

On the day before the contest the hand pump for transferring gasoline from the pontoon tanks to the main tank had been sticking on the R3C-4 racer. It was a standard pump and was replaced with a similar pump Cuddihy had brought along in case of an emergency. The new pump was tested and considered satisfactory, and Cuddihy started the contest feeling satisfied that all was well with the R3C-4.

One minute later Ferrarin took off in the Macchi. By this time Bacula had completed his first lap, averaging 209.58mph (337.42km/h). This was slower than Doolittle's speed in 1925.

The first realization that the contest was going to be Italian dominated was when De Bernardi completed his first lap at 239.44mph (385.5km/h). The Americans were not yet far behind, however. Cuddihy was now averaging 237.76mph (382.79km/h) and had turned lap two at 241.61mph (388.99km/h). Schilt, after a slow first lap of 224.17mph (360.91km/h) was somewhat steady at about 232mph (373.52km/h).

At the conclusion of his third lap, Ferrarin had completed 93.17mi (150km), but as he crossed the home pylon it was obvious his engine was not operating satisfactorily. Ferrarin left the course and circled beyond the hangars, coming in for a landing into the wind with his engine throttled back to idle. His oil temperature had risen rapidly, and he wisely set it down, having flown for 23min, 37.2sec. On inspection the problem was found to be a broken oil line.

It was noticeable how much wider the Italians were taking the pylon turns. The Curtiss racers were following the turning system set up by Jimmy Doolittle in 1925, coming quite close to the pylons in their turns. The Italians chose to fly wide and in some cases were about 200yd (183m) from the pylons. If De Bernardi had cut closer like the Navy pilots, his time might have been faster.

On his third lap Cuddihy noticed his fuel gauge down to 25gal (94.75ltr) and started operating the hand pump to bring the fuel up from the pontoons. But the gauge kept showing the main tank decreasing, and so Cuddihy just pumped harder. The pump was having no effect on replenishing the main tank and on the seventh lap it ran dry and the V-1550 stopped running. He had completed two-thirds

Ferrarin's M.39 being prepared for the 1926 contest. The three Macchi racers had large white race Nos. 1, 3, and 5 on their bright red fuselages. *A. Coccon*

of his last lap and was running a close second place. His right hand was swollen and blistered from continual pumping and on inspection after beaching, both tanks were full. The V-1550 engine was running very well for the part of the contest that it ran. This was the second time Cuddihy had been forced down on his final lap almost in sight of the finish line.

De Bernardi's speed gradually increased on each lap, although his fastest lap was number three at 248.520mph (400.117km/h). On his sixth lap he came by the home pylon considerably higher than earlier. His oil temperature gauge indicated an overheating problem so he climbed up to 600ft (183m) in an effort to cool the engine. Then on his last lap he came down low and shot across the finish line for a lap speed of 247.202mph (397.995km/h). Schilt came in second with a steady 231.36mph (372.49km/h). Bacula came in third at 217.962mph (250.919km/h), and Tomlinson in the Hawk came in fourth averaging 137.019mph (220.601km/h) and a full lap behind Schilt. For a standard fighter put on floats, the Hawk's speed wasn't bad.

The complete results of the contest by lap speed and resulting average are as follows:

Lap Speeds

Lap No.	De Bernardi	Schilt	Bacula	Tomlinson	Cuddihy	Ferrarin
1	239.443mph (385.503km/h)	224.172mph (360.917km/h)	209.584mph (337.430km/h)	137.312mph (221.072km/h)	232.427mph (520.718km/h)	234.631mph (377.756km/h)
2	247.071mph (397.784km/h)	232.056mph (373.61km/h)	217.410mph (350.03km/h)	141.429mph (227.701km/h)	241.611mph (388.994km/h)	243.012mph (391.249km/h)
3	248.520mph (400.117km/h)	232.902mph (374.972km/h)	218.062mph (351.08km/h)	140.116mph (255.587km/h)	240.991mph (387.996km/h)	237.582mph (382.507km/h)
4	247.103mph (397.836km/h)	233.164mph (375.394kɪn/h)	222.664mph (358.489km/h)	136.763mph (220.188km/h)	238.575mph (384.106km/h)	—
5	247.886mph (399.097km/h)	232.225mph (373.882km/h)	220.370mph (354.796km/h)	137.557mph (221.467km/h)	242.160mph (389.878km/h)	—
6	248.492mph (400.072km/h)	232.785mph (374.784km/h)	215.574mph (347.074km/h)	132.587mph (213.465km/h)	241.199mph (388.330km/h)	—
7	247.207mph (398.003km/h)	232.514mph (374.348km/h)	222.070mph (568.789km/h)	133.366mph (214.719km/h)	—	—
Average	246.389mph (396.686km/h)	231.403mph (372.558km/h)	217.962mph (350.919km/h)	137.019mph (220.607km/h)	239.494mph (385.585km/h)	238.425mph (383.864km/h)

The NAA held a banquet at the Hotel Monticello in Norfolk on the evening of November 13. NAA President Porter H. Adams officially turned over the massive Schneider Trophy to the Italian team. Approximately 300 attended and cheered on Mario De Bernardi as he stood to receive the gold plaque as a symbol of his performance in the contest. In reply to the ovation, De Bernardi spoke in his native tongue, which was translated by Commodore J. L. Callan, USNR, who was on duty as liaison officer to the Italian team. Lt. Frank Schilt received a silver plaque for second place. Mario Castoldi of Macchi and Ettore Ferretti of Fiat, designer of the As.2, were there as well. It must have been with pride that De Bernardi sent a telegram to Benito Mussolini: "You order to win at all cost has been carried out." Back came a reply: "To you and your fellow teammates, Italy sends her greatest applause for the superb victory." The US magazine *Aviation* wrote, "We were overconfident." The Curtiss company cabled Macchi and Fiat companies congratulating them on their victory.

The Italians had demonstrated their mastery of structural problems in a high-speed seaplane racer. They deserved all the credit they would get. For the five originally built M.39s, Italy had a good plan and preparation for this year's contest attempt. Both Macchi and Fiat had incurred high costs, but they did finally get support from Mussolini and Gen. Italo Balbo, an Italian aviator and politician. The first two M.39s had the 590hp Fiat A-22 engine installed and were designated as practice machines and airframe proof test vehicles. The first flight was flown by company test pilot Romeo Sartori on June 6. But the first flight of an M.39 with the Fiat As.2 engine was toward the end of August. The team pilots trained at the Schivanna Air Station on Lake Varese which was near the Macchi factory.

Fiat had studied and tested the Curtiss CD-12 in 1925 prior to its being installed on the Macchi M.33. It then designed a V–12 engine designated A-20, which became the A-22 having a rating of 550hp and 590hp for takeoff power. The next development was the 750 and 800hp A-25. But this powerplant was too large for Castoldi's M.39 being built for the Schneider contest. Since the A-22 dimensions were suitable for the new racer, the concentrated ef-

fort went to upgrading this engine. Changes involved increased bore and stroke, rpm, compression ratio, plus other improvements. This became the As.2, which was the engine used in the Schneider contest.

The propellers for the Italian machines were Reed forged duralumin. Those on the Curtiss racers were the R type. Italy contracted with Reed to meet their engine specifications. The Italians used new B.G. Midget spark plugs as did the R3C-4 in its V-1550. The Curtiss V-1550 used a Splitdorf magneto while the Hawk used the standard Scintilla magneto.

Since the Packard V-1500 was the only American engine that was different from those used the previous year, and it had some features worth mentioning. Being geared, it put the propeller shaft in the middle of the engine allowing much smoother cowling and some propeller efficiency increase.

The bearing load was a high 35,000psi, which yielded excellent results. Weight of a complete cylinder was 9.5lb (4.32kg) and it developed nearly 60hp. Valve springs were unique. Instead of the double arrangement of the concentric springs, a series of small piano-wire springs were arranged in planetary fashion around the valve-stem guide. There were seven springs to each valve and each spring was located over tubular guides welded to a lower fixed washer. The upper ends were secured in an annular groove of a movable washer. This had been used with perfect results on Packard racing engines, eliminating breakage problems at extremely high engine speeds. The reason is that the small-diameter springs had a natural period of vibration much higher than the conventional valve-spring system, so the destructive "dancing" of the springs is avoided.

Italy used the M.39 to attempt to set a world speed record in 1926. It achieved 282mph (454km/h). Of the five machines built—MM-72, 73, 74, 75, and 76—three had the As.2 800hp engine and two had the A-22 550hp engine and slightly larger wingspan for transitioning to the high-speed floatplane system. Two were destroyed in crashes with pilots Lieutenant Borra and Vittorio Centurione. The other three were used as trainers for the newer racer being developed. The Macchi M.33s MM.48 and MM.49 were sold to the Regia Aeronautica and used at Sevola Alta Velocita (an Italian company that trained pilots for seaplane operations) as trainers for modern flying boats.

Two crewmen crank the inertial starter on Lt. W. G. Tomlinson's F6C-3 before the start of the Schneider contest. *A. W. Yoskin Collection.* Above left, Maj. Mario De Bernardi being beached after winning the speed contest in the M.39. *A. Coccon.* Top far left, Commandante Marchese Vittorio Centurione, the Italian team captain in the M.39 trainer on Lake Varese. On September 21, he was killed when he stalled the M.39 and it crashed into the lake. *A. Coccon.* Center far left, the M.39 trainer with its cowling removed showing the Fiat As.2 engine. *A. Coccon.* Bottom far left, the only remaining M.39, now in a Milan museum. *A. Coccon*

119

Chapter 12

1927 Venice

British Determination and Italian Complacency

The question of annual or biennial contests came to a head during December and January 1927. The FAI called a special meeting in Paris on January 25, 1927, where a decision was reached between the three countries involved: the United States, England, and Italy. The NAA wanted the contest held in 1928. Italy wanted it in 1927, and England backed Italy, opting for the biennial events to start in 1927. Britain by this time had had two and a half years of development since the 1925 defeat and saw an opportunity to put their experience to practice.

There was a flurry of activity in Italy, with the Aero Club of Italy occupied mostly with preparations for the contest. Everything was made much simpler by choosing Venice for the site for the third time, since all of its pros and cons were already known to all contestants. With American participation questionable and France not participating, this contest was shaping up as a two-nation affair. The course in the vicinity of Lido was much different this time, however. It stretched along the two islands form Porto De Lido to Porto De Chioggia and to a pylon off the beach of Lido De Sottomarina making it a long, straight run of 15.4mi (24.7km). The course was 80.5mi (50km) and had to be lapped seven times. The Excelsior Palace Hotel was again the start and finish.

The American Effort

The government was about as forward and determined in pulling out of the Schneider contests as they had been when they first invaded it in 1923. On February 9, 1927, Curtiss Dwight Wilbur, then Secretary of the Navy Department, released a statement that the United States would not be entering the Schneider contest. To send a full service team to Italy would involve construction of new racers and engines and would cost over $500,000. This would require curtailing funds from other important service activities. Congress had not provided for any more seaplane racer aircraft, but Wilbur expressed hopes that a private American entry would be ready. The NAA made a blanket entry for three machines.

In the final weeks of 1926 the Navy laid out a tentative plan in which machines, equipment, and personnel would be sent to Italy on an aircraft carrier. This would provide facilities and reduce financial obligations to any civil entrant. This plan never got past the discussion stage, but it allowed the Navy to claim it was fostering support for racing as best it could. Behind the scenes in Washington, D.C., the high-level heads of government were convinced that they had gotten all they had wanted to get out of racing and felt that competition and continuance would not be commensurate with increasing expenditures. The unfortunate tendency of the US government, after they had accomplished something worthwhile, was to sit back and assume they were the best and could not do any better, not realizing they had merely set a standard for someone else to beat. Once realized, this cold fact struck the

The Kirkham-Williams on slide rails coming out of the hangar. Navy Lt. Al Williams is in the cockpit checking controls and connections with the crewmen looking on. *Hirsch Collection*

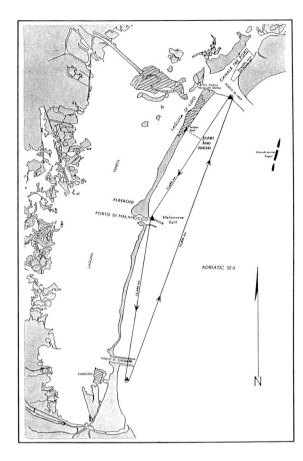

The Schneider contest course for 1927. Below, the Kirkham-Williams machine with its cowling off showing the big Packard X-2775 engine being readied for launch and taxi tests. The X-2775 was built from two V-1500 engines mounted on a common crankcase and produced 1,200hp. *Hirsch Collection*

industry like a hammer blow. The US aviation industry had backed itself into the biplane corner and couldn't come out of it without tremendous effort and money.

The Kirkham-Williams

After the US government announced officially that it did not intend to support the 1927 Schneider contest and that it would not have an entrant, a group of businessmen—concerned about the lack of interest when the United States had the trophy within its grasp—provided $100,000. This was to build a racer capable of retaking the trophy and establishing another speed record. Thus on March 24, it was announced that a group of New York sportsmen were donating $100,000 toward the Schneider racers. An American win in 1927 would put the trophy in the United States permanently.

The aircraft was basically designed by Charles B. Kirkham who created the original K-12 engine designs for Curtiss Aircraft Co. and established his own Kirkham Products Corp. on Long Island, New York. Another influence was Navy Lt. Al J. Williams who was to be the pilot and who contributed much of his time and money toward the new biplane racer. Kirkham and his associate designers had considered a mid-wing monoplane but Williams was adamant that it should be a biplane. When details were released on the racer it was the highest-powered single-engine biplane in the world.

From many angles the Kirkham-Williams machine looked like a king-sized Curtiss racer, having been designed and engineered by men still working for Curtiss. The Packard Motor Car Co. contributed the engine on a loan basis, along with technicians. Many components and various parts were contributed by US component manufacturers. The sponsoring consortium opened doors for hardware manufacturers, and much labor was contributed.

The Packard X-2775 engine consisted of two 650hp V-1500 units, one upright and one inverted, mounted on a common crankcase. It formed a four-bank X-type power unit delivering 1,250hp. The X-2775 was a remarkable engine in many respects. Its dry weight was 1,475lb (670.45kg), and its compression ratio was 7.5:1, which could be increased. It drove an 8.5ft (2.59m) two-blade metal propeller

without gear reduction. The 1,250hp Packard, as it was, overshadowed what Italy and Britain had available.

The wingspan of the upper wing was 29ft, 10in (9.09m) with wing area of 142sq-ft (13.19sq-m). Area of the lower wing was 75sq-ft (6.97sq-m) and span was 24ft, 3in (7.39m). The overall length was 26ft, 9in (8.15m), but fuselage length was 22ft, 9in (6.93m). The pontoons were 21ft, 3in (6.48m) in length and 3ft, 4in (1.01m) at the widest point. They had an 8ft (2.44m) spread and both carried fuel. The aircraft was of all-wood construction and plywood covered. The oil radiator was in an outboard section of the lower starboard wing, holdling 15gal (68.18ltr) of oil. The wing radiators carried 35gal (159.08ltr) of water, and 60gal (272.7ltr) of fuel was stored in the pontoons. The conventional tail unit, with fairly large dorsal fin and rudder, was wire braced. Floats were attached by four large streamlined struts diagonally braced. There were two spreader bars and the forward flying wires were attached to the floats.

All test work was done over Port Washington, New York. New of this machine caused concern in Europe. Although its speed with floats was unknown, it was publicized as having flown 322.6mph (519.39km/h) on a speed run test in a landing-gear configuration. Its potential speed with floats could only be estimated. The lift section between the wheels in the land version seemed unnecessary.

The British Effort

In 1926 the Air Ministry decided to extend their program for developing high-speed seaplanes. With this objective they placed orders with Supermarine, Gloster, and with Col. W. A. Bristow for a machine that was to be built by Short Brothers, using the Bristol air-cooled radial Mercury engine. And from Napier the sturdy Lion engine was to be further developed.

The Glosters were covered by Specification 5/26, the Supermarines by S6/26, and the Short-Bristow by 7/26. Also, toward the end of 1925 the Air Ministry asked the National Physical Laboratory (NPL) at Teddington, England, to employ the Duplex tunnel for conducting tests on quarter-scale models of the upcoming S.5 and Gloster IV racers. Four in all were tested for calculating drag.

Supermarine S.5 being readied for its first test flights. Note the short oil coolers on the fuselage. *A. W. Yusken*

When the British began considering the engine program for the 1927 Schneider Trophy contest, they made a study of machines used in the 1925 contest. Immediately there was a divergence in expert opinions as to what the best form should be. Some wanted the Rolls-Royce vee-type and some wanted the broad-arrow Lion engine. Still others felt the radial type had more reliability.

Under the guidance of Capt. G. S. Wilkinson another study was made of the 1925 machines by Napier, with particular attention to the following criteria: the frontal area had to be smaller; the engine was to help streamline the fuselage and reduce its size, especially behind the propeller; a maximum possible increase in power needed to be achieved; and the engine weight would need to be kept as low as possible consistent with reliability. Engine redesign to reduce fuselage drag would provide a greater speed increase than just increased power alone.

Wilkinson had joined Napier in 1912 and in 1914 was appointed chief of the drawing office. In 1915 he moved to the Royal Aircraft Factory in Farnborough and was put in charge of the engine drawing office there. Wilkinson was responsible for the design of highly successful air-cooled engines. In December 1917 he joined the staff of the Aircraft Manufactur-

ing Co. (AirCo), in charge of the engine department developing a high-horsepower air-cooled engine. He returned to Napier in 1921 as chief engineer and went about developing the Napier Lion engine.

A study drawing was made of a fuselage of the smallest size possible that could house pilot and engine. No consideration was given to installation of tanks, pipes, controls, instruments, engine mounts, and so on. Then the engine redesign was initiated, with the objective being to cause as little interference as possible with the ideal fuselage shape.

Cylinder heads of the broad-arrow Lion engine obviously had to project out beyond the fuselage and so they were made as small as possible with a smooth exterior so as not to require additional external cowling. Cowling plates could be attached to fair-in between heads and in front of and behind the cylinder head covers.

Mounting of the engine auxiliaries was altered so that no extrusions were present to cause interference in the fuselage lines. Magnetos were removed from the rear of the engine where they increased the engine width, and moved to the front of the engine. They were mounted almost parallel to the crankshaft so that they were inside the cylinder-block fairings, and were lightweight and capable of running at very high speeds.

Water-cooling systems were altered so that all pipes and connections were inside the theoretical fuselage shape. The water system was arranged so that water flowed in a natural direction circulated by a thermo-syphon system when the engine was idling and the water pump was ineffective. The outlet pipe was placed at the highest point at the front of the engine and taken down along the vee bottom between cylinders. Tests with a standard Lion engine were run with engine inclined upward and downward 25deg from level. When preliminary design was completed and dimensions fixed, a model of the fuselage was made for drag comparisons with other aircraft.

Concurrently with engine configuration design work, experiments were carried out to increase power output. Higher compressions such as 10:1 and increased rpm were tried and found possible, which resulted in a considerable increase in horsepower. But this increase caused a great strain on the ignition system, particularly on spark plugs. A number of different types of spark plugs had been developed and there were several problems to face: the high gas pressures and temperatures called for exceptionally good joints between various components of the plugs and minimum surface exposed to the gas; the small insulating surfaces made it necessary to pay attention to engine design and fuel used to avoid deposits and consequent leakage; plugs also had to be much shorter to avoid bulges on the cylinder head cowls; a special type of cable terminal was necessary to reduce the projecting terminal of the electrode; and finally, experiments and tests were made on pistons and rings to minimize the amount of oil passage and to keep spark plugs clean.

The makers of plugs and magnetos were heavily involved in the development of the Lion.

Research on propellers lagged behind engine development, so the engine was built in both geared (VIIB) and non-geared version (VIIA). However, the gear ratio was not very high, and in the end, tip speed losses were not totally eliminated. By that time the airframes had already been designed by Supermarine and Gloster, and in the forming of reduction gearing it was important not to necessitate any alteration of their airframe designs. Overall height had decreased by 2in (50.8mm) and frontal area was reduced by 4.25sq-ft (0.395sq-m) in the VIIB.

The Lion VIIB's engine gearing was unsuitable for the fuselage shape used so a double-reduction gear type was adopted having a single layshaft. This made the propeller and crankshaft coaxial. The layshaft was placed above the propeller shaft and fit inside the fairing of the center cylinder head. The drive was taken from the crankshaft to the idler countershaft and back to the propeller shaft. This meant transferring power through two separate gears, thus creating a small power loss, but the extra engine rpm made possible more than compensated for it. The outcome was that on the same airframe an average speed of roughly 10mph (16.1km/h) greater was achieved by the geared engine. The geared Lion engine performed very well in between overhauls. It was originally expected to last only 2hr, but was found to last 15hr between overhauls and half of that was at actual high-speed flying time.

By 1927 it was realized more than ever by the aircraft industry that there was more to be had from the Schneider Trophy contest than the mere adding of a few miles per hour to an annual record. Both land and sea aircraft were benefiting in design and performance—to a large degree from experience gained in the contests.

Both America and Italy had demonstrated the value of government-subsidized aircraft and of approaching the contest as a disciplined military operation using well-trained service pilots. However, in Britain the RAeC did not have the ability or the power to organize a successful team. That had to be the prerogative of the Air Ministry. Therefore, Sir Hugh Trenchard made a number of presentations before the Treasury to argue the advantages. Finally, on May 13, 1927, the Air Council gave authority to participate. In anticipation of this, the Air Ministry had formed an RAF High Speed Flight team and test operation at Felixstowe on October 1, 1926 with Sqdn. Ldr. Leslie J. Slatter as commander. Officially it was not connected with the Schneider Trophy contest, but pilots were carefully selected and began training for the 1927 contest.

Supermarine S.5

The Supermarine S.4 was a leap forward over the three Sea Lions for achieving a streamlined racer. Its failure provided some valuable lessons in design. Supermarine provided three wind-tunnel quarter-scale models for the NPL Duplex test lab. Two were low-wing models, one with W-struts bracing the wing and floats with spreader bar between floats. The second was wire braced from and between fuselage-to-wing-to-floats. The third model was a high gullwing blending into the fairings behind the outer cylinder banks.

The problems that Mitchell and all other aircraft designers had to face in any given new design were reduction in aerodynamic drag, overall weight, and acceptable water handling. Comprehensive wind-tunnel testing was accomplished on models of all British entrants at the NPL. The results obtained using the Reynolds numbers—a conversion system for windtunnel model testing, summed up as a re-

Top, a second S.5 on the slipway. The S.5's oil coolers now have five channels and extend farther aft. *S. Hudeck.* Center, Flt. Lt. Sidney M. Webster standing up in the S.5 cockpit, waiting for motor launch hookup and tow. *A. J. Short.* Bottom, the Gloster IVA just after it was built. The long wing span shown was later reduced after flight tests indicated a shorter span would suffice.

sistance factor of psf at 100ft/sec—were 9.3 for the S.4 fuselage and 6.6 for the S.5 fuselage.

Ten different float designs, and three different flight models were tested as Mitchell attempted to reach perfection. The Reynolds number for the floats was reduced from 5.0 on the S.4 to 4.43 on the S.5. All this was described in Reports and Memorandums 1300 of the Aeronautical Research Committee.

The S.5 cross-sectional area was reduced some 35 percent simply by tailoring the Lion engine to the airframe. Fuel consumption was 55gal (208.5ltr) per hour while oil consumption was 4gal (15.2ltr).

The fuselage was of monocoque duralumin construction including engine mounting. Four continuous members of longitudinal framing from engine to fin were of light flanged channel section. Heavy plate frames carried the wing root spars. The tail horizontal stabilizer and fin were built into the fuselage. Engine frames were of 16-gauge flanged channel 2in (50.8mm) deep and wide with stiffening plates. The smaller S.5 was approximately two-thirds the size of the S.4.

The all-wood wing panels were of plywood-faced built-up spruce ribs and compression ribs with two box spars and a heavy diagonal box member near the tip to resist torsion loads and reduce the aileron flutter problems that had destroyed the S.4. Tips and edges were of laminated spruce and ash. Two bolts at either spar root connected each wing panel to the top and bottom plates of the center section. The joints were faired by long dural fillets. The vertical stabilizer was built of two spruce spars and built-up ribs with edges laminated with 3/32in (2.4mm) plywood covering. Elevators were of a common box spar similar to the stabilizer. Rudder was covered with 1/25in (1mm) sheet ply, but ailerons and elevator were 3/32in (2.4mm) ply. All controls were operated by two counterweight flexible cables running in fiber fair-leads. Pilots stated that when flying with full throttle the lateral balance was so perfect that the ailerons were not required to counteract engine torque. All exposed duralumin was anodized to prevent corrosion.

The primary reason for lowering the wing on the fuselage was to improve pilot visibility. The high-wing gullwing gave lower resistance (drag), but the calculated loss in speed was only about 3mph (4.83km/h). Selecting the system of wire bracing for wings was done for several reasons. The unbraced (full cantilever) wing was very high in structure weight and needed to be thick at the wing root. The wire-braced wing reduced structure weight by 24 percent for the S.4 and 36 percent for the S.5. The end result was that a 12 percent improvement gave a 40mph (64.4km/h) increase. It was getting harder to squeeze large speed increases out of an airframe. Reginald Mitchell chose an RAF-30 airfoil section (symmetrical of median thickness).

About 70 percent of the drag of a high-speed wing is from skin friction. The wing radiators on the American machines had external corrugations. On the S.5 this could almost double the surface area and could increase drag by about 30 percent. Therefore, after much experimental work and testing, radiators with a flat outer surface were produced for the S.5. The greatest difficulty was to strengthen the outer surface skin to enable it to withstand the heavy air and expansion loads.

The wing radiators were of 40-gauge copper and covered almost the whole upper and lower surface of the wing. They were built in 8.5in (215.9mm) wide sections and consisted of two sheets rolled to wing airfoil form and sweated together. The outer sheet was smooth and the inner sheet was corrugated to form water passage channels. The complete radiator was formed by overlapping sections at the edges and sweating them together, then inserting eyelets to bind the sections together and form a bearing for fasteners. Water troughs were sweated together at leading and trailing edges; the trailing edge was the inlet and leading edge was the outlet. The troughs were formed at the end of the edge into a pipe that connected to the main water pipe by rubber connectors. Each radiator was a self-contained unit and could be removed and repaired independently. Flush vents and drains were incorporated. Wing flexing on steep turns at first caused radiator weeping or minor leaks. These leaks were corrected with a common sealing compound.

There was no room in the fuselage for fuel, so it was placed in the starboard float as a torque offset load. It worked both on water and in the air. It also lowered the C.G. of the airframe, giving better stability. The frontal

area of the floats was reduced about 14 percent from the S.4 floats through reduction in reserve buoyancy. The S.4 had a 55 percent reserve and the S.5's was 40 percent. The floats were single-step, constructed of duralumin and steel. The starboard float with its tinned-steel fuel cell was slightly longer than the port float, but this was only on aircraft number N-219. The float shell was 18 gauge on the bottom and 20 gauge on the topside. Inspection doors were fitted at 3ft (0.92m) intervals. The starboard float was mounted 8in (203.2mm) farther from the airframe centerline than the port float.

Fuel passed from the float tank via the engine pump to a header tank in the cylinder-head fairings aft of the engine. It was then gravity fed to the carburetor. Overflow returned to the main tank float by gravity as well. The distance the fuel had to be lifted could be handled by the fuel pump in level flight. However, in steep turns with centrifugal force against it the engine would be starved of fuel so the small header tank would feed the engine. Back on level flight, the fuel pump would replenish the header tank. Oil coolers were of 26-gauge tinned steel 7in (177.8mm) wide and 11ft (3.36m) long, mounted on each side of the fuselage.

Oil passed through one radiator into a filtering tank and back through the other radiator to the engine. Since the air does not follow the fuselage surface smoothly but is churned up and already somewhat heated from passing over the engine, the oil radiators first used on N-219 had to be enlarged. Oil temperature leveled at 125deg (52deg C) during the contest.

Gloster IV, IVA, and IVB

H. E. Preston was assistant chief engineer and designer of the detailed improvements on the Gloster IV series. He and Henry Folland still favored the biplane configuration. By blending the various components where they joined, a 40 percent reduction in head resistance over the Gloster III was achieved. Blending of the upper wing into the Lion engine fairings and joining the lower wing at a 90deg angle not only improved the drag characteristics, but also allowed a 15 percent increase in lift. Estimated speed increase was a whopping 70mph (112.7km/h). So the Gloster IV evolved into a gullwing sesquiplane in which infinite care had been taken to reduce drag.

While the three machines were basically alike the Gloster IV (N-224), the IVA (N-222), and the IVB (N-223) had several detail

Angle view of the Gloster IVA showing oil radiators and details of the long, slender floats. Left, a Gloster IVB and IVA in preparation for shipment to Venice following the IVA's wing-span reduction. *J. D. Canary*

127

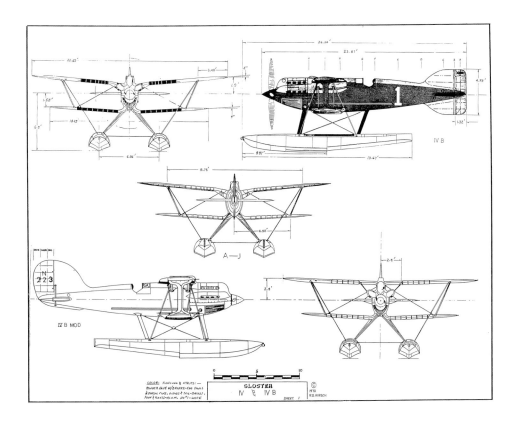

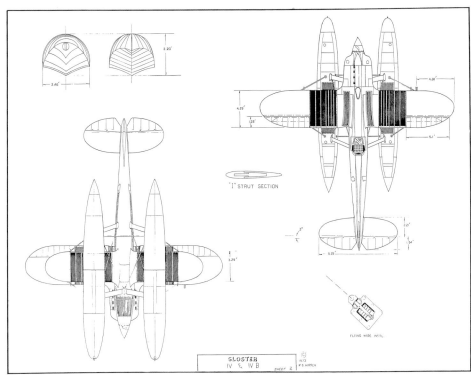

changes. The tail units were not all the same, however. N-224 had the large ventral fin above the fuselage similar to the later model Gloster VI, and the other two (IVA and IVB) had an above and below fin arrangement that was discovered to give a high-speed yaw. To minimize the sensitivity of high speed on the controls, the Gloster IV models had a patented variable control system. The stick transmitted at a 3:2 ratio for high speed where three linear travel units of stick produced two linear movements on the control surfaces. For low-speed flight the ratio was reversed to 2:3, giving greater control surface movements for a given stick movement. Selection was controlled in the cockpit by the pilot.

Wings were constructed of wood, as was the fuselage aft of the engine mounts. The fuselage was of monocoque construction, with ash longerons. Skin was dual diagonal strips in opposite directions. When shipped to Venice, N-223 had bronze wings, cylinder-block fairings and tail unit, and a white No. 1 painted on the sides of its Cambridge blue fuselage. N-222 was the same color, except it had red, white, and blue stripes on the rudder. The Gloster IV and IVA housed the direct-drive Lion VIIA engine with propeller diameters of 6.75ft (2.06m) and 7ft (22.13m). Gloster IVB (N-223) had the geared Lion VIIB engine with propeller diameter of 7.71ft (2.35m). Wingspan on the Gloster IV was 26.63ft (8.11m) while the IVA and IVB had a 22.63ft (6.9m) span, giving wing areas of 164sq-ft (15.24sq-m) and 139sq-ft (12.91sq-m).

Gloster designed their own floats, spending considerable time on the aerodynamic and hydrodynamic requirements. After many tests with various designs they ended up with a shallow vee-bottom, single-step duralumin float that did not incorporate fuel tanks. Fuel was entirely in the fuselage in tanks aft of the engine.

Surface radiators were of corrugated copper with brass for strength at the leading and trailing edges. They were made like a sleeve and slipped over the airfoil surface and fastened with brass ferrules. These and the ones on the upper surface of each float between the two attachment struts, provided 125sq-ft (11.61sq-m) of radiating area for cooling. The oil cooling was with a radiator-tank combination on the underside of the engine-forming part of the cowling.

Weight and Speed Differences

	N-224 (IV)	N-222 (IVA)	N-223 (IVB)
Weight empty	2,072lb (843kg)	2,447lb (1,109kg)	2,613lb (1,185kg)
Gross weight	2,780lb (1,261kg)	3,130lb (1,419kg)	3,305lb (1,499kg)
Stalling speed	76mph (122km/h)	97mph (156km/h)	99mph (159km/h)
Maximum speed	265mph (426.4km/h)	295mph (474.7km/h)	289mph (465km/h)
Flight duration	1.1hr	1.1hr	1.1hr

All three machines were delivered from Sunningend to Calshot during July and August of 1927 for their primary or preliminary flights. All flights were of short duration. N-222 arrived at Calshot on July 29 and was only flown 40min before being shipped with N-223 to Venice on August 16. These two were eventually shipped back to Felixstowe on October 4, and on to the Gloster factory on February 21, 1928. Then all three Gloster IVs were modified in March of 1928 into practice machines for the next High Speed Flight team. Speed was still about 280–285mph, but the 200lb (90.5kg) taken from the gross weight made it possible to reduce landing speed by 8mph (12.9km/h). The vertical stabilizer and rudder configuration of N-224 was used in the modification of N-222 and N-223, and it did eliminate a high-speed yaw problem for these two aircraft.

N-222 was looped and rolled by Lt. S. M. Kinkead and was considered by Britain to be the first high-speed racer to be used for aerobatics.

Short-Bristow Crusader

At Bristol, Roy Fedden designed a new air-cooled radial engine based on the Jupiter and named it the Mercury. It had the same bore but an increased stroke and higher rpm. It was running on the Filton testbed by spring 1925 and showed promise of around 950hp. Fedden went to the Air Ministry with a brochure on the Mercury and an old 1924 Jupiter-powered floatplane design of the Schneider type made by Frank Barnwell, then Bristol's chief engineer. He was awarded a 13,000 contract to build three upgraded Mercury engines for the 1927 Schneider contest.

The Bristol Mercury engine was a 9cyl air-cooled radial engine normally rated at 500hp. It did produce 960hp on the test stand on short runs but was limited to 810hp due to ig-nition problems and carburetion induction starvation cutting the engine off at intervals. Col. W. A. Bristow, an aeronautical engineering consultant, was one of the driving forces behind the Short-Bristow Crusader, but overall design was basically accomplished by Wilfred G. Carter who came from the Hawker Engineering Co. and who became intrigued with the idea of a radial-engine racing floatplane. By spring of 1926 the design was far enough along to submit to the Air Ministry, so Bristow and Carter tendered the design in the strut-braced version and Specification 7/26 was written to define it. Contract No. 674206/26 was awarded to the men, and the prototype

Bristol Crusader at the Rochester ramp on the Medway. Note the stress-wire attachment and Reed-type stamped-metal propeller.
Blandford Press

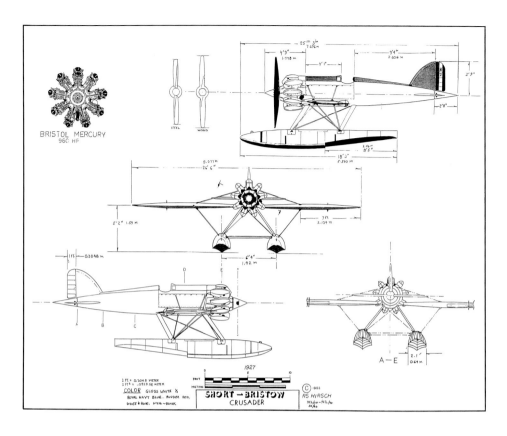

BRISTOL MERCURY
960 HF

SHORT–BRISTOW
CRUSADER

COLOR GLOSS WHITE &
ROYAL NAVY BLUE, RUDDER RED,
WHITE & BLUE, N.226 ~ BLACK

© 1988
RS HIRSCH

1927

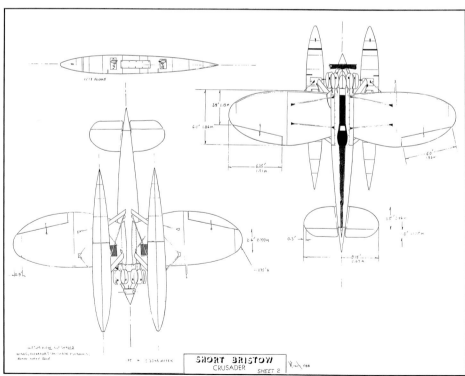

SHORT BRISTOW
CRUSADER SHEET 2

was to be designated N-226. Engine developers John D. Siddeley and Roy Fedden were also persuasive in obtaining the airframe development contract. A quarter-scale model was tested in the NPL Duplex wind-tunnel at Teddington, but drag was too high. Carter made major changes reducing the span by 1.5ft (.455m), replacing the struts with streamlined wires similar to those used on the S.5, and adding cylinder helmets for the engine.

The Crusader was built by Short Brothers at their seaplane works at Rochester under contract A.M. 674206/26. Short Brothers were already building floats and hulls and could easily take on the task. C.T.P. Lipscomb took on the design details and tooling and Arthur Gouge headed up the drafting work. In 1927 the Crusader was allotted Short serial number 736, but was not given an index number. The philosophy behind the design was low weight—a 12 percent reduction over liquid-cooled engines—and reliability of the air-cooled engine. However, this was offset by the engine frontal area drag which was equal to the entire drag of the S.5.

While the airframe was being detailed the Mercury engine was being bench tested. By mid-February of 1927 as the airframe was nearing completion, the Mercury was transferred to the Royal Aircraft Establishment at Farnborough for some final adjustments and checks on carburetor problems. In March it went to Rochester to be installed in the airframe and on April 18, construction of the Crusader project was completed and assembled and it was launched on the Medway that afternoon. Since test flights were not authorized by Rochester Air Ministry, a taxiing test and water-handling program were scheduled. On April 19 it did undergo taxi testing and handling at speeds up to 63.25mph (101.83km/h) on the step for a half mile. Then after being moored to test water tightness of floats, the Crusader was dismantled and shipped by road to Felixstowe.

On May 4 the Crusader was towed out into the Orwell waters. The engine was started up and Bert Hinkler took off easily from the water. He was clocked in two passes averaging 232mph (373.52km/h). Coming in to land he touched his port float hard enough to snap the machine to port, buckling the float struts slightly and slacking the bracing wires. When the machine was repaired and ready for service, the tricolor was painted on the rudder and the original blue on the strut fairings was painted white. On the next flight test, spark plugs limited the engine output to about 790hp instead of the 960hp it was designed to achieve. Consequently, it recorded only 225mph (362.25km/h). Trials were plagued with spasmodic engine cutout. The second of three engines ordered produced only 750hp at 2500rpm.

Two days after testing, H. M. Schofield flew the Crusader from Dovercourt to Felixstowe. He just cleared the water and climbed out when the engine quit, then cut in with a loud backfire. Somehow he came to rest on the water without damage. The Crusader was then stripped for modification and engine change with induction intake improvements, special spark plugs, and larger fuel tank in the starboard float to provide range for the Schneider course. Frank Abell flew it next, and in opening it up to 240mph (386.4km/h), the backfiring was repeated. He was able to throttle back and return to Orwell and land without trouble.

The Crusader was of composite construction, predominantly of wood. The wing was 28ft (6.53m) to start with but was reduced to 26.5ft (8.08m), modified to a sharper leading edge. The planform was elliptical, very pronounced the maximum chord thickness at half span where the flying and ground wires were attached. Ribs were of spruce and skin was mahogany sheet and covered with silk, then doped and finished with a white paint. Ailerons were fabric covered and actuated by cable. Fuselage was monocoque with spruce frames and two opposite diagonal sheets of mahogany. Elevator and rudder were also fabric covered. The duralumin floats developed by Gouge in the Short Brothers' seaplane tank gave 78 percent buoyancy reserve, which reproduced excellent water performance in the test area.

From 1923 on, all successful teams had been organized and run by service personnel. Therefore, the two contest teams were government backed and run in the same manner as a military operation. In England by mid-July, the whole flight except for the Crusader had moved to Calshot. However, the race machines were not fully tested and there was much

groundwork yet to do, so the pilots spent time practicing on older machines.

Finally on August 17 the first consignment, the S.5 (N-219), the Gloster IVA (N-222), and the Crusader left for Venice on the SS *Heworth*. Ten days later two more S.5s (N-220 and N-221) and a Gloster IVB (N-223) left on the SS *Egyptian Prince* from Malta where they were transferred to the aircraft carrier HMS *Eagle*. The teams would be in Venice about three weeks before the contest. The advanced members of the British team, L. H. Slatter and O. E. Worseley, arrived in Venice on August 30. On the thirty-first the *Heworth* docked at San Andrea, a small island at the north end of the lagoon opposite the main shipping approach to Venice.

Facilities were better than the team expected, but the squally weather offset their progress by curtailing flying for almost a week. Kinkead, Sydney Webster, and Schofield arrived by train during that week and all pilots were accommodated at the Excelsior Palace Hotel on the Lido beach. Ground crews resided at the San Andrea non-commissioned officers mess. Air Vice-Marshall F. R. Scarlett was in command of the overall operations of the British team. Pilots and aircraft lined up as follows: Webster in the S.5, Kinkead in the Gloster IVB, Worseley in the S.5, and Schofield in the Crusader. The Cru-

The Crusader being eased into the water for float and taxi tests at Felixstowe, England, before the first mishap. Notice the blue wooden propeller and dark struts. *Blandford Press*

sader was not expected to fly, so Schofield also had the non-geared Gloster IVA as a possible back-up mount. The Crusader was slower than the others so it was being flown in practice to save engine time on the contest aircraft.

On Saturday, September 10, Slatter made the first S.5 flight at Venice at about 11:00am and after a few local turns, set out and covered the full course. Shortly after, Kinkead took off in the Gloster IV and finally made a speed run along the beach. On September 11, Webster made a flight in the S.5, and Schofield prepared for his first Crusader flight at Venice. He'd already had several rides back in England. After the ground team, mechanics, and Air Ministry inspector completed their checks, Schofield climbed into the cockpit and the shoulder lid was closed and locked.

The engine quickly came to life on the first startup and Schofield started to taxi out for takeoff. He began by opening and closing the throttle in intermittent power surges to test the machine's water-handling characteristics, then he headed out into the lagoon. Loaded for the first time with a full fuel load for a complete course run, the machine was a bit sluggish. The weather was hot, too, which amplified the sluggishness. It took a long run on the step before the machine showed any signs or willingness to lift off. Eventually Schofield broke clear and held it down to about 15–30ft (4–9m) above the water. As he started to nose up, a downdraft gust of wind dropped the starboard wing. Schofield corrected automatically, but the result was a fast further roll to the right and the wing went suddenly over beyond the vertical with the wing tip striking the water. The machine tumbled and disappeared in a fountain of spray, suddenly plunging into the sea at about 150mph (241.5km/h). When the fuselage hit the water it broke in half at the cockpit. Schofield hit the water with such force it ripped his clothing and tore off his boots.

Schofield regained consciousness in the water and swam to the floating tail and clung to it until he was rescued. He had no broken bones and suffered only facial injuries from the frame of his goggles. For two days he was limping and using a cane, and he sported lots of black and blue marks. Not surprising, that ended that day's flying. The cause of the mishap wasn't known until about a week later

when the Crusader's forward half was salvaged from the Grand Canal. From the cockpit forward, the wings and fuselage were fairly intact. The magnesium alloy crankcase had almost completely disintegrated, but the control cables to the ailerons were intact and clearly showed what happened. It was found that during the re-rigging at Venice the two turnbuckles connecting stick to aileron had the wrong halves connected, crossing the controls. Therefore, Schofield's failure to visually check all controls was his downfall. On September 12 Italo Balbo, undersecretary of state for aeronautics, visited Schofield in the hospital and conveyed to him condolences from Benito Mussolini as air minister and from Italian aviators in general.

Italy and its Macchi M.52

The disruption of Italy's aircraft industry in 1926 due to the all-out effort to create the M.39 was not to be repeated in 1927. During December of 1926 it was decided to develop the M.52, a cleaned-up version of the M.39, rather than create a new design. This should limit cost and speed up the production program. Mario Castoldi, given a promise from Fiat that more power could be developed from the As.2, started considering the refinements. The contract stipulated the M.52 be capable of at least 292mph (470km/h). Castoldi figured the M.52 could be made to top 300mph (482.7km/h). He could reduce wingspan and also the horizontal tail surface. He could also reduce the fuselage hump, improving pilot visibility, and sweep the wings back 10deg giving better yaw stability. Floats could be reduced in length and volume to the minimum commensurate with sufficient buoyancy.

Muzio Macchi was in the United States during the 1925 contest and no doubt kept his eyes wide open. He watched the American and British machines compete with his own company's M.33 flying boat, and noted the clean lines of the British floats. They made little splash and so the British aircraft did not porpoise on landings like the Curtiss racers. He also made note of the clean lines of the S.4 and noted that the American Curtiss float struts were the cleanest and of a sound design. All he observed no doubt influenced the M.39 design. Machines were constantly in the process of evolution and anybody who copied everybody

and achieved a better result was making progress.

Tranquille Zerbi completed the As.3 drawings and they were received at Macchi's Varese factory by the end of February 1927. Fiat had increased the bore and stroke to 5.7in (14.5cm) and 6.9in (17.5cm) and pushed the compression ratio from 6 to 6.7:1. The new engine was expected to produce 1,000hp, and weight was reduced to 950lb (430.35kg). The Italians were aware that the British had some of their engine parts made in France by Gnome and Lorraine, so the Italians had their crankshafts forged in the Krupp factory in Germany to ensure that its specifications were not leaked to the British. The frontal area was slightly reduced, affording better streamlining at the propeller area.

The two-blade, metal, Reed propeller was 7.62ft (2.33m) long. Material for five new engines had been ordered by March 11, 1927. As the five new As.3 engines were being test run, problems showed up from the higher compression ratio and combustion chamber redesign. Catastrophic breakdowns resulted in scrapping and replacement of complete engines.

The M.52 fuselage was made to fit the As.3 engine's smaller frontal section. The windshield was smaller in the frontal area and was hinged at the front to provide easier cockpit access. It had a span of 29.97 ft (8.98m) which

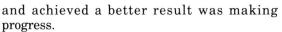

was 11.25in (28.6mm) less than the M.39, and area was reduced by about 10sq-ft (0.93sq-m). Weight was reduced by 132lb (60kg). Wing-chord thickness was 10 percent, not accounting for the angle of sweepback. The length was 23.42ft (7.14m), and fuselage length was 22.03ft (6.71m). Wing area was 143.2sq-ft (13.3sq-m) and weight was 2,618lb (1,187kg) empty.

While construction of the three M.52s was proceeding at Varese the two M.33s and four M.39s were returned to the Macchi plant for upgrading and maintenance in preparation for their use as practice machines for the Italian team.

The Italian team was led by Maj. Mario De Bernardi under the command of Colonel Tacchini and included Capt. Arturo Ferrarin, Capt. G. Guasconi, Capt. Frederico Guazzetti, and Lieutenant Salvattore.

All pilots assembled at Varese on May 16 and began their flying in older aircraft. One month later Lieutenant Borra crashed and was killed while making his first flight in the long-span M.39. He stalled the machine while practicing a turn. It rolled over into an inverted position and struck the water.

The first M.52 was flown the first week of August by Mario De Bernardi. The second and

Two of the M.52s on a pontoon barge being readied to move out at Venice. Some pontoon rafts were self-powered and some were towed. Left, the second M.52 being launched from its pontoon on Lake Garda with Capt. Arturo Ferrarin in cockpit. There were three M.52s at Varese and Lake Garda. A. Coccon

third were flown during the next ten days. The same engine problems found on the test stand surfaced during taxi and test flights. One problem was that Zerbi used magnesium pistons, a new design that had not been bench tested due to a time factor. The higher compression ratio and increased combustion temperatures were causing misfiring. There were two possible causes for this. One was that a correct spark plug was not developed in time, and the second was that the Italian aircraft industry did not have the same fuel additive expertise that Britain had for using ethyl and tetraethyl lead along with benzol. De Bernardi played a major role in efforts to improve reliability. The magnesium alloy used was only 70 percent the weight of aluminum alloy and so could provide higher rpm with less strain.

Castoldi was also building the M.52R (bis) while the Italian team was practicing in their M52s at Varese, but it didn't progress fast enough to be ready for the Schneider contest. It was to be flown by De Bernardi, but it did not get airborne until February 1928 when De Bernardi made two flights. This smaller racer was 20–25mph (32–40km/h) faster than the M.52s and De Bernardi, on March 30, 1928, at the Lido in Venice made six runs over a 1.86mi (3km) course averaging 318.623mph (512.776km/h).

On September 9, the Italian team moved to Venice and practice flying resumed. They spent most of their time practicing a new cornering technique developed on the lake. This was a climbing turn and then diving back down on the new leg. Italy's preparation for the contest was admirable. The hangars for the Italian and English entries were located on the shores of an inlet opposite to each other so that while the crews could exchange friendly courtesies easily, they also could have complete privacy when it was desirable. One other good feature was that the public was kept away from the hangars, which made for much better conditions for the crews. The presence of Benito Mussolini and party gave formality to the occasion. His presence was an indication of interest taken by Italy in the service's flying teams.

Gen. Italo Balbo was present with a large staff of officers from the Regia Aeronautica, Italy's air force. Before the contest he presided at a luncheon given by the Air Ministry at the Excelsior Palace Hotel at Lido in honor of the participants. About 300 guests attended and the representative of the NAA was honored by being seated at the guest table between Gen. Francisco De Pinedo and Air Vice-Marshal Sir W. Sefton Brancker. General Balbo and Sir Philip Sassoon, British undersecretary for air, were the only speakers, both paying graceful tributes to contest teams. Sir Philip flew to Venice for the contest, leaving England at 9:50am and arriving at Venice in the late afternoon barely in time for the luncheon. The rivalry between the two teams was felt everywhere.

Air Vice-Marshal Sir John Higgins, who was air member for supply and research, and Air Vice-Marshal R. F. Scarlett were probably the most vitally concerned officials present since they bore the final responsibility for the success of the British venture. Castoldi and Balbo pretty much did the same for Italy.

On September 21, Kinkead was coming in to land in the Gloster IVB when the propeller spinner came off and was struck by a propeller blade. The lost spinner could be easily remade and replaced, but the propeller blade was damaged, and the propeller shaft also showed effects of the impact. This caused much extra work on the part of the ground crew for the next two days. These were two days of favorable weather, so much serious practice over the course would have been possible had Kinkead not been left sitting and watching. The machine was readied for the navigability test on Friday, September 23.

The Trials

Shortly before 9:00am on Friday, Webster i S.5 N-220, Worseley in S.5 N-219, and Kinkead in the IVB N-223 were towed on their floats to position for navigability trials. They were told the Italians would be an hour late. The wait was long for the anxious group, but just before 10:30 they received permission to proceed. Just as Kinkead was starting up, tugs towing the slope ramp barges carrying the M.52s came into the channel from the San Andrea naval air station. It looked close for a minute but Kinkead got off and the Italians, seeing the action, moved over to the side of the channel. Although starting late, the Italian team completed their tests in good shape, impressing the British by how well their Macchis handled on the water and how easily and cleanly they lifted off. In the air, the scarlet Macchis were clearly fast and responsive to controls. Crowds on the beaches saw almost none of this but those aboard the US carrier *Eagle* and escort vessels had a good view. A good contest was shaping up.

As the six machines lined up at anchor for the flotation test, all was calm and crews were relaxed since Saturday was free to attend to last-minute checks and adjustments. However, late in the afternoon came the shocking announcement that Webster had been disqualified by crossing the start line incorrectly. As he passed the start line on the step, a wave from a nearby ship momentarily put the S.5 in the air. The S.5 was prepared for flight early Saturday morning and in conjunction with the rules, Webster made a second attempt and completed the tests without incident. The S.5 was then gone over with careful scrutiny. All that was needed now was decent weather on Sunday.

The Contest

By Sunday, Venice had been invaded by throngs of would-be spectators all keyed up for the spectacle. Having admired the American's handling of the 1926 contest, the Italians had also arranged a good public-address system as well as a large scoreboard to record lap times of each contestant. The enthusiasm of the Italians was immense. Venice was draped with banners, posters, flags, and tapestries, and the trophy itself was in St. Mark's Square for display. The state railway system was allowing half fare to all Venice and vicinity stations from anywhere in Italy. Thousands of tourists overran the streets for several days and the canals were overcrowded with gondolas. Since Friday, huge crowds were scrambling for a place on the ferries to the Lido beaches and the hotels, which already had become chaotic.

On Sunday morning, September 25, Venice was awakened by the loud flapping of unfastened shutters from an almost gale-force wind. It quickly became apparent that it would be impossible to hold the contest under such conditions. It was not until noon, however, that the official announcement confirmed what was already a foregone conclusion. The contest would not be run on Sunday, but would be held on Monday, weather permitting. The postponement was just one more in a series of

unfit flying weather delays that had considerably hampered preparations. The disappointed throngs of spectators flocked back across the lagoon to Venice, having had their excursion spoiled.

The Italian weather forecasters predicted on Sunday evening that the weather wouldn't clear for at least two days, so the pilots relaxed and the drinks were plentiful. Monday morning's weather was only marginally better. It was overcast and there were fairly large swells in the gulf, but the wind had subsided and the canal and lagoon were calm. Since the starting point was on the Adriatic side of the lido, the committee was hesitant in ordering the start. Finally, after consulting with pilots it was announced that barring any deterioration in the weather, the contest would be held.

On Monday noon, the weather was still unpredictable. By this time the crowd was estimated at about 230,000. Private parties were everywhere and various vantage points on the hotel roofs were overcrowded. The crown prince of Italy was watching from the balcony of the tower. Finally the British team was told to line up off the mole at Porto De Lido by 2:00pm. The Italian team received the same orders. At 1:40pm the British machines on floats were towed gently by rope down the channel from San Andrea to the starting position. They were followed by the Italian ma-

Captain Ferrarin getting the M.52 hooked up for tow on its floats after a Venice flight. Col. Mario De Bernardi's M.52 had race No. 2. *Hirsch Collection*

chines on their barges. The sight of all six machines lining up raised emotions among spectators.

This year the competitors would be making a flying start. Each would have a warning signal 5min before start time, and the second signal indicated takeoff. There then would be a 10min allowance from the second signal until the machine had to have dived across the starting line at the Excelsior Palace Hotel and then onto the course.

At 2:29pm, after the 5min warning gun was fire, the starting gun broke the hush of expectancy on the beaches and at the hotels. Kinkead in the Gloster IVB moved out from the assembled area, pushed the throttle wide open, and took off. The contest was finally on as he executed a climbing turn into position for his dive across the mole and lined up for the starting point. He soon flashed past the Excelsior Hotel with a penetrating roar of the Napier Lion engine and headed down the beach toward the Porto De Malamocco light and on toward Chioggia. After his turn and as he headed back toward the Porto De Lido pylon turn, Kinkead found it difficult to see and line up on the distant pylon so he dropped down to below 100ft above the water, rising slightly only to clear the mole. His half-circle turn was smooth and lined him up perfectly for the next leg. His first lap was clocked at 266.5mph (428.8km/h).

Kinkead was followed by De Bernardi before he reached the Porto De Lido turn. After takeoff, the Macchi headed for the starting line at about 200ft (61m) and although it seemed to be traveling very fast, it was leaving a trail of black smoke. The characteristic sound emitted by the Fiat engine was more crackly than the Lion and seemed noticeably rougher, but on the straight the Macchi looked superior in speed. At Chioggia, De Bernardi cornered with a climb to about 600ft (183m) and then dove back down on the northward leg toward Porto De Lido. This drew cheers of applause from the crowd at Chioggia who were mostly Italians. His first lap was posted by the race officials. It was 1/2sec slower than Kinkead's time, but he had lapped in almost 15sec less than Kinkead so his speed was actually about 275mph (442.5km/h). He was going to be hard to beat!

The next to fly was Webster in his first full-load takeoff, which he managed very cleanly.

He did not drop down low nor did he corner as sharply as Kinkead in the IVB, but he looked as fast as De Bernardi on the straight legs. His first lap was almost exactly as De Bernardi's, which promised a close contest. Guazzetti, then Worseley, and finally Ferrarin all followed at the same intervals and the course was becoming a confused spectacle in which it was almost impossible to keep up with the status of each contestant. but Ferrarin's participation was short-lived. As he crossed the starting line his engine backfired, emitting a puff of smoke and then a large belch of flame. It started missing intermittently and Ferrarin banked sharply behind the Excelsior Hotel and headed for the sheltered waters of the lagoon.

During the confusion and while all eyes were on Ferrarin, De Bernardi's engine started running rough near Chioggia and then failed on the northward leg, throwing a rod through the Fiat engine's crankcase. De Bernardi was trying to make his way back to San Andrea but went down in the haze on the sea surface, which somewhat hid the action from the Lido. His absence was not noticed until he did not show up for Lap 3. He was picked up by a patrol boat from HMS *Eagle* and was towed to the naval base at San Andrea. Now the two As.3-powered Macchis were out of the contest and the slower As.2 machine could win only if it was the lone survivor. Guazzetti in the Macchi was lapping about 10mph (16km/h) slower than Worseley in the slowest of the British machines.

According to the British timers who were keeping their own score, Kinkead's second lap was faster than Webster's first and on his third lap he was doing 247.5mph (398.5km/h), but then his times fell off on the fourth and fifth laps. On his sixth lap Kinkead also pulled out and headed for San Andrea with a vibration set up again by a failed spinner. Webster and Worseley were lapping about 272mph (437.92km/h). With his third lap his best at 275.8mph (444.04km/h). Guazzetti was about 11mph (17.71km/h) slower.

At the end of Guazzetti's sixth lap a punctured fuel line squirted raw fuel in his face. Momentarily blinded, he took a very wide turn and barely cleared the Excelsior Hotel but managed to put the Macchi down on the lagoon. Webster, now coming across the finish line on his seventh lap, kept right on going toward Chioggia and then back on the northward leg and wound up making an extra lap. It had started to rain on his fifth lap and in concentrating to stay on course he wasn't sure he had flown seven laps. By that time the huge crowd on the beach was already thinning out. Webster averaged 281.86mph (453.80km/h), winning the contest. His speed was 3mph (4.83km/h) faster than the existing world speed record. Worseley averaged 273.01mph (439.55km/h), placing second. Despite haze and rain squalls, their speed was only 3.5 percent below the machine's maximum speed.

After the elation of Venice—regarded as the pinnacle of achievement for the members of the RAF High Speed Flight team—and the many receptions held, came the sobering return to the everyday routine of service life. The team was disbanded and members were returned to their original units.

On November 4, 1927, De Bernardi of Italy set a new world speed record at 297.76mph (479.2km/h) over a 1.86mi (3km) measured course, thus demonstrating that the Macchi was every bit as fast as Britain's Supermarine S.5. Fiat had been working on the As.3 engine, correcting pistons, compression, fuel makeup, and ignition, and it now ran as well as the As.2. Then again on March 30, 1928, De Bernardi set another world speed record of 318.57mph (512.69km/h) in the Macchi M.52R (bis), which was smaller and more powerful than the M.52. The M.52s were then put to work as trainers.

In retrospect, 1927 was a year in which seaplanes made new progress in the field of aerial service but with such strides in engine reliability, landplanes were now stretching across the oceans to other lands. The James D. Dole race to Honolulu, the Lindbergh crossing of the Atlantic, the Clarence D. Chamberlin flight to Germany with Charles Levine, the Lester J. Maitland flight to Honolulu from Oakland, and Commander Byrd and Bert Acosta's almost successful flight to France's coast were only some of the epochal flights achieved that year.

On April 14, Lt. Guage R. Henderson established an altitude record for seaplanes of 22,178ft (6,764.29km/h) in a Vought Corsair, and on April 23, Lt. S. W. Calloway set a speed record for a 1,105lb (500kg) load over a distance of 62mi (100km) at 147.263mph (237.093km/h), also in a Corsair. Then on May 21, Lt. Rutledge Irvine set a seaplane record of over 621.1mi (1,000km) averaging 130.93mph (210.80km/h) in the same Corsair. Jacques Schneider's contest was stimulating progress.

Regardless of how much the Americans admired Italy's 1926 Schneider Trophy victory, there was much criticism of the US effort in the American press. Newswriters condemned the US defeat and subsequent failure to enter a naval team for 1927. The Bureau of Aeronautics had asked for funds to construct entries. They were refused, however, which let the Navy off the hook. Newswriters hinted that naval pilots were not fit to represent the nation in the Schneider Trophy contest. The squabble over selection of a third pilot and subsequent crash of one of the US entries at the Norfolk race caused much comment in the news. Writers contended that the United States had been beaten at its own game (this was referring to the 1923 contest when the United States invaded the Schneider contest with a military team).

New problems were brought on by the high performance of these aircraft and as speeds would increase, these problems surely would become more acute. A blackout phenomena was reported by all pilots flying around the pylons. Medical opinion was that this momentary blindness during flight turns at high speeds was caused by blood draining away from the optic nerve due to centrifugal force. Although they were forewarned, the contestants found these blackouts to be alarming, and they spent considerable time developing techniques to allow minimum radius turning just on the twilight of blackout. Another problem was the torque reaction of new, high-powered engines and racing propellers while accelerating for takeoff. These new problems that arose as speeds were being pushed upward were a new challenge to the aeronautical engineers of all nations.

Capt. Frederico Guazzetti taxiing out for navigation tests. He will taxi from Canale Tre Porte to the Porto de Lido canal for takeoff. *Hirsch Collection*

Chapter 13

1929 Calshot

All-Out Italian Effort

Immediately after the 1927 contest the question of annual or biennial competition was again raised. Since designers and aircraft builders were entering new areas of technology, the biennial was favored. The question was resolved at an FAI meeting held in Paris on January 5, 1928. It was a historic event in that it was attended by Jacques Schneider, despite his failing health. He came to congratulate the RAeC on their team's victory at Venice. The two-year contest separation was unanimously agreed upon.

Following a meeting held on February 29, 1928, the RAeC then made a preliminary announcement that the 1929 contest would be held at some date between August 24 and October 5. More information was to be announced when the committee had worked out the details.

Seven weeks after this meeting the news of the death of Jacques Schneider was released. He had died on May 1, 1928, at Beaulieu-sur-Mer near Monte Carlo while recovering from an appendicitis operation. He did live to see seaplane speeds go from about 85mph (136.77km/h) to 318.57mph (511.66km/h), to become the world's fastest machines. However, he died before seeing Britain become the final holder of the trophy bearing his name, or of seeing the extent to which he had advanced maritime aviation. He did see the beginning of a new generation of high-speed aircraft of historic importance. The Schneider contest had developed so disproportionately that his death passed almost unnoticed.

The RAeC finally released some information on how the start of the contest would be organized: "The zero hour on Saturday, September 7 will be 2:00pm. The starting ship will be the monitor HMS *Medea* which will be moored probably in the neighborhood of Calshot. It will signal to each machine, giving permission to take off by a gun and by hoisting the national flag at the masthead. On receipt of the signal each pilot is allowed 10 minutes in which to rise and cross the starting line at Ryde pier in flight. If he crosses the start line before the expiring of the 10 minutes he will be timed from his actual crossing of the line. If he takes more than 10 minutes he will be timed as if he had actually crossed the line at the 10 minutes time. Thus, if a pilot takes 11 minutes from the firing of the gun until he crosses the line, one minute will be added to his actual flying time.

"There will be an interval of 20 minutes between each starting gun. There should normally be only two machines on the course at a time, never more than three. If seven machines start, as seems possible, the last will get off at 4:10pm and the contest will be over before 5:00pm.

"The committee wishes to emphasize the distinction between 'delaying' the start from minute to minute, and 'postponing' the contest from day to day. At 1:00pm on Saturday, red flags will be hoisted at all stations around the course and so long as they remain flying, the race has not been postponed to the next day, though the start may be delayed while waiting

S.6 N-248 with its engine idling while the aircraft is being pushed to the water. This machine had the float radiators on the top forward part of float. Later they were moved to the sides of the fuselage, similar to those on N-247. *Hirsch Collection*

The Schneider contest course for 1929. Bottom right, the Mercury was developed from the 1927 Kirkham-Williams racer. Using the same engine, fuselage, and floats, the Mercury evolved as a mid-wing, wire-braced monoplane. Its cleaner lines gave expectations of well over 300mph. With cowling off, showing ram-air intake and reduction-gear housing, Al Williams in the cockpit is waiting for the starter crank to be hooked to the propeller hub. *Hirsch Collection*

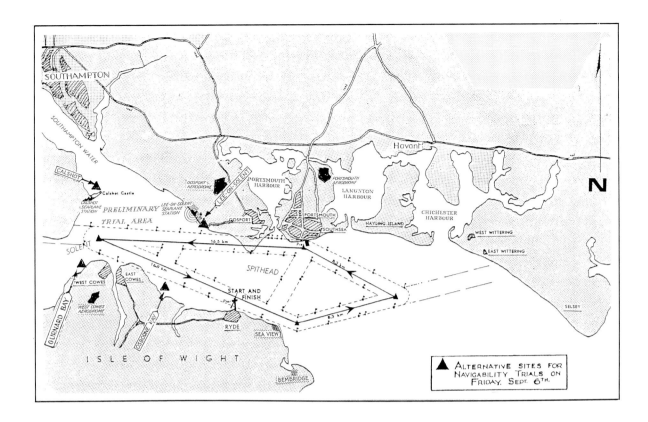

for weather improvement. Spectators should note this. Rumors are apt to get about when the start is delayed that the race has been postponed. However, as long as the red flag is flying, such rumors should be disregarded. The Committee will not postpone the start until all hope has been abandoned of completing the race on that day. Once a postponement has been decided on, the red flags will be hauled down and blue flags will be hoisted in their place. The race will be flown anticlockwise and all turns will be to the left."

Initially ten machines were entered in the 1929 race, plus one possible from Germany's Dornier. Of those entered there was one from America and three each from France, Italy, and England. France eventually announced its entries would not be ready in time. Italy asked for a one-month delay, and the US Navy, in the last weeks before the event, pulled back its support of the Kirkham-Williams machine and backers.

The American Effort

In the United States the situation was almost the same as it was in 1927. The higher levels within government had no interest in the contest and once again the effort was left to private enterprise. Well, . . . almost.

The Mercury

The beautiful Mercury racer was now a mid-wing monoplane and was designed, or redesigned, in the Navy's Bureau of Aeronautics. It was built at the Naval Aircraft Factory at Philadelphia under extreme secrecy, and was funded by generous individuals. A non-profit company was floated and named Mercury Flying Corp. to finance development and construction. Lt. Al Williams again was to be the pilot. He was a guiding spirit and most of his personal funds went into the project. Wind-tunnel models were tested at the Washington Navy Yard—right under the noses of those who had influenced the halting of the 1927 project. Aeronautical engineer John S. Kean of the Navy Yard supervised construction of the Mercury racer.

The Mercury was developed from the 1927 Kirkham-Williams racer. Many of the fuselage and float components were from the 1927 biplane, but the single wing was set at mid-fuselage position close to the thrust line. The ma-

chine was extremely photogenic from any angle. The fuselage was a deep oval section forward and tapered aft of the cockpit with the headrest blending into the upper stabilizer half.

The wire-braced wing was constructed of wood, with plywood skins. Ailerons were aluminum as were the rudders and elevators. Fuselage and tail unit were still all wood. Floats were typically Navy: although large and with a single step, they rode deep in the water. Reserve buoyancy was low since the machine ended up 400lb (181kg) overweight. Engine cowling and floats were of aluminum.

The 24cyl X-form Packard engine had been used in the Kirkham-Williams racer. It was to have minor modifications to improve maximum power and was to be capable of up to 1,500hp. To cool this large powerplant, radiators were placed on the wing and uniquely on the float bottom to cool the engine while taxiing on the water, where insufficient air mass is traveling over the wings. While in the air, it made no difference. The Kirkham-Williams' engine was rated at 1,100–1,200hp and car-

Frontal view of Williams standing up in cockpit, being towed back in from an unsuccessful takeoff. Notice the Hamilton Standard propeller and depth of floats in water. *Hirsch Collection*

ried the float biplane to 290mph (466.9km/h). Thus, 1,500hp in the Mercury monoplane gave all indications that it would be highly competitive. The old engine was installed, however, about the last two weeks of July and first half week of August, when test work was being done on the Santee Wharf of the Annapolis Military Academy.

Because of the Mercury's pontoons sitting deep in the water and the lower 1,100hp availability, Williams had many frustrating attempts to become airborne. Torque produced a tendency to bury the left wing tip while taxiing below hump speed and the use of rudder and ailerons increased drag loads just enough to prevent the machine from getting on the step and airborne. As a last resort Williams just left the controls in neutral and let it correct itself. Propeller damage from spray occurred on many takeoff attempts, or whenever the engine was throttled back at the end of a taxi run. Williams stopped this by cutting the

The Bernard HV.41 with 12cyl Hispano-Suiza engine on Lake Hourtin near Bordeaux, France. The HV.41 actually was completed after the HV.42 because of modifications to eliminate the Lamblin radiators on the float struts. *B. C. Kavelaars*. Right, the Fiat C.29 with As.5 engine uncowled. Although it is on a dolly, it was only being moved to a position for engine run-up.

engine switch as he throttled back, so that the propeller would stop rotating in the spray.

Spray was so bad on takeoff run attempts that Williams would cover his goggles until speed was enough to get up on the step. On August 18, Williams finally lifted the Mercury off the water and was airborne for a few hundred yards. It was the Mercury's only flight. He kept the machine 8–10ft (2.4–3.1m) off the water and then set it back down because of a fuel pressure drop, bending the propeller in doing so.

The Packard Motor Car Co. had promised to provide the 1,500hp engine for installation during the trip to England. But the Navy—by then interested in the program but recognizing its problems—pulled back its transport support in a face-saving move, leaving Williams and his backers high and dry. The only American possibility was canceled.

The French Effort

France had not entered as a competitor since 1923 but this year it was determined to make a special effort to win the 1929 contest. Prestige of a victory seemed essential in that

The Fiat C.29 open cowled, with a mechanic making some adjustments. Note the engine cradle and plumbing provisions for tight cowling. Left, a frontal view of the Fiat C.29 showing its small frontal area and floats. Its 1,000hp As.5 engine gave it a speed of 347mph (558.32km/h). *A. Coccon*

Side view of Macchi M.67 showing its clean, elongated lines, which were developed from the M.52. Note the chin oil cooler on the fuselage side. *Hirsch Collection*

its aviation industry had virtually come to a standstill as compared to those in the United States and other countries. After the Gordon Bennett race ended in a French victory, France became complacent and then somewhat dormant. Therefore, to reverse this trend, the Ministry for Marine in early 1928 ordered four racing seaplanes for competition in the Schneider contest. Two were to be from the Societe des Avions Bernard and two from Societe Anomyme Nieuport-Delage. The Gnome-Rhone, Renault, Fueman, Hispano-Suiza, and Lorraine engine companies also received orders to develop and produce new racing engines for the Schneider races.

The Ministry for Marine also set up a new training base at Etang De Berre on Lake Hourtin near Marseilles for the French Schneider team. Commander Amanrich, Adj. Florentin Bonnet, and Sadi Lecointe were retained to undertake the acceptance trials of the Bernard and Nieuport-Delage competition machines. The pilots chosen for training as the Schneider contest team were: Captain Marty, 32nd Regiment, Dijon; Lt. Paul Retourna, 34th RA, Bourget; Lieutenant Adjutant Doer-

nev, 2nd RA, Strasbourg; Chief Sergeant Baillet, 2nd RA, Strasbourg; Sergeant Dumas, 3rd RA, Chateauroux; Sergeant Goussin, 38 RA, Thionville; and as back-up, Adjutant Chief Raynaud, d'Istres.

Bernard HV Racers

The Bernard Company was founded in 1916 with associates Louis Bleriot, Marc Birkigt, and Louis Bechereau, plus founder Adolphe Bernard. It also became Societe Industrielle des Metaux et du Bois (SIMB), and high speed was a guiding principle. Bernard Aircraft Ltd was also incorporated under the Companies Act, 1929, in Britain, with Gabriel Borel and Adolphe Bernard as managing directors.

The Bernard company's designers, Roger Robert and S. G. Bruner, produced designs for two twin-float, mid-wing monoplanes and ended up building three that were similar. The first was designated HV.40, the HV standing for Haut Vitesse or high speed. It was powered by a new Gnome-Rhone Mistral engine, a development of the British Jupiter engine, producing 600hp at 2350rpm. With power limited to 600hp and the large frontal area of the 9cyl radial arrangement, it hardly seemed this seaplane was intended for anything more than a training machine for the racing team. Bernard engineers certainly had Short Crusader performance data available.

Development of the HV.40 and HV.42 continued through 1928 and testing went on into 1929. The third machine, HV.41, which was slower but steadier in development was flown in November of 1929—too late for the contest—by Antoine Paillard, chief pilot for Bernard. As far as was known, there was only one HV.40 built and flown but there were two HV.41s and two HV.42s delivered to Etang De Berre. These were the first to look like competitors, even though they were not up to the performance expected at Calshot.

All of the Bernard HV series had a wing with a thick inner section, similar to a full-cantilever design, which passed through and became part of the fuselage center section. Although there were no ground wire stress requirements from fuselage to wing upper surface, it did have flying wires from floats to wing. Its center-section structure was multicellular. The vertical members were made up of laminated plywood with stringers on top and bottom made with spruce, also plywood covered. The wing outer panels were built up with the conventional two-spar construction, with the front spar being the main and heavier one. Ailerons were aluminum and were hinged to an additional extended spar attached to the rear spar via stringers and short butt attachments. Wingspan on the HV.40 was 28.54ft (8.7m) with an area of 107.64sq-ft (10sq-m). Overall length was 24.31ft (7.41m). The HV.41 and HV.42 had a span of 30.18ft (9.2m) and an area of 129.17sq-ft (12sq-m). Fuselage length was 23.62ft (7.2m), and overall length was 26.21ft (7.99m).

The fuselage forward section was basically the engine mounting attachment to the wing center section and floats attachment blocks. From the aft surface of the center section the remaining fuselage including cockpit was attached. It was built up with the sides consisting of spruce and plywood girders, with spruce frames and interconnecting plywood. The fuselage was contoured with a slight downward slope into the integral vertical stabilizer which was all wood and of cantilever structure. The cockpit opening was at the trailing edge of the

wing, with pilot accommodations extending into the wing center section.

Floats were made up of duralumin and included integral fuel tanks. They were of a single-step vee-bottom design, which became standard for almost all seaplanes of that era. The two struts attached to a duralumin frame, forming the base of the wing center section.

Wire bracing was used between floats. The HV.42 had wrap-around Lamblin radiators mounted on the upper area of the wide, streamlined struts. The HV.41 had finned radiators running beneath the fuselage. Floats were almost as long as the fuselage at 19.93ft (6.075m), giving an overall length of 26.22ft (7.99m).

By the summer of 1929 the Bernard and Nieuport-Delage airframes were completed and waiting for the new engines. A great amount of development effort by Hispano-Suiza went into a variant engine named 18-R. It was an 18cyl inverted-tee engine of 1,680hp at 2400rpm, with compression ratio of 10:1 and 80deg between each bank of cylinders. Hispano-Suiza also had a V–12, water-cooled engine of 900–1,000hp called the Special.

Nieuport-Delage ND.450

The second company ordered to develop and build two machines was Nieuport-Delage. Type designation was ND.450 and it was a clean, low-wing conventional monoplane con-

The M.67 MM-105 at Calshot, England. It was distinguishable by its three-blade propeller. The three banks of cylinders of the Isotta-Fraschini Asso 18 are also very distinct. *Hirsch Collection*

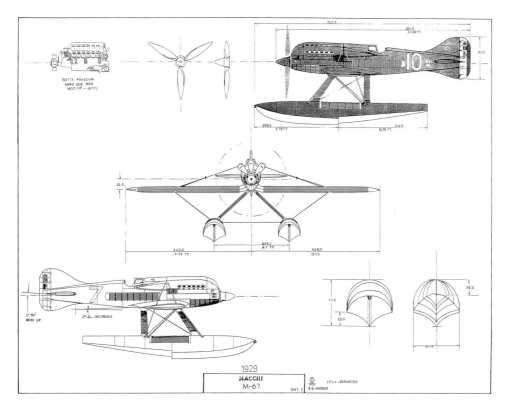

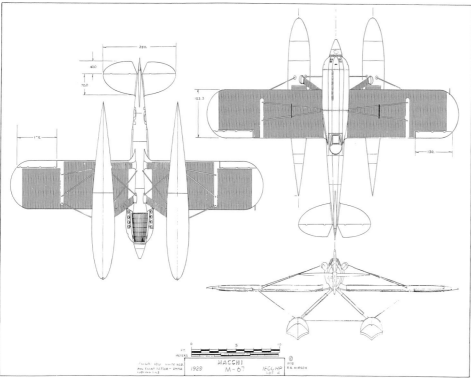

figuration designed for the geared Hispano-Suiza 18-R engine. It was an all-wood aircraft with a slim, deep-section fuselage, with the pilot headrest melding into a fairly large dorsal fin and a broad oval rudder. The cantilever horizontal stabilizer was narrow chord, as were the elevators. Wings—unlike the Bernards—were thin sections and wire braced from fuselage to floats with wire bracing between floats.

The first engine installation on the ND.450 had a two-blade propeller installed. Original wingspan was 31.82ft (9.70m) and the mean chord was 5.25ft (1.60m). Later this span was reduced to 29.59ft (9.02m). The wing's trailing edge was straight and it had an 8deg swept-back leading edge on the large wing and 10deg on the short wing. With short wings, ND.450 was later redesignated ND.650. Floats were shorter than those of Bernards, but the reserve buoyancy appeared just as good. They were of a two-step design, with the first step at the mid-point and the second step about three-fifths aft.

In about August of 1929 the ND.450 received its engine and the machine was shipped to Hourtin for its first flight.

Efforts were made to bring some of the team to a base on Lake Hourtin near Bordeaux, but pilots could only train on older hacks while Sadi Lecointe and Florentin Bonnet stood by to test the new racers whenever they became available. (Bonnet was to test the Bernards and Sadi Lecointe was to test the Nieuports.) On August 6, 1939, Bonnet was killed in a crash attempting to loop his Nieuport 62 trainer, which had problems similar to those being experienced by the contest machines and engines. (The HV.40 and HV.42 had been tested with low output development engines, and the three engine manufacturers—Gnome-Rhone, Hispano-Suiza, and Lorraine—were not ready to supply high-compression racing engines.) That tragedy, coupled with the facts that Bernard did not have the machines ready to dismantle for shipment to Calshot and Nieuport-Delage was still waiting for engines, led the French to withdraw from the contest. France formally withdrew from the Schneider contest on September 5, 1929.

But France was not quitting entirely. In the spring of 1930 Lorraine devoted a special fac-

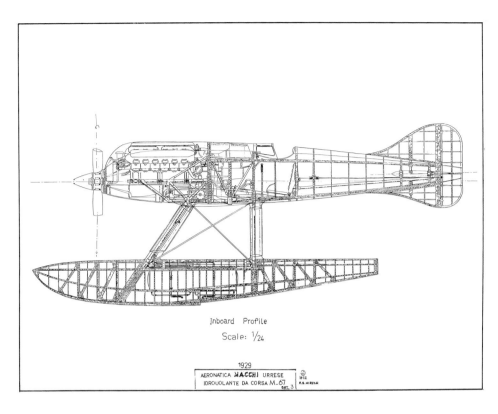

Inboard Profile
Scale: 1/24

1929
AERONAUTICA MACCHI VARESE
IDROVOLANTE DA CORSA M_67
SKT. 3

tory to produce a water-cooled, 12cyl, geared, and supercharged engine designated Radian. However, none were delivered to Bernard in time for installation on contest aircraft. France, not able to show at Calshot, was preparing for 1931.

The Italian Effort

Italy's defeat in 1927 following their triumph only one year earlier was a traumatic shock. Most of the negative press releases and fingerpointing were aimed at Fiat. Gen. Italo Balbo with concurrence of Benito Mussolini demanded changes and reorganization, and also full military backing. All of the leading aircraft manufacturers were asked to become involved.

The high-speed training establishment was assembled at Desenzano on Lake Garda because of better expected weather than at Lake Varese, transportation availability, team accommodations, and its remoteness for better security. The eight pilots chosen in the first selected group all had some high-speed experience. They were: Capt. Giuseppe Motta, Capt. A. Canaveri, Lt. Giovanni Monti, Lt. Remo Cadringher, W/O Tomaso Dal Molin, Sgt. Maj. Francesco Agello, Sergeant Major Huber, and Sergeant Major Gallone.

All but two of the pilots would go to Calshot. The Solent race course was laid out on Lake Garda to practice on. Three M.52s and

the smaller M.52R as back-up were the basic high-speed practice machines, plus the remaining M.39s.

The reorganization precipitated four new and different types of high-speed machines for the Schneider contest. Designs were chosen from Macchi, Fiat, Piaggio, and SIAI. Because of many types under development, the Italians felt they were in as strong a position as Britain had been in for the 1927 contest. But complexity of designs chosen brought about problems, and the Italian team had to wait until August for deliveries of contest machines. They then had to contend with the unflyable weather of the changing fall season. Almost all of the setbacks for the companies came less than a month before the contest and only about ten days before they were due to pack up and depart for England. Although the SIAI S.65, Fiat C.29, and Piaggio-Pegna P.C.J. were considered as nonstarters, only the Piaggio was not shipped to Calshot.

Fiat C.29

From the unreliable As.3 engines that were considered the downfall of the 1927 Italian ef-

Above left, a Macchi M.67 taxiing out to a safe takeoff position. A motorboat and steamship can be seen in background. Pilots had to put up with the wash from these watercraft, which could upset a seaplane on its takeoff run. *Hirsch Collection*

M.67 MM-105, with Lt. Giovanni Monti in the cockpit after a test run. The low-lying floats indicate a full fuel load. Above right, Lt. Remo Cadringher moving out for takeoff in Macchi M.67 MM-103 after it was released from its pontoon barge. The crew motor launch is in the foreground. This was a rare occasion when the Southampton waters were devoid of steamships passing through. *Hirsch Collection*

fort, Fiat produced a new As.5 1,000hp, water-cooled V–12 engine, which Fiat claimed had the best power-to-weight ratio of any water-cooled engine. The As.5 proved reliable during test runs. When he designed the new Macchi racer, Mario Castoldi used an Isotta-Fraschini engine, so the Fiat company simply designed its own airframe for the new engine. It was designated C.29.

Fiat planned to build four machines. The first was likely a stress static example and the second was probably a machine with the original tail configuration and open cockpit of the first flight vehicle. It is not known whether this machine became MM-129 or if MM-129 was the third machine built. If it was modified into MM-129, then only three of the proposed four were built. MM-130 was the machine shipped to Calshot and MM-129 was destroyed on Lake Garda.

The original C.29 had wire-braced vertical and horizontal stabilizers. Its rudder was contoured, mostly above the horizontal flight surfaces. Both MM-129 and MM-130 had full-cantilever cruciform tail unit. The C.29 was the smallest of the 1929 Schneider race planes and the only one with an enclosed cockpit, made possible by its sliding windshield capa-

ble of being moved fore and aft. The first flyable machine was delivered to Lake Garda during the first week of August and was the third of the new designs to be delivered to the team at Desenzano. On about August 10, it made its first flight with Sgt. Maj. Francesco Agello, who was the smallest of the team pilots.

The C.29 fuselage was a mixture of wood and metal construction with four steel-tube longerons which were connected and stiffened by steel-tube diagonals, internal braces, and stress wires inside the longerons. Spruce formers provided the fuselage contour. The dorsal and later ventral fins were integral to the fuselage frame. The fuselage cover was with aluminum sheet. The horizontal stabilizer, elevators, and rudder were framed in spruce and covered with aluminum. The engine mounted to two metal girder beams that were braced and supported by diagonal steel tubes attached to the fuselage bulkhead. Detachable aluminum cowling panels tightly enclosed the engine.

The wing was small. Its span was only 21.72ft (6.62m). The left wing section was 11.09ft (3.38m) and the right was 10.63ft (3.24m). The wing held deep-finned radiators on its upper and lower surfaces covering a relatively small area inside the flying wires attachment. The wing was of medium thickness with sharp leading and trailing edges. It was built up of two light-alloy spars machined to their required shape and connected by compression tubes and wire braced by diagonal drag wires. Ribs were of spruce and were attached to fittings for aileron attachment. Ailerons, like rudder and elevators, were wood ribs and spars covered with aluminum. Each wing half was attached to the fuselage by socket joints attached to the engine girder beams and bulkhead.

The C.29's Floats were constructed of wood and aluminum covered with a single-step, deep vee bottom and rounded top. Four steel struts with aluminum streamlined covers connected the floats to the fuselage just inside the wing socket joint. The floats were wire braced. The fuel tanks were between the fore and aft steel struts. The propeller was a two-blade, ground-adjustable, metal unit of 6.5ft (1.98m) diameter.

The C.29 MM-129 weighed 1,984lb (900kg) empty and grossed out at 2,557lb (1,160kg), giving it a wing loading of 29.69lb/sq-ft (145kg/sq-m). The fastest timed speed accomplished by the C.29 was 347mph (569.08km/h) at Lake Garda.

After the C.29 had been flown several times and timed on speed runs, there were some minor changes made to the floats. The machine was returned to service and it was again flown. Agello flew it around the Lake Garda course and it appeared to handle well, but just as Agello was setting down on the water there was an engine fire, probably from backfiring. The rescue boats arrived immediately and put out the fire. The pilot was not burned and the C.29 was quickly towed to the maintenance area where it underwent preparations for more testing.

Within a few days the machine was ready and Agello prepared to take it up again. For some unknown reason the little Fiat would not lift off, and it was brought back to check the floats and controls. On the second try Agello still could not get it airborne, but on the third try the machine made a very short run on the step and leaped into the air. Instead of climbing out, however, the machine suddenly slammed back down onto the water, collapsing the float struts and allowing the propeller to rip big gashes in the floats. The fuselage settled into the water and began to sink. Rescue boats arrived quickly and pulled Agello—un-

conscious and floating on his back—out of the water. He had been shaken up but was only bruised. MM-129 sank before lines could be brought out to salvage it.

MM-130 was shipped to Calshot but not flown since it was in back-up status. The Fiat C.29 is one of the few Schneider racers in Italy that survived World War II and it is on display near Milan.

Macchi M.67

The M.67 was the third derivative of Mario Castoldi's well-proven configuration, the first being the successful M.39. Its general appearance was similar to its predecessors but like Supermarine, Macchi had to scale up the size to handle a heavier, more powerful engine. Castoldi chose the Isotta-Fraschini Asso, which was an 18cyl, broad-arrow, water-cooled engine of about 1,600–1,800hp driving a three-blade propeller and designed by Giustino Cattaneo. Three machines were built, MM-103, MM-104, and MM-105. Construction began in 1928, but the first M.67 was not delivered until August 1929. A principal external difference between the M.67 and its two predecessors was that the M.67 had a straight wing and the machine was longer and more slender in appearance. It also had two long, slender wood floats, each having an aluminum fuel tank.

Another noticeable difference was the three banks of cylinders in long cowlings extending

Savoia S.65 in its final stages of assembly after shipment to Calshot. A second truss from the float to the stabilizer boom was added for extra strength. The oil coolers on side of cockpit must have made the pilot uncomfortably hot in flight. *J. D. Canary*

back to the cockpit, defining the contour of the
forward half of the fuselage. There were three
oil-cooling radiators, one under the chin of the
fuselage and one on each side under the cockpit. The fuselage was of composite or mixed
construction. Forward of the cockpit, metal
was used in the engine bay, support cradle,
the fuel tanks support, and a rigid mount for
the wing and floats attachment. Aft of the
cockpit, construction was mainly of wood, including the full-cantilever integral tail unit of
the typical Macchi cruciform configuration.

The wing was conventional, all-wood, two-
spar construction with plywood covering and
attached metal radiators. A major consideration in design was the dissipation of the
tremendous heat that would be generated by
the 18cyl engine, so the wing had every possible bit of surface covered top and bottom with
engine-coolant radiators. Only the wing tips
and plywood-covered, metal-rib ailerons were
not covered with a radiator surface. The radiators had small fins to provide additional cool-

ing surface. There also were radiators on the
upper surface of the floats between the fore
and aft struts on MM-103 and MM-105, and
the struts themselves had wraparound radiators. The floats were wire braced to the wings.

The M.67 had a wingspan of 29.47ft
(8.98m), the left wing was 7.02in (180mm)
longer than the right wing. Wing area was
145.65sq-ft (13.531sq-m). Length was 25.02ft
(7.63m) overall and fuselage length was
22.69ft (6.92m), floats were 20.32ft (6.14m),
and gross weight was 4,750lb (2,152kg), which
was 1,410lb (641kg) greater than the M.52.

Weather kept flying to a minimum and
training and testing was at a slow pace. Six
days after the first flight of the M.67 at Lake
Garda, Capt. Giuseppe Motta made his first
flight, followed by several subsequent flights.
Motta also had been involved in attempts to
get the Piaggio P.c.7 airborne and was considered the only pilot that was familiar with the
machine. Weather again kept flying down and
it wasn't until August 22 that Motta again

took the M.67 (MM-104) for some high-speed runs around the course. While rounding a corner, he entered a high-speed stall, plunged into Lake Garda, and was killed instantly. The exact reason for his losing control was not known, but some observers suspected that he was overcome by exhaust fumes entering the cockpit.

Ventilators were then fitted to the other two machines just before being shipped to Calshot on August 29. On September 4, Lt. Giovanni Monti made the first M.67 flight from Calshot to Spithead beyond Ryde. His takeoff was clean with a good run on the step, although he had swerved after being balked by a motor launch running across his path. Most of his flight was far out past Ryde, probably to limit observers onshore from obtaining estimates of his speed. He landed in about 10min with a broken flying wire and taxied to the ramp.

On September 5, Lt. Remo Cadringher attempted to take the other M.67 up for its first flight and encountered problems. He couldn't prevent the port float from digging into the water as he opened the throttle and his machine just kept turning in a series of arcs over the surface of The Solent. The M.67 couldn't be made to get up on the step or unstick. It was brought back and some rigging adjustments were made as well as shifting some weight and additional fuel to the starboard float to solve the problem. Cadringher eventually got the machine airborne. The Asso engines in both machines would not run smoothly at full throttle, so the full-throttle stops were retarded to bring the rpm down from 3000 to 2800, where the engine seemed to run smoothly.

Savoia S.65

Of the four new Italian Schneider types intended for the 1929 contest, only three actually were shipped to Calshot. The Savoia S.65 was one, and it was the most unusual. It was, for that period, a far-sighted design and quite revolutionary. The aircraft was designed by Alessandro Marchetti, who attempted to obtain the power of two engines with the frontal area of only one engine, and at the same time resolve the problem of propeller torque.

There had been previous push-pull tandem-engine Schneider contestants with the Savoia

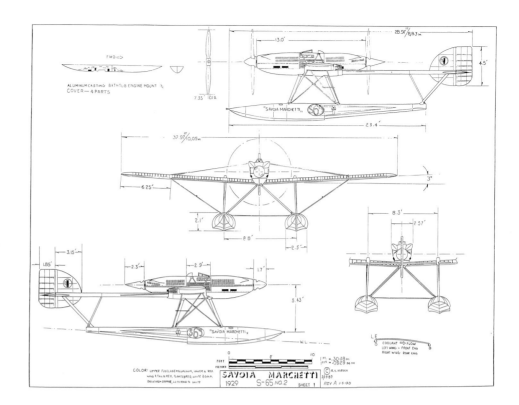

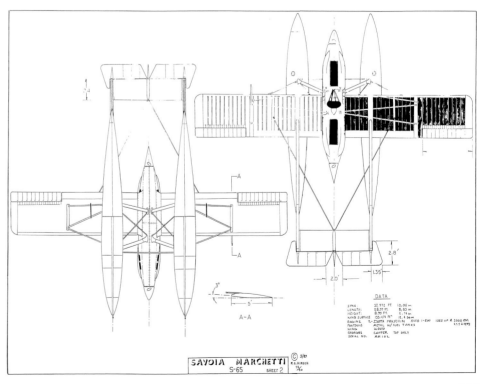

propeller would benefit from the forward propeller already having accelerated the airstream, thus allowing it to increase still further the velocity of the whole air flow. Also, it would allow use of smaller diameter—thus more efficient—propellers. During testing, however, it proved to be almost impracticable to synchronize the rpm's effectively, which seemed to adversely affect the aerodynamic stability.

The Savoia was a low-wing, twin-float, twin-boom monoplane with an unconventional fuselage that consisted of two short engine nacelles and cockpit. The nacelles covered two Isotta-Fraschini Asso water-cooled V–12 engines of 1,080hp at 3000 rpm, each driving a two-blade metal propeller of 7.35ft (2.24m) diameter. The central fuselage also provided a 2.9ft (0.884m) cockpit between the tandem engines, which showed up in flight tests to be far from ideal. Oil coolers were flush-mounted on both sides of the cockpit. The fuselage shell was only 13ft (4.524m). Front spinner was 1.7ft (0.52m) and the rear one was 2.3 ft (0.7m), making a total of 17ft (5.18m) for fuselage length. Overall length was 28.97ft (8.83m).

The entire lower quarter of the short fuselage was a cast-aluminum bathtub engine mount, bolted together in four sections. The cockpit was mounted on the bathtub casting and four steel struts connected it to the all-metal floats. The bathtub also contained the two wing panel spar joints. The floats were a narrow 2.5ft (0.76m) and extremely long at 23.4ft (7.13m), with the aft sections attached by vee struts to the two narrow booms extended from the wing spars to the horizontal stabilizer. The vertical stabilizer, which was cruciform shaped at Calshot, was mounted on the horizontal stabilizer centerline.

The wing was wire braced as were the floats. The tail unit was laterally braced by a stabilizing wire running from the wing spars through the booms to the tail. The wing was rectangular in form, with a small 90deg radius rounded tip at the leading edge. Most of the upper surface was covered by copper radiators fastened to the plywood skin and with internal troughs to carry the water to and from the engines. Construction was all-wood, with two spars and ribs fabricated of spruce and ash. Ailerons were fabric covered as were the horn-

S.22 in 1921 and in 1923 the Latham, both flying boats. But by 1929, highly streamlined small racer configuration, with a special supercharged engine were the trend. On the S.65, however, the concept was that the rear

balanced elevator and broad-chord rudder. Wing area was 133.424sq-ft (12.395sq-m).

Only one S.65 was built by SIAI at Sesto Calende during 1928 and 1929. It was numbered MM-102. This machine was completed by midsummer of 1929, but had problems with overheating during engine run-in and taxi tests. Flight-test trials are not known to have brought results, but MM-102 was shipped with the rest of the machines to Calshot. However, there were fuel system and overheating problems at Calshot and the S.65 did not make it to the navigation and float-test trials, but stood down with the Fiat C.29. Once back in Italy, the S.65 underwent flight trials again through 1930, with expectations of development improvements for 1931 competition. But as flights were resumed, some engine problems were corrected while new problems surfaced. The longitudinal instability became acute, and on one test flight W/O Tomaso Dal Molin was killed in a crash during a high-speed run for a speed record. He was said to have been the only team pilot small enough to fit into the cockpit. Speed of the S.65 was said to be well over 350mph.

Piaggio-Pegna P.c.7

Giovanni Pegna's last of the Piaggio-Pegna Schneider trophy racer designs was the most revolutionary of all the Italian projects. Humorous comments in the news referred to it as a flying submarine. The P.c.7 was far beyond any of Pegna's earlier advanced projects. Some writers claimed it bordered on the fantastic, with too many revolutionary design features and with no vestige of reality.

Pegna tested models of his designs in the Pegna wind tunnel. His first design concept was the P.c.1 which was a combination of airframe and boat hull with a tractor propeller, driven by an extension shaft, on the nose. The propeller was kept out of the water during taxiing, takeoff, and landing by tilting the engine 15deg upward. When the P.c.1 became airborne, the engine with its propeller would be hydraulically lowered back to the line-of-flight. In 1924, airframes were constructed for the P.c.2 using a Fiat engine and a slimmer fuselage and the P.c.3 using a Curtiss D-12 engine, but not covered. They were conventional two-float machines with wings that were thick at roots but tapered off sharply to tip. Neither showed advantages over the Curtiss R3C-series racers, and Italy did not file an entry for 1924.

The P.c.7 was first laid out to use a 1,000hp Fiat engine. But Pegna switched to an 800hp Isotta-Fraschini water-cooled V-12 engine driving a two-blade metal propeller for flight and a two-blade variable-pitch hydro-propeller that could be decoupled from the engine and feathered in flight. The engine was placed well back into the fuselage with clutch connection to the long propeller shaft. Another clutch and shaft mechanism was mounted on the rear of the engine to drive the hydropropeller. It in turn was to drive the machine through the water until it was moving fast enough for the hydrofoil to lift the airframe clear of the water so the pilot could clutch in the aero-propeller. The thrust of the aero-propeller would then pull the machine until liftoff speed was attained. Then the hydro-propeller would be automatically declutched. The clutches and transmission gears were designed by Fiat.

A large vertical lever on the left side of the cockpit operated push-pull rods connecting the two clutches via bell cranks and rocking levers. Another system was connected to a hydro-propeller bell crank and pitch-change mechanism to the propeller. On the right side of the cockpit there was a cable and push-rod system connecting the aero-propeller shaft brake to keep the propeller from turning while moving forward on the water. The same lever through another attached lever also controlled a rubber valve closing the air intake for the carburetors. The engine then breathed through the cockpit hatch.

The P.c.7 was a high-elliptical-wing monoplane with watertight wing and fuselage structures. Conventional floats were replaced by a set of three hydrofoils, two forward and one aft. The two forward hydrofoils were attached to broad-chord cantilever struts. Both hydrofoils offered a small amount of lift in the air at angles of attack above 3deg, such as during takeoffs and landings. But any water contact below the 3deg line of flight would be hazardous. Water touchdowns would have to be with the nose high and the hydro-propeller running. The slightest negative angle of the hydrofoils when in contact with the water would produce negative pressure 800 times that of when they were in air, and would force

Top, the Savoia-Marchetti crew moving the S.65 back into the hangar after an engine run-up. A Supermarine S.6 is in background. The Savoia drew a lot of attention and much speculation, but didn't fly. Bottom, the Piaggio-Pegna P.c.7, last of Giovanni Pegna's attempts at building a winning Schneider racer. It was the most advanced design of all the racers, but Pegna just didn't have time to complete its development. The P.c.7 was dubbed "the flying submarine" by the press. *B. C. Kavelaars*

tried the Forlanini hydrofoils on a seaplane. In 1912 a Farman seaplane with Guidoni fluid wings added under the wings operated successfully and smoothly on the water. In 1916 a seaplane was built in the Milan Isotta-Fraschini plant with vee-shaped hydrofoils from wing floats to fuselage hull. In 1917 there were at least eight different designs of hydrofoils proposed for seaplanes, and some were built and tested.

There were some problems with carburetor and exhaust openings and the oil radiator, all of which needed improvement and functional timing. Pegna finally put the air intake holes on top of the fuselage instead of the sides of the hull. He also cooled the oil by water from the principal radiators by means of a tubular radiator within the hull. The P.c.7 could not be made to function sufficiently for flight training and would not be ready for Calshot. It was temporarily abandoned by Piaggio and the Italian Air Ministry. However, piloted by Dal Molin, the P.c.7 rose on its hydrovanes at the angle as expected, but for lack of time, takeoffs were not tried. Tests were continued in mid-1930 but there were too many problems to be solved, and the Air Ministry eventually canceled its contracts.

The British Effort

The excitement of Britain's win at Venice had barely died down and the matter of biennial competitions was just settled when Britain's RAeC made the preliminary announcement of the 1929 contests on February 29, 1929. There were still decisions on the venue to be made by the committee, but the race would once more be held over The Solent between Isle of Wight and the mainland. After Flt. Lt. S. M. Kinkead's fatal accident in 1928, Britain's High Speed Flight had been re-formed and moved to Calshot.

In June 1928, Flt. Lt. D'Arcy Grieg had tried to beat De Bernardi's speed record of 318.5mph (512.5km/h) in S.5 N-219, but his four runs' average was only 319.57mph (514.19km/h). This was not the full 1 percent increase required by FAI. Clearly, Britain would have to do better. The recognized suppliers of high-speed racing seaplanes were Gloster and Supermarine. Both of them were approached to develop new aircraft capable of significantly higher speeds.

the nose under and the machine would tumble over.

The idea of using hydrofoils on seaplanes was not new. They were tried by Calderara, Crocco, Forlanini, Guidoni, and in 1911 Pegna

Gloster VI

In November of 1927 Henry P. Folland and Howard E. Preston began the design of a Gloster IV successor designated Gloster V, which was intended for the 1929 Schneider contest. It also was a sesquiplane design and was to use the new Napier Lion VII-D of 1,320hp at 3600rpm. It weighed 300lb (136kg) more than the previous model due to a newly added supercharger.

Wind-tunnel tests of the Gloster V model showed great promise of well over 350mph (563.5km/h). However, it was discovered in the mock-up stage that the Napier engine interfered with the upper wing main spar as it passed through the fuselage. Redesign was required, but any repositioning of the wing further jeopardized both the pilot's vision and the clean lines of the original design, and would result in loss of speed.

Instead of redesigning the Gloster V, Folland and Preston began designing a new monoplane, the Gloster VI, in May of 1928. It was of composite construction of wood and metal with multi-spar, multi-rib wood wings of spruce. Two layers of spruce skin covered the overall wing structure, with an additional layer added to the high-stress areas. The fuselage was all-metal, semi-monocoque construction with oval formers and flush-rivetted aluminum skin.

The floats were made by Gloster. They were flush-rivetted aluminum and contained the main fuel tanks. The floats were single-step vee bottom, similar in appearance only to those of the Gloster IV. They were connected

S.6 N-247 launched from the slipway at Woolston. It was then moved out to the Supermarine pontoon for delivery to Calshot. *S. Hudek*

to the wing root by steel-tubing struts covered by aluminum fairings. Two engine-driven fuel pumps raised the fuel from each float tank to a 2gal (7.58ltr) tank in the fuselage that gravity-fed fuel to the engine.

The flat-surfaced radiators were very think in cross section and were fitted to the wing on top and bottom. The oil was cooled by a circular oil cooler and tank combination that completely wrapped around the fuselage behind the cockpit and flush with the fuselage. There were additional flat-tube oil radiators on the upper surface of the floats. When it was needed, oil could be sent through this system via oilways in the leading edge of the four struts and then to the fuselage cooler tank and back to the engine.

The wing was semi-elliptical, with the wing root being thinner than the mid-section with the widest chord. This provided lateral control improvement at low speeds. The reverse taper also induced less drag at the wing root, where fuselage drag creates interference. Streamlined stress wires fastened from the floats and fuselage to wing at the widest and thickest section. The three banks of cylinders were

blended in with the general, as they were on the Supermarine S.5. The fuselage, wing, and empennage were painted gold and the radiators were copper. Floats were light blue except for the copper radiators.

Construction of the two machines, N-249 and N-250, was completed in July 1929. N-249 was delivered to Calshot on August 12 and N-250 five days later. The first flight was made on August 26 in N-249, but Sqdn. Ldr. A. H. Orlebar only reached about 30ft (9m) in altitude before the engine quit. Engines in both airframes were ground tested. On late afternoon, on August 31, Orlebar got one flight on N-250. Within the next five days, N-249 and N-250 were flown by the High Speed Flight pilots. Newswriters reported that the Gloster Aircraft Co. had never produced a better example of aircraft construction. It was an outstanding example of high standards in their workshop, and the design was highly praised, as were Folland and Preston.

Supermarine S.6

The Napier Lion, which had been the main British competition engine since 1919, was reaching a point of no return in new developments. Horsepower increases sufficient enough to warrant development could only be had through supercharging. The output of an engine depended on the air mass it could consume within a given time and for a given displacement, and a supercharger provided the most reliable means of constant air mass pressure.

Napier considered the Lion sufficient for many more years of commercial products. They therefore declined a contract offer from the Air Ministry to provide a supercharged engine for the S.6. After some prodding, Napier later changed their minds for the Gloster VI. Rolls-Royce, through Henry Royce himself, accepted an invitation to design a new engine of high power, specifically for Supermarine's Schneider contest aircraft. So the design of the new engine was begun by Royce and A. G. Elliot at West Wittering in November 1928. It was eventually named the "R" engine and was guaranteed to produce 1,500hp.

The Rolls-Royce Buzzard (2,237.8ci or 36.7ltr) was the starting point in the R engine's design. It produced only 825hp at 2000rpm. Supercharging was the key to power increase. James E. Ellor, an expert on super-charging, was brought into the firm by Royce. F. R. Banks of the Associated Ethyl Co. also was brought in, and his special fuel mixtures allowed maximum use of the 6:1 compression ratio.

On May 14 the R engine was producing 1,545hp at 2750rpm for 15min. By July 23 it completed a 60min run, producing 1,615hp at 3000rpm, and by August 27 it ran for 80min, giving 1,800hp at 2850rpm and, for a short run, 1,900hp at 2900rpm.

Reginald J. Mitchell consulted with Maj. R. J. Bulman who was responsible for engines at the British Air Ministry and then began his design of the S.6 while the R engine was still on paper. The S.6 was Mitchell's first all-metal racer, and two were built: N-247 and N-248. It had a semi-monocoque fuselage with forty-six internal section frames spaced 6 and 8in apart. Although of metal, the wings had the same two-spar construction with ribs of diaphragm webs with lightening holes and flanges of extruded angle sections. Wing radiators were of 24 gauge continuous aluminum sheets instead of copper strips as on the S.5, and the sheets were rivetted together, with 1/16in (1.58mm) spacers to provide for the water cavity. These were fastened to the wing structure by screws and covered the entire wing surface except ailerons. Wing area was 145sq-ft (13.47sq-m).

The tunnel-like windshield ran straight back, and the forward-blending cowl came to a point between the engine cylinder-head cowlings. Oil cooling and fuel tankage had to be recalculated and redesigned for the larger and heavier engine. Oil was cooled by being circulated through coolers that ran the full length of the fuselage on both sides, then up the vertical stabilizer and down into an oil filter tank. It then ran down to another oil cooler along the belly of the airframe and back to the engine, giving the maximum possible cooling surface.

The forward float struts had to be repositioned farther forward on the fuselage to help support the larger and longer engine. The floats were of Supermarine design with fuel tanks in the center position of each float. The right float was 1.05ft (0.32m) longer than the left float. The right float carried 58gal (263ltr); the left float carried 48gal (218ltr) of fuel.

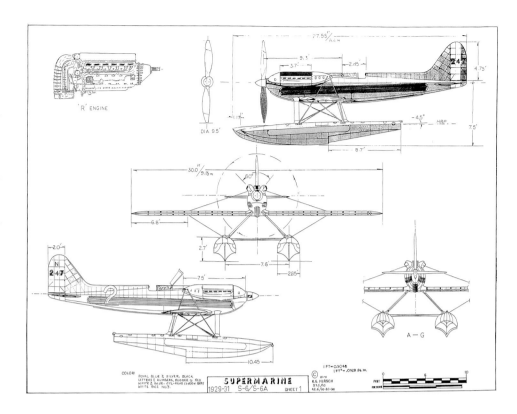

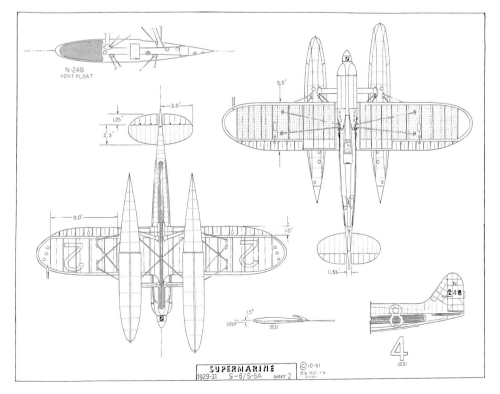

S.6 N-247 after delivery at Calshot. This machine had radiators on the side of the floats which allowed water cooling during taxiing. *Hirsch Collection*

water to Calshot. There it was delivered to the RAF High Speed Flight team. N-248 followed in about eighteen days since it had been completed about August 15.

Preliminaries and Trials

N-247 was flown to Calshot on August 10 by Sqdn. Ldr. A. H. Orlebar, who commanded the re-formed High Speed Flight team. At first, the S.6 would turn in circles when the engine was opened up because the rudder could not counteract the engine's torque. The first takeoff was made possible by transferring most of the fuel to the right float. Later, the right float was lengthened and fuel capacity increased to 90gal (341ltr), while the left float gas capacity was reduced to 25gal (95ltr). Also, the C.G. was moved forward by the added fuel. Small ram-air intakes were added to the wing tips to assist internal cooling. The float radiators also were installed at this time.

Sunday, August 18: At 6:00pm the sea had calmed down, although there were some rain clouds at various points on the horizon. Orlebar had the R engine in the S.6 run up, and then he climbed into the cockpit. The S.6 was launched and towed out toward Lee-on-Solent. The Bristol starter was then used from the launch pontoon to get the engine started again. Orlebar headed into the wind and took off. There was a little more wind to help him as compared to the preceding Monday, when he made a run of 31sec. He climbed a few hundred feet and did gentle left turns, banking moderately. After a couple of circles between Calshot and Cowes he made two right turns near the Isle of Wight (IOW). He disappeared in the evening mist near Ryde, and each time he came back over Calshot he was faster and banked more sharply as he got used to the machine. The last time over Calshot he was very fast and put the machine into a vertical bank. After 27min he landed and was towed in. This was his fourth flight with a total of 1.5hr in the machine.

Monday, August 19: F/O H.R.D. Waghorn was selected next to fly the S.6. It was a calm morning with an almost glassy sea and scattered clouds. Waghorn went out at 6:30am, first taxiing about to get used to the controls. He then made a very good takeoff run, climbed out at a few hundred feet, and did several vertical banks plus high-speed runs. He came in

Gross weight was 5,771lb (2,617kg) giving a wing loading of 40psf (195.29kg/sq-m). N-247's floats had a short wing stub near the rear of the floats to act as a hydrofoil to help produce lift on takeoff and a planing function for softer sink on landing. They were removed immediately after the first taxi tests. N-248's floats had radiators on the top front surfaces; N-247's had them on each side near the waterline.

The two S.6s were built together at the Woolston factory when the R engine at Derby had run 100min, delivering 1,850hp. The first fuselage (N-247) had the frames completed by April 20 and skin was fitted on by May 11. By June 10 the entire airframe was virtually completed and by June 21 an R-engine mockup was installed for load tests which were still being done with sand bags.

On Monday, August 5—just one month before the contest date—the first completed S.6 (N-247) was launched into the water for the first time. After some onshore engine running it was taken in tow by the Supermarine launch and towed down the Southampton

slow and made a good landing. He was airborne for 34min. Before Waghorn alighted on the water, F/O Richard Atcherley took one of the Gloster biplanes up for a flight; it had just been returned to serviceable status. After the flight, the ground crews used the Gloster to practice moving a machine on and off the pontoon barge. When that was over, Orlebar climbed in and flew it around the course while D'Arcy Grieg practiced his maneuvers in a Flycatcher. At 3:30pm Flt. Lt. George H. Stainforth went up in a Flycatcher.

Tuesday, August 20: Atcherley had his first flight in the S.6. He practiced taxiing for about 15min, then he took a long run for his takeoff. He appeared to have handled it well and after returning he made a perfect landing.

Wednesday, August 21: The Gloster IV, sporting a new enclosed canopy installed for

Rolling the two S.6s out at Calshot in questionable weather. N-248 had race No. 4. Left, H.R.D. Waghorn climbs into S.6 N-247. It will then be moved onto its pontoon barge, from which it can be launched and operated on its floats.

team practicing, was flown by the team pilots. Atcherley made his second flight in the S.6 at 11:25am, trying out a new propeller. After a couple of aborted attempts he got off in a very short run. The engine began to miss in steep banks and Atcherley returned in 6min for a smooth landing. The S.6 seemed to touch down very smoothly for a racer and to pull up quickly on takeoffs.

At 3:30pm Waghorn made his second flight in S.6 (N-247), taking a long, smooth run on the step before gently lifting off. After circling around a few times he dived over Calshot and onto the Southampton 1.86mi (3km) course for a couple of all-out runs, passing very low over the pier. It was quite noticeable that the Rolls-Royce engine had a much less ear-splitting sound than the shriek of the Napier when running all-out. Those observers on the ground— many of whom had flown—had never seen anything traveling so fast. Most of the great bursts of speed ended in spectacular climbs. Waghorn then flew over Calshot Castle with the engine idling (almost), and then S.6 floated down with absolute steadiness at a ground speed of about 95mph (152.95km/h). Waghorn landed after 38min of giving a beautiful exhibition of flying.

The Gloster VI was then run up on the slipway and lowered into the water with Orlebar in the cockpit. As he was being readied to taxi, the ship *Mauretania* came around the corner from The Solent as the S.6 was being towed in. By the time the water had calmed down the wind became too gusty, and the Gloster was hauled back onto the slipway and shut down. About 7:40pm Orlebar decided the water was smooth enough to justify taxi trials. Again, he was just clear of the slipway and had started to taxi when another large ship appeared from The Solvent. The Gloster VI again was tossed about, bending the propeller. Orlebar shut down the engine and was towed back.

Each day there was only one comparatively short period of time in which conditions were just right for taking the racing seaplanes off the water; if for any reason that period of time was missed, the day was wasted. On Thursday morning, August 22, conditions were doubtful, so Orlebar had the new Gloster loaded on a pontoon barge and dispatched to near Lee-on-Solent, and he followed in a small, fast boat. Upon arrival he found the sea there also too rough, and the machine was towed back. The Gloster remained on the moored pontoon barge all day but by 7:00pm, flying time was declared to be over. By now the second Supermarine S.6 (N-248) had arrived from Woolston. Its engine had by then accumulated 2.5hr of flying time, which was exceptionally long for a racing engine.

The advance guard of the Italian team arrived consisting of a small party of airmen, warrant officers, and one technical officer. They traveled to their hangar, closed the door, and nothing more was seen of them. The crates that had arrived earlier contained the two Macchi M.52s. An RAF armed guard was posted outside the hangar each night.

Friday, August 23: The wind was so strong that the machines were not even taken out of their hangars. Shortly after midnight the Rolls-Royce engine on N-248 was run up. Viscount Hugh Trenchard flew into Calshot from Cattewater and inspected the High Speed Flight team. It was also the day Britain received the sad news that Italian pilot Capt. Giuseppe Motta had been killed on Lake Garda in an M.67.

Saturday, August 24: Although the sun was shining most of the day, the wind was still too strong, tossing whitecaps on the waves from the horizon right up the Southampton water, precluding any flying. Later in the day there was some interest generated when Orlebar took the Gloster VI (N-249) out on taxi trials for a short time. Later in the afternoon one of the M.52s was wheeled out to the run-up ramp and the engine was started up. After a full run-up check, however, it was wheeled back into the hangar.

Sunday, August 25: Due to Sunday worship services, there was no flying in the morning. The second Gloster VI (N-250) arrived in the afternoon and was being assembled in the hangar. Now, two Supermarine S.6s and two Gloster VIs had been delivered at Calshot. In early afternoon the weather was perfect at Calshot but was rougher in mid-Solent. Orlebar sent Glosters N-249 and N-250 on pontoon barges quite a distance east of The Solent and followed in his motor launch. D'Arcy Grieg, Waghorn, and Atcherley went out in a speedboat to watch. The Solent was thick with sailboats, yachts, and speedboats.

Orlebar climbed into the cockpit of one of the N-250. After being started up and having the machine put into the water, he put it through a short run on the step and then headed southwest and opened the throttle. Within 30sec he came unstuck. It looked beautiful, flying about 30ft (9m) above the water for about 0.75mi (1.21km) before the engine sputtered. Orlebar put it back on the water and the engine stopped. Speedboats dashed up to the machine and the other pilots slowly took it in tow back to the slipway. Onshore, Napier mechanic Tullin soon had the engine running again, but the machine was put back in the hangar. Meanwhile, Orlebar had gone back to N-249, still on its pontoon barge, and eventually got it into the air. After some circling and steep banks, he flew it four times up and down the 1.86mi (3km) course, but not at full throttle.

After flying the Gloster VI, Orlebar was able to also make a flight in S.6 N-248. The S.6's stalling speed with full load was 110mph (176.99km/h). Its R engine ate up 2gal (7.58ltr) of fuel per minute, and the course was expected to take 60min or 120gal (454.8ltr). Since the 115gal (435.85ltr) available was insufficient, the S.6 engines would have to be run under 2950rpm, developing only 1,850hp.

Monday, August 26: A heavy mist covered the area throughout the morning. The afternoon breeze that cleared it out became too brisk for the new racers, so only the training machines such as the Avrocet and Flycatcher were used. No other flying took place. The Italian team kept pressing for a twenty- to thirty-day postponement. S.5 N-219 and S.6 N-248 left for Woolston for some adjustments. The constant flights of the S.6s between Calshot and Woolston for minor repairs, engine changes, and adjustments were made mostly by carrying the aircraft on pontoon barges towed by motor launches. During this period, the aircraft sustained various small bumps and dents, and there was never enough time to pound them out.

Tuesday, August 27: This day was bright and sunny but with the sea much too rough for racing seaplanes; there was no flying. The Schneider Trophy Committee held a day-long meeting and in the late afternoon drafted a reply to Italy's request for a short postpone-

Top, the modified Gloster IV being launched for one of the team's practice flights. N-223 was one of the three usable practice machines. Bottom, Gloster IVA N-222 being eased down into the water from the slipway. These became very useful machines to the High Speed Flight team. Note how closely the ocean liner passes the active course waters. *Hirsch Collection*

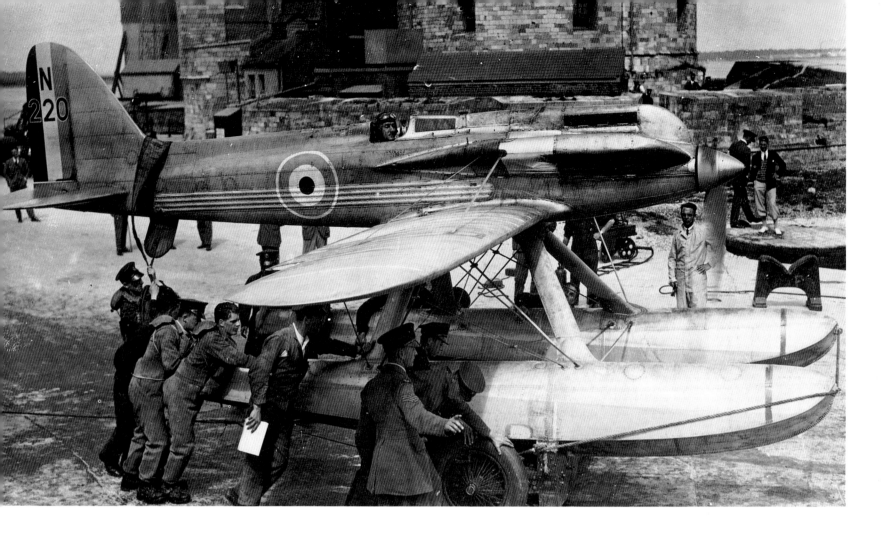

N-220 was assembled at Calshot and moved to the water slipway for flight tests. Part of the Calshot Castle is visible in background. *S. Hudek*

ment. After the death of Motta, the Italian Air Attache in London had contacted the RAeC and officially requested the postponement. From the RAF base at Calshot at 6:00pm the RAeC issued a pronouncement. It said the organizing committee's unanimous decision was that the date was fixed and could not be changed except on a day-to-day basis due to weather. This ruling was sent to the Italian Air Attache.

The smartness and cut of the Italian team's uniforms and the strict discipline to which they were subjected was apparent, compared to the baggy uniforms and relaxed discipline of the RAF. The Italians brought their own food supply, their own chefs, and their own doctor who set down strict rules of conduct for the team. They could not drink or smoke, nor fraternize with British women. Team members had to be in bed by 10:00pm every night. They also took the multitude of the British team's pranks with good nature.

Wednesday and Thursday, August 28–29: Both days had weather that dictated no flying, so there was little activity.

Friday through Tuesday, August 30 to September 3: Just one week before the trials, Italian General Balbo arrived and took over command of the team. On Saturday, August 31, Orlebar again flew N-250. The aircraft handled satisfactorily but the engine cut out on turns and occasionally in level flight. D'Arcy Grieg and George Stainforth flew both Glosters during the next five days, but Napier could not find the cause of the engine cutout. The decision was made to withdraw the Glosters, and the S.5 (N-219) was substituted. There was little other activity for the next three days, but a lot of last-minute adjustments were made on the machines.

Wednesday, September 4: The day was hot, and a morning haze had covered the entire area. The supermarine S.5 (N-219) had returned from Woolston along with the S.6 (N-

248). During the morning the Savoia S.65 was wheeled out of the hangar and one engine was run up, then it was taken back into the sheds. Orlebar took off in a Flycatcher to check out the weather on the course. The Italian pilots had been practicing on the course in the M.52, now painted black to distinguish it from those machines that would compete. Then Monti made the first flight in an M.67 and landed without incident. Dal Molin then took the M.52R up but fouled a float on a floating hazard on takeoff, ripping a gash about 6in (0.15m) long in the float close to the step. Water could be seen streaming from the float as he climbed out. When he came back in to land all available motorboats rushed to the machine to stabilize it until it could be put on a pontoon barge and brought ashore.

Thursday, September 5: Another hot day with the morning mist almost as thick as a London fog. By 10:00am it had cleared enough to fly and Dal Molin took the M.52 up for a look at the course. He came back and landed opposite Calshot in Southampton water. At 1:45pm Stainforth took the Gloster N-250 out for his first flight in it, and with a full load of fuel. He only remained aloft for 5min, and then it was returned to the hangar.

About noon Sir Samuel Hoare (British Air Minister), Sir Philip Sassoon (RAeC chairman), and Viscount Hugh Trenchard were present. Viscount Trenchard, the undersecretary for air, was flown around the course. A little later in the afternoon a twin-hulled Savoia S.55 came in at Calshot from Italy and was greeted by General Balbo, the Italian team commander. The S.5 was taken out to fly by D'Arcy Grieg but the engine stopped and flight was abandoned.

In the early evening Stainforth took the Gloster VI (N-250) up for about 20min and landed in almost darkness. A fuel starvation problem had occurred and it was traced to the fuel pump. The contest team's pilot selection was finally released in the late evening. The order of start was to be as follows:

Aircraft	Registration	Race	Pilot	Reserves
S.6	N-247	2	Waghorn	Stainforth, Gloster VI (N-249;N-250)
M.52R	—	4	Dal Molin	—
S.5	N-219	5	D'Arcy Grieg	Agello, M.52
M.67	103	7	Cadringher	—
S.6	N-248	8	Atcherley	—
M.67	105	10	Monti	—

Friday, September 6: The cool mist of early morning was appreciated after two previous hot days. Weather was excellent for navigability and flotation tests and competitors were ready at 7:00am. The Supermarine S.5 had been substituted for the Glosters since both of them had the same engine breathing problems. The Gloster VI was clearly the faster machine, but it was doubtful that it could sustain the course, so both had been withdrawn.

The first machine out was the M.67 (No. 10) and flown by Monti. It was followed a few min-

Tomaso Dal Molin being brought ashore after the Schneider contest. The M.52R placed second ahead of the reworked Savoia S.5. *A. Coccon*

utes later by Dal Molin in the M.52R (No. 4). By 8:00am both machines were on their pontoon barges being taken toward Calshot lighthouse, which was southeast of where they would undertake the navigability trials. They were followed by the second M.67 (No. 7). The two S.6s and S.5 were next to go. They had been on their pontoon barges since 7:50am.

There was a line of boats marking the lane down which the machines had to land and taxi, but a shift in the morning wind necessitated a change in the course. The marker boats were directed to new stations and they moved with some difficulty and confusion; several high-speed boats found themselves in the new landing area and had to be cleared out. By 9:15am, however, Waghorn in the S.6 (No. 2) was given the signal to start.

Waghorn got off well and after making a circuit he came in to land toward the lane and made an excellent landing. But then he slowed down too quickly and too much, sinking down into the water to the float's waterline and causing water to spray over him in sheets. The judges by then were watching his speed very closely, but he got away again without difficulty. On the second landing he did not let the machine sink but kept it on the step. After a final circuit Waghorn taxied across the finish line and headed toward the mooring buoys.

The rest of the contestants followed one by one, the M.52R following Waghorn. All passed their tests without difficulty, except for the M.67 (No. 10). It sort of chased its tail until a Navy boat came barging across the area, creating ripples that broke the machine loose and it finally got off. Landing and taxiing was roughly from south to north but takeoffs were toward the east. The busy waterway of The Solent was somewhat of a rude shock to the

Italians after the tranquility of their training on Lake Garda. No. 10 had not been in the air before the navigability trials. It was distinguishable by its three-blade propeller, in addition to the race numbers, which couldn't always be seen.

For the 6hr mooring test the machines were all returned to Calshot and tied to buoys for their protection from the elements in the little bay north of the station and Calshot Castle. The passing of high-speed boats, however, kept creating waves, which at times constituted a risk. At about midpoint of the watertightness test S.6 N-248 was beginning to develop a list. R. J. Mitchell was contacted and gave his opinion that the machine would remain afloat for the next 3hr, which it did. At about 6:00pm the 6hr mooring test was completed and the last of the machines were returned to their hangars to make ready for the Saturday contest.

Part of the routine maintenance and checks was replacement of spark plugs. On the S.6 (No. 2), one of the plugs removed showed white metal on the electrode. The mechanic showed it to the technician, Flight Officer Moon, who quickly called A. C. Lovesey of Rolls-Royce. It was decided to change the cylinder block, which was permitted by the rules. It was fortunate that a group of Rolls-Royce production fitters who had worked on the R engine were in various Southampton hotels. They were waiting to join the Supermarine design staff which would board the SS *Monarch*.

All of the fitters were speedily rounded up and began the difficult task of a block change with the engine still in the airframe, and without special equipment. Their skills and determination brought about many innovations and by morning the engine was run up satisfactorily. The old engine had a badly scored cylinder wall, broken rings, and a damaged piston. It was believed that the slow 450rpm idling caused a lack of lubrication and seized the rings.

Lovesey decided not to fly No. 2 with the repaired engine before the contest. When Orlebar arrived at the hangar he was surprised to find himself confronted by a bunch of grimy and exhausted mechanics, most of whom he had never seen before. Shortly after, Waghorn showed up and they were told the whole story

by Moon. On contest day the Schneider Committee went over the facts and confirmed that the rules had not been broken; No. 2 was ready for the contest.

The SS *Monarch* was docked at the Southampton docks early Saturday morning. It was chartered especially for the Supermarine Aviation Works design staff for viewing the contest. At 11:00am the vessel departed for a position just off Osborne, IOW, but it eventually anchored inside the course between Ryde and Cowes about 2mi (3.2km) from Oxford.

The Contest

Nearly a million people were expected to witness the great international seaplane contest for the Schneider Trophy. The race took place on Saturday, September 7, 1929, off the IOW. Most of the spectators were lined up at the seven vantage points for the navigability trials. Two land airports at Hamble and East Cowes and a seaplane station at Cowes were reserved for visitors. The Spithead area inside the course was zoned for various vessels ac-

Pilot Lt. Col. Mario Bernasconi and ground crew, with the M.52 perched on its dollies. This machine was painted black at Calshot to distinguish it as a training aircraft. A. Coccon

165

cording to their size. The vantage points were: Portsmouth, Southsea, Stokes Bay, Hayling Island, Lee-on-Solent public enclosures along the sea front, Ryde pier head, Cowes and East Cowes (IOW) turning point of the course, St. Helens (IOW) Puckpool Park.

On Saturday morning, September 7, the little town of Ryde (IOW) presented a gay spectacle of people and flags. The weather was perfect with a light easterly wind of about 10mph (16.1km/h) that swept away the early morning mist. Although a haze could be seen over the distant horizon, Portsmouth and Southsea were clear. The turning point pylon off West Cowes still was not fully visible in the slight mist, but the Sea View pylon was clearly visible. Far-off Hayling Island was also obscured by a slight haze which would disappear by afternoon. The contest was scheduled for 2:00pm.

Excitement of both participants and spectators mounted by the hour. This year the

Gloster VI, launched from the slipway and being readied for takeoff. The ship in the background was typical and its presence, as well as others, often forced cancellation of takeoff. Right, S.6 No. 2 with A. C. Lovesey, Flight Officer Moon, and Rolls-Royce fitters making a final check on the engine right-bank replacement, just prior to the 1929 contest. *Hirsch Collection*

RAeC members had surpassed themselves in making arrangements to keep spectators informed of the race's progress. It was the largest crowd ever to assemble for a Schneider contest.

A southeasterly wind dictated where the starting ship, HMS *Medea*, would be positioned. After lunch, Britain's Orlebar and Italy's Bernasconi went out on a launch from Calshot to settle on the takeoff run and to position their pontoon barges beforehand. They decided on an area at the mouth of Southampton water, directly opposite Calshot. The starting and finishing line was opposite the Ryde pier. The pier head was all ready for the many visitors expected, charging 3 shillings admission, but the pier remained somewhat empty since the public could enjoy the spectacle just as well from the beach promenade. The timekeepers were perched in a small enclosure on the pavilion's roof at the pier end. By 1:30pm, four pontoon barges had been towed out to the starting point; one for each British machine and one larger pontoon for all three Italian machines.

At 1:40pm the crew of Waghorn's S.6 (No. 2) started filling it with hot oil. At 1:50 Lovesey got into the cockpit. In a couple of minutes, he started the engine and ran it at full throttle for almost 2min. Then he left the cockpit and Waghorn took his place. At 1:58 the pontoon barge was placed facing the wind and Orlebar signaled for launch. At precisely 2:00pm the boom of the starting gun on the *Medea* was heard, along with a visible puff of white smoke. Two minutes later Waghorn crossed the starting line. Using full-right rudder and aileron to keep the left wing inches above the water he started about 70deg right of the direction of the wind and the direction he would be facing when on the step. Up to 30mph (48.3km/h) the cockpit was enveloped in spray, but from 40–50mph (64.4–80.5km/h) it subsided, and he was slowly moving into the wind and onto the step. As he reached hump speed he came directly into the wind, and at 110mph (177.1km/h) he lifted off. The contest was on!

Tomaso Dal Molin was up next, but there was a 15min gap between takeoffs; this meant Waghorn would have completed the course by the time Atcherley could take off. Waghorn was holding at about 200ft (61m) leaving a faint trail of smoke, denoting a rich mixture for cooler running. The multitude of ships and

boats of all sizes and shapes helped to obscure the turn pylons, and the first lap was by guess. Otherwise, the first lap would give a fair indication of the speeds that could be expected in the contest. A trio of three dots approaching and growing larger soon became visible as being the S.6 completing Lap 1. It roared across the line and disappeared toward Sea View and Hayling Island marker boats. Waghorn's first lap speed was 324mph (521.32km/h). His second was 329mph (529.69km/h); his third lap was 331mph (532.91km/h). His fourth lap dropped back to 328mph (528km/h), but his temperature gauge stayed at 203deg (95deg C). The air in the cockpit was hot, but fresh cool air from the ventilation tube kept his face cool and provided comfortable breathing.

About one minute before Waghorn entered his fourth lap Dal Molin lined up the M.52R, took off, and flashed by the starting line with the screaming high pitch of the Fiat engine. The closeness of the two on the course and the S.6 overtaking the older Macchi was the only semblance of a race. As Waghorn approached

Italian team, left to right: Lt. Remo Cadringher, W/O Tomaso Dal Molin, Sgt. Maj. Francesco Agello, Lt. Giovanni Monti, and Lt. Col. Mario Bernasconi, in front of the M.52. *A. Coccon*

The M.52 trainer, with the pilot coming down the ladder to the float from its cockpit. He would then be carried on the shoulders of a crewman to shore, and the plane would be beached on a dolly. *A. Coccon*

Dal Molin, they began to appear close together. Then the S.6 passed the Macchi, and the progress made between 1927 and 1929 could be seen in the passing. The M.52R clocked 286mph (460km/h) on its first lap, indicating that it would provide an interesting match with the Supermarine S.5. Shortly after Waghorn crossed the start-finish line, D'Arcy Grieg flashed by in the S.5 on his first lap. Dal Molin was flying very low on the straightaway but sort of skidded and slipped upward on the turns. As the two completed each lap, the Macchi was steadily being clocked about 2mph (3.22km/h) faster than the S.5, even though the D'Arcy Grieg's turns were smoother, with less deceleration.

While Dal Molin was still lapping, Remo Cadringher took off in the first Macchi M.67 (No. 7). Shortly after his climbing turn, Cadringher flashed across the start line with an ear-splitting scream from the Isotta-Fraschini at about 50ft (15m). He followed Dal Molin in the M.52R but did not appear to be catching up at a very fast rate. When Cadringher approached his second lap with his engine smoking, Dal Molin was still ahead

of him. As Cadringher neared the West Cowes marker boat he pulled up from his 50ft (15m) level and swung wide around the boat, cut across the middle of the course and over the many boatloads of observers, and headed for Calshot—obviously retiring from the contest. His lap speed was only 284mph (457.24km/h), which was 2mph (3.22km/h) slower than the M.52R.

A few seconds after D'Arcy Grieg had crossed the finish line in the S.5, Richard Atcherley crossed the starting line in S.6 No. 8. He flew behind the pavilion with the time-keepers sighting him on a line with the Ryde church tower. On his return he flew in front of the pavilion (seaward side) to start Lap 2. It was obvious his flight path on the course was erratic and his first lap was only 302mph (486.22km/h). But his speed improved dramatically on and after his second lap. By Lap 6 his speed was 331mph (532.91km/h) and his Lap 7 speed was 332mph (534.52km/h). Atcherley had his goggles ripped off by the wind blast when he tried to push them up onto his helmet and wipe the takeoff spray from his eyes. With gloves on both hands and with one hand on the stick, he could not get his second pair of goggles up on his head. He flew the course with his head ducked down inside the cockpit.

The last to start was Giovanni Monti in the second Macchi M.67 (No. 10), crossing the line almost over the pavilion. Along the Hampshire shore Monti was only 20–30ft (6–9m) off the water. As Atcherley and Monti approached the end of Monti's first lap both were flying farther south than the other pilots, crossing the pier at Ryde, well behind the pavilion. Then as Monti passed the Sea View turning point he kept going straight, then quickly slowed down and landed. Motorboats rushed to the scene and one of them quickly brought Monti to shore while the boats towed the Macchi back to Calshot.

It was soon announced that Monti's Macchi had burst a water pipe and that he had been badly scalded. His only lap was 301mph (484.6km/h). A short time later came the announcement that Atcherley had cut inside the Sea View turning point and was disqualified from any position in the contest. On Lap 6 and 7, however, he had set a 31.06mi (50km) and 62.12mi (100km) speed record, and had turned the fastest lap of the contest. The final contest positions were then Waghorn as the winner,

Dal Molin in second place, and D'Arcy Grieg in third place. Sir Philip Sassoon, RAeC chairman, presented the trophy to Waghorn at a formal banquet aboard the SS *Orford*. Also attending was General Balbo who stated that in 1931 Italy would be better prepared. Two potential Italian winners, the Fiat C.29 and Savoia S.65, had not flown in the contest.

On September 10, just three days after Britain's victory at Calshot, Viscount Hugh Trenchard released a statement from his office as chief of the British air staff to the secretary of state for air, through Air Vice-Marshal Sir John Higgins: "Frankly, I am against this contest. I can see nothing of value in it. Development of high-speed machines will continue under scientific research, but the expense of the Schneider contest was all out of proportion to its value." At the end of 1929, Viscount Trenchard relinquished his post as chief of the British air staff. The air member for supply and research added that the contest was bad from the service viewpoint; bad also from the viewpoint of efficiency, and bad for RAF morale as a whole. It was felt in government high offices that the expenditures could no longer justify the rewards. This ran in parallel to the government's position of 1926–1927.

On the same September 10, George Stainforth flew a Gloster VI (N-249) on four passes over a 1.86mi (3km) course to establish a world speed record of 336.23mph (540.99km/h). The beautiful Golden Arrow machine was not to be denied at least some glory. Later on the same day, however, Orlebar in an S.6 (N-247) averaged 355.8mph (572.48km/h) over the same course. What was significant about this event was that the S.6 had an advantage of about 750hp over the Gloster VI but only beat its time by 19mph (30.59km/h). It was a great tribute to the aerodynamic cleanliness of Folland's design.

Two days after the speed record, Orlebar tried a second time to raise the record. His average speed was 357.7mph (575.66km/h). Thus, the High Speed Flight team had raised the world speed record three times in two days. But it was in the aftermath of this success that the British Air Ministry and Air Council announced they wanted no more to do with the Schneider Trophy contest. This news came as a shock to the aviation industry and to the public. It raised angry responses from those concerned with aviation and national prestige. The government's attitude was more precise: they simply would not allocate the necessary money for support of the 1931 contest, saying that it was wrong to allocate funds for prestige purposes rather than for Britain's practical needs.

Lieutenant Monti standing up in cockpit of his M.52R after the contest, and being towed in to the beaching area.
A. Coccon

169

Chapter 14

1931 Calshot

Not-So-Grand Finale

A tentative decision made early in January 1930 by the British RAeC and discussed at the mid-January 1930 FAI meeting ruled that the entry deposit for the 1931 Schneider contest would be 5,000 francs per machine. The FAI left the close-out date to be settled at a later meeting. Both Italy and France plunked down the money for three machines. However, the RAeC on second thoughts raised the amount to 200,000 francs per machine and returned both France's and Italy's deposits with a letter to the FAI stating they could not accept deposits that were not in compliance with their prescribed conditions. Also, the close-out date was set for July 31, 1930.

In March 1930, Supermarine Aviation inquired of the Air Ministry if the two S.6s would be lent back to them and if the work necessary to increase the horsepower of the R engine would be charged against normal engine development. They were determined to get another 25mph (40.25km/h) from the two machines. The Air Ministry's answer was that it was not possible to lend either machines or pilots for the next contest.

On July 16, the Aero Club of Italy sent copies of their contest entry and the British refusal to accept to the secretary of the FAI. They accused the British of flouting the authority of the FAI since the 5,000 francs was agreed on in the January meet. They also stated that if the British could not organize a contest without such ridiculous conditions, that Italy would be ready to incur all expenses of holding the meet in Venice and that there would be no forfeit-deposit required. Along with the letter, Italy sent 16,500 francs for both entrance fee and guaranteed deposit for all three machines. France sided with Italy and did the same.

The FAI tried to resolve the impasse and held another meeting on September 12, where they ruled that the RAeC must attend a further meeting on November 30 to hear all arguments and finalize a set of rules. Lt. Col. Mervyn O'Gorman argued for Britain that the FAI had no power to alter any rules drawn up by the RAeC. Italy's delegate, General Piccio, and France's delegate, Capt. De L'Escaille, took the opposite view, claiming their deposit had been in order.

Throughout the year a quarrel ensued between the RAeC and French and Italian clubs. Britain maintained stubborn indifference, claiming that what they did was legal and binding. By December 1930, the French and Italians reluctantly paid the 200,000 franc deposit. Once again the contest would take place in the Spithead/Solent area between August 31 and September 19. Specifics would be announced later.

On January 21, 1931, in the House of Commons, Sir Philip Sassoon asked Capt. Peter Macdonald, the undersecretary of state for air, if he was aware that without the Air Ministry's organization and cooperation it would be impossible to compete in the 1931 Schneider Trophy contest, which Britain had only to win once again to keep the Schneider Trophy. Macdonald replied that, after a careful review,

Supermarine S.6B S-1595, with the larger floats and higher-pitch propeller. In the background is the Calshot Castle. *Hirsch Collection*

S.6B S-1596 and S.6A N-247 sitting on their dollies for public inspection prior to contest time. *Hirsch Collection*

there could be no departure from the policy set in October 1929. Their decision against official participation in the contest had not been made for financial reasons alone, but also for reasons of policy and principle. This did, of course, contradict what James Ramsay Macdonald, the prime minister, pledged in a speech on September 7, 1929, when presenting the trophy to the High Speed Flight team. Macdonald said: "We are going to do our level best to win again."

So far the RAeC had promises totaling £22,000, far short of the estimated 100,000 needed to enter and run the contest. The government was not enjoying the negative publicity the *Daily Mail*—a stalwart supporter of aviation—was carrying in its headlines about its do-nothing attitude. Throughout the year

of 1930 a battle had ensued on the floor of the House of Commons, with the conservative opposition party constantly taunting the socialist government for its insistence on relying on private enterprise while urging state intervention and participation with funds made available from private sources.

At a meeting with Sir Philip Sassoon, Comdr. O. Locker Lampson, and five members of Parliament on Tuesday evening, January 27, Prime Minister Ramsay Macdonald was asked to reconsider. He agreed, stating he would make a statement at the next House meeting. Before the upcoming meeting, however, Lady Lucy Houston removed all doubts by sending Macdonald a telegram with a guarantee of £100,000, which would be immediately forthcoming. On January 29, Macdonald made his promised statement, but instead of the usual opposition, he expressed his opinion that the RAF should be authorized by the government to defend the Schneider Trophy. The check was delivered to Sir Philip Sassoon, and he lost no time in placing it onto Macdonald's desk.

The government publicly, although sheepishly, thanked Lady Houston. It ended up that she paid not only for the two machines (S.6Bs), but also for the entire cost of preparations, including testing maintenance, housing and, feeding RAF officers and men, down to such things as their telephone calls to family and friends. She also paid for the patrol boats sent out by the admiralty to control the course.

For a quick reversal, in the House of Commons on February 11, Capt. Peter Macdonald was asked about the High Speed Flight of the RAF. He stated that it had been in continual existence since the last contest, engaged in research work using the Schneider high-speed machines, plus some others. He also understood that the team for this year's race had been chosen and was in training. The Air Ministry then announced that Sqdn. Ldr. A. H. Orlebar had again been given the command and would take charge of administering the team.

By March 12, 1931, the Air Ministry formally announced that the following pilots had been selected to begin special high-speed flight training right after Easter: Flt. Lt. E.J.L. "Freddie" Hope, Flt. Lt. Frank W. Long, Flt. Lt. John N. Boothman, Flt. Lt. George H. Stainforth, A.F.C. Lt. R. L. "Jerry" Brinton, F/O H. H. Leech, and F/O Leonard S. Snaith.

From these men the final team of three would be selected as contestants. Additional officers required for support were Flt. Lt. W. F. Dry, engineering officer, and F/O M. F. Tomkins, stores officer (supply officer).

Nine racing machines were at the disposal of the High Speed Flight team during the training periods: two S.6Bs, two S.6As, two S.5s, two Gloster VIs, and one Gloster IVA. In addition there was an Armstrong-Whitworth Atlas, and a Fairey Firefly and Fleetwing as hack machines.

By August the date was set for the contest: Saturday, September 12, with start time of 12:30pm, coinciding with high tide. The White Star Line furnished the SS *Homeric* for the club's official ship.

The 1931 contest was to be different from the 1929 event: the preliminary trials were to immediately precede the speed runs to form one continuous contest. The preliminary trials would consist of takeoff and climb to 150ft (45.75m), landing, and taxiing for about 2min; then the contestant would proceed to the start line and take off for the speed contest. The preliminary trial and speed course areas were separated for safety reasons. Each competitor was to be started by a signal gun from HMS *Medea*; a flag would be hoisted 5min before each gun firing and hauled down upon firing. Each competitor would be allowed 30min to carry out preliminary trials. Any time beyond the 30min was to be added to the contestant's speed time.

On August 3, the Aero Club of France notified the RAeC that eight pilots, seven officers, and sixty-seven service mechanics would arrive at Calshot on August 26 under command of Capt. De Corvette Amanrich. Pilots included Captain Marty, Captain Vernhol, Lieutenant Retourna, Adjutant Chief Reynaud, Adjutant Chief Doernaer, Adjutant Chief Baillot, Sergeant Dumas, and Sergeant Goussie. Calshot provided for nine French seaplanes.

The Italian pilots were to arrive on August 12, and the remainder on August 26. They were to be Maj. Guglielmo Cassinelli, Lt. Pietro Scapinelli, Lt. Stanislao Bellini, Lt. Ariosto Neri, and W/O Francesco Agello.

But the contest had already been adversely affected by several accidents. On July 30, Lt. Georges De Vaisseau Bougault, one of the original French team, was killed at the Berre training base near Marseilles in one of the Bernard seaplanes while on a training flight. The cause was believed to have been a broken propeller. Then on August 2, Capt. Giovanni Monti of the Italian team was killed while practicing over Lake Garda in one of the five M.C.72s. While on a high-speed run, he dove straight into the misty lake instead of leveling off. Earlier on July 3, Flt. Lt. E.J.L. Hope flying S.5 N-248 had a cowling part come loose and cut his ear. He decided to set down on The Solent. As he landed, about 300ft (91.5m) from the Royal Holland liner *Gelria*, he was flipped by the wash from the liner, bounced into the air, and capsized in about 50ft (15.25m) of

All three of the contestants out on their dollies being set up for inspection and publicity photos prior to the contest. The lead counterbalances can be seen on the rudder and ailerons on No. 7. This was to dampen any control-surface harmonics, a phenomenon that was then called aileron buzz. *Hirsch Collection*

water. He sustained injury to his eardrum and was grounded by the team medical officer. A buoy was dropped to mark the spot where the machine sank. It was later raised and reconditioned.

British training machines originally included two S.6s, two Gloster VIs, one modified Gloster IV, an S.5, and a few hack machines. Italy had the M.39, M.52, M.52R, and an M.67. France depended on Bernards and Nieuports, most of which were not serviceable.

The French Effort

After France's failure to provide entries for the 1929 contest, preparations continued for the 1931 event. The government and aero-industry were intensely criticized for allowing such a gap in expertise and experience to occur from years of nonparticipation. It was going to be difficult, but the French Air Ministry responded by placing orders with Dewoitine for two HD.412 racers with Lorraine Radium engines, a Bernard HV.220, and two Nieuport-Delage ND.650s. They hoped to

achieve 390 to 400mph. Bernard also made a start on an HV.320, but it went no further than configuration layout. The new racers were to be built for new engines by Lorraine, Renault, and Farman, engines that would be in the 2,300hp class.

The bickering over the forfeit-deposit and the French procrastination in paying the deposit and entry fees most likely had something to do with the slow progress in manufacturing the machines. An on-again, off-again attitude of government can all but kill a time-dependent project.

The Nieuport-Delage machines did not move from the drawing boards into hardware until December 1930, mostly because the engine manufacturer failed to deliver the 18-R engines on time. The first of the two ND.450s began flight testing about mid-February at Hourtin on the Gironde, and also north of Bordeau. This place was the French team's earlier training area. Actually, from September 1929, the Hourtin base was used primarily by contractors for flight testing. Sadi Lecointe was to

do a flight test of the ND.450s, since most of the team's pilots had little or no flying time in seaplanes.

On November 15, 1929, Antoine Pillard, chief test pilot for Bernard, flew the HV.41 with a specially boosted Hispano-Suiza engine. The HV.40, HV.41, and HV.42 were machines developed for the 1929 Schneider contest. The general configuration of HV.42 was modified, including a new, geared, inverted-T, 18cyl engine and a wing with surface radiators. It was designated HV.120-01. This became an interim machine, while a newer design, HV.120-02, was developing. Test flights of the HV.120-01 were completed by March 1930 by Paillard and the machine was delivered to the high-speed group by May. The

ungeared HV.120-02 followed a month later. They remained at Hourtin.

By 1930 the flight training base had been established at Etang De Berre on the Cote D' Azur, just west of Marseilles with Captain Amanrich in command. Twelve pilots from French fighter units were selected for training, but this dwindled to eight. The only fast machine available for all eight pilots was the HV.41. The two Bernard HV.120s were still at Hourtin, undergoing propeller testing by Paillard until he became ill with peritonitis. He died on June 15, 1931, at the age of 34. This was a setback for Bernard, but by July 1930 most of the pilots had flown the two HV.120s and they were at Berre before 1931.

Propeller problems hindered the direct-

The S.6B up on the pontoon barge with its handling crew. At left is Sqdn. Ldr. A. H. Orlebar's motor launch carrying him and Boothman. When in position, Boothman will climb in and take off. S. Hudek

Vickers-Supermarine S.6B S-1595 was one of two S.6Bs built; the other was given serial S-1596. These aircraft were powered by a Rolls-Royce R engine that produced 2,600hp, which was 700hp more than the 1929 R engine had produced.

drive HV.120-02 progress, but Jean Assolant made several high-speed flights at Etang De Berre. It was becoming the only machine with any chance of taking part in the contest. But performance of the S.6 in 1929 meant a plateau of about 400mph (644km/h) would need to be reached. Takeoff problems persisted due to the lack of controllable-pitch propellers and several diameters and pitch angles were tested. But these always affected the efficiency at high speed, and 320mph (515.2km/h) was the highest speed achieved. The larger diameter propellers were damaged by spray from the floats, so a three-blade propeller was tested. It produced too much torque for efficient takeoff, however. De Vaisseau Bougault did most of the testing. In search of more speed, the second of the two HV.120s was sent back to the factory for wing-area reduction.

After a series of tests of the Nieuport-Delage ND.450 and some team practice flights, the machine was returned to the Nieuport

company for overhaul on July 22. While alighting on its flight from Lake Hourtin to Paris it crashed into the Seine River. The pilot, Fernand Lasne, was not seriously injured, but the ND.450 needed major repairs. Since the high-speed machines provided very little training and the second ND.450 had not been tested by Sadi Lecointe, and with the two most qualified pilots dead, the two civilian pilots, Jean Assolant and Sadi Lecointe, were becoming the most likely to fly the contest.

The final list of French pilots entered by the aero club were Sadi Lecointe, Assolant, and Vernhol, finalists, and Retourna, Baillot, and Dumas, substitutes.

The Nieuport-Delage ND.650 was a modified ND.450 having the Hispano-Suiza 18-R engine and reduced span by 3.21ft (0.98m). It was returned to Hourtin for testing by Sadi Lecointe but by the last week in August, it still had not lifted off the water. Floats were changed but showed no difference in performance. However, on September 3, Sadi Lecointe managed to get the ND.650 in the air and made some speed runs. The machine was credited with a speed of 329.2mph (530km/h). Nieuport planned to dismantle the airframe and transport it to Cherbourg, France, then take it to Calshot on a French naval vessel. But the mediocre speed achieved, continuing propeller problems, and direction instability influenced a change of plans.

On July 30 the geared Bernard HV.120-01 crashed into the lagoon at Berre and Lieutenant De Vaisseau Bougault was killed. There were several theories as to how, but no salvaged material proved the exact cause. He was the only service pilot competent in both types of Bernards. Trials were temporarily suspended at Berre. On August 9, French Air Minister Dumesnil flew to Marseille for Paris to visit the seaplane station on the Etang De Berre and to inspect the French team. Since the death of De Vaisseau Bougault a cloud of pessimism had settled over French hopes for being competitive in the 1931 contest. Also, the Bernard HV.220 and the Dewoitine HD.412, both with a Lorraine Radium engine, were still in construction and not ready to fly.

On return to Paris, Dumesnil stated he would decide soon whether France would enter the contest. As late as August 28 the British Air Ministry received an official notification saying that France would compete for the Schneider Trophy and that French Air Minister Dumesnil would arrive off Calshot in the light cruiser *Foch* about September 8 or 9 and remain there through the contest.

The machines that had been flown up to mid-August had not exceeded 328mph (527.75km/h). Also, the four new machines being built—which might have been competitive—were behind schedule and there was doubt as to whether any would be ready in time. On September 5, France confirmed it would not compete.

The Italian Effort

At a meeting on October 22, 1929, the Italian government met with leading aero engineers at which plans were discussed for the construction of new machines for the 1931 contest. It was chaired by Colonel Bernasconi, captain of the 1929 team. General Balbo's review of proposals and concepts brought the re-

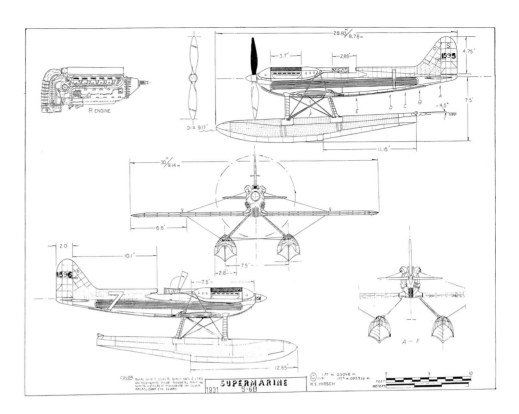

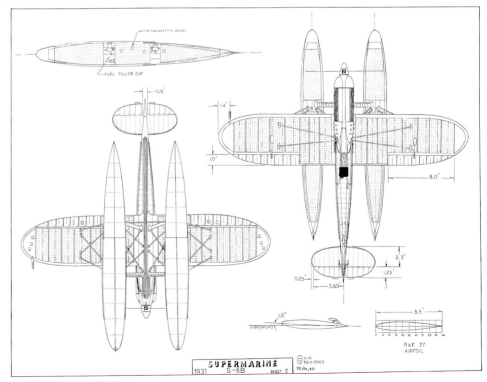

S.6B with Flt. Lt. F. W.
Long standing by and
watching Boothman
make his rounds of the
course. Note the
newsreel truck and
photographers. *Hirsch
Collection*

sponse that scattered resources among several companies, as was done in 1929, would be a mistake. Thus, combining Fiat engines with Savoia-Marchetti airframes was the preferred plan for 1931. Both companies were anxious to work together again.

Fiat put an engine project together by combining two 1,500hp As.5 engines back-to-back, each geared to a coaxial propeller shaft with one rotating inside the other. Thus each propeller rotated in opposite directions. Both shafts ran forward within the vee area of the forward engine above the crankshaft casing. The engine was a V–24 with a displacement of 3,050ci (50ltr) and 11ft (3.353m) in length and drove two 8.5ft (2.59m) propellers at 2000rpm. By dividing the high engine output between two propellers, use of smaller diameter higher efficiency propellers was allowed. The engine was designated As.6 and was designed by Tranquille Zerbi.

The As.6 was designed to function as a single engine and had a single induction system, but each propeller and its engine were mechanically independent except for throttle connection. The supercharging and fuel induction

systems for both engines were geared to the rear engine. It was rated at 2,850hp, but within three years, output would reach 3,000hp.

Advantages of the As.6 were twofold: it had the power of two engines with the frontal area of one, and each counter-rotating propeller canceled out the torque effect produced by the other. Propeller pitch was ground adjustable. The Fiat As.5 used in the C.29 had achieved a high degree of reliability, so much was expected of the As.6. The M.C.72's designer, Mario Castoldi, had been impressed by the torque elimination concept of the Savoia S.65, but he thought it was essential to bring the propellers together at the front to improve stability and propeller synchronization. The new Macchi design was designated Macchi-Castoldi M.C.72.

The M.C.72's wings and tail planes were similar to the M.67's, but the fuselage was longer and slimmer. The fuselage was of mixed, or composite construction, with metal used for the forward fuselage and cockpit and wood from there aft. The tail units were full-cantilever and wood-veneer covered. Wings were wire braced and of two-spar duralumin design and almost fully covered with flat-tube surface radiators over its bi-convex, almost symmetrical, airfoil section. Additional radiator surface covered the top of floats and all four flat struts. Even more radiator surface was installed on the fuselage sides aft of the cockpit during the summer months when it was felt the engines were running too hot. Oil-cooling radiators were on the fuselage top and bottom directly behind the propellers. Five machines were built, each with small variances. Production numbers were MM-177 through MM-181. Maximum takeoff weight was 6,409lb (2,907kg). All-metal floats were built and tested along with wooden floats, but the metal ones reduced top speed by 9.3mph (15km/h), so wooden floats were selected and attached to broad-chord steel streamlined struts. Each float contained pressurized fuel tanks that raised the fuel to two small gravity-fed tanks directly behind the induction system.

A second high-speed pilot training project was started at Desenzano early in 1930 under the command of Col. Mario Bernasconi, with ten new pilots selected plus the two pilots Monti and Agello who had elected to stay on.

Most of the training was done on the old Macchi M.52s through the first half of 1931. However, they still flew an M.39 and an M.67. The Savoia-Marchetti S.65 had attempted a world speed record on January 18, 1930, and crashed into Lake Garda killing Dal Molin, the only successful Schneider pilot still in training. The main theory at the time was that Dal Molin was overcome by fumes and heat.

Italy was not finding the going easy. Fiat's new As.6 engine was proving to be a handful with the air induction and fuel mixture in ground and flight testing. Spark plug mismatch was thought the problem, but proved not to be. Since the rear engine produced power to run the induction compressor, it delivered less power to the propeller than did the front engine. This made the synchronization of propeller rpm difficult. The problem was solved by ground adjusting the front propeller

pitch angle. General Balbo cast the first doubts of Italy's participation on April 29, 1931, in his presentation on Italy's air status in the Italian Chamber meeting. Pilot efficiency would not be a problem, but the machines would have to be thoroughly tested before Italy would go to Calshot.

The first M.C.72 arrived at Desenzano in June 1931. Monti was chosen as pilot for the initial testing. The first takeoff was straight, as the aircraft handled almost like a landplane. However, the flight was not much more than 2min old before the engine began sputtering and backfiring into the induction system, and Monti was forced to bring it back in. More flight testing was done, but whenever the engine was brought up to power, shortly thereafter backfiring would commence, some being violent. There was danger of a backfire causing an explosion in the supercharger section. Despite the carburetor problems, the

M.C.72 attained a speed of 375.2mph (604km/h).

On August 2 the Italian Schneider contest plans received a tragic setback. Monti made a clean takeoff in the M.C.72 and throttled back to get into position for making a low-level pass over the maintenance area so engineers could better hear the backfiring for themselves. With the throttle fully open he overflew the area at a very high speed; the aircraft pitched up and then nosed down, making a quarter-turn spin, and dove into the lake. An investigation found that a bearing failure caused the contra-rotating propellers to break up. However, Muzio Macchi, who witnessed the accident, was not convinced of that theory. By this time the second M.C.72 was being flown by Lieutenants Bellini, Neri, and Scapinelli, and Warrant Officer Agello. The third machine was being prepared for flight.

General Balbo insisted on witnessing further trials and arranged for a visit on August 20, but weather forced cancellation of his flight until August 23. Neri flew the demonstration for the general and more were planned but again the weather closed in and the flights were postponed. Then on August 28, fishermen on Lake Garda recovered the body of Monti. It showed many body burns, indicating fire in the cockpit. General Balbo returned to Rome stating that he could not confirm with certainty that Italy could be ready to take part in the contest this year. Time was quickly running out.

Both the French and Italian teams were in deep difficulty as the established contest date drew near. Both aero clubs approached the RAeC on September 3 pointing out their problems and requesting a postponement. They both cited the precedent created by the Americans in 1924. Only nine days away from the contest date, the RAeC refused to consider any postponement, other than from day to day due to weather, and replied to both clubs without hesitation. It cited all the elaborate preparations that had already been made and the large expenditures incurred, including a grant by Lady Lucy Houston so that the race would go forward. Britain insisted that they would carry out the program alone, if necessary. However, they hoped France and Italy would be able to compete. France and Italy both notified Britain that they would not compete.

Then on September 10, two days before the contest, Italy—smarting from the British refusal and anxious to set a speed record Britain's S.6B could not touch—put one of the M.C.72s through a record run. Pilot Bellini was trying to exceed the 394mph (633.95km/h) previously accomplished by Neri. Bellini made several successful runs over a marked course, then cut back on power and flew over the Desenzano base. He then turned left to the lake and opened up the throttle crossing the water at a very high speed. But instead of pulling up he flew straight into the shore on the other side of the lake with terrific impact, scattering parts in all directions. A burned sleeve from Bellini's uniform was found 1.86mi (3km) from the impact point, indicating an explosion in the air intake induction system, which then set fire to the fuel in the gravity-feed tank. After that, all flying and record attempts with the M.C.72 were abandoned. Two of the three completed M.C.72s were destroyed, and no further development was made on the aircraft for quite some time.

The British Effort

By the end of January 1931, only seven months before the contest, development began on the Vickers-Supermarine–Rolls-Royce S.6B. Its appearance was similar to the 1929 S.6 machines, but the S.6B was designed for greater power and to carry greater loads of fuel and oil. The oil and water cooling was improved and more efficient. The fuel load in the floats was redistributed to balance the increased engine torque and the floats were redesigned with better water-handling and unsticking characteristics. All control surfaces had mass balances installed to eliminate the flutter experienced on S.6 N-248. The S.6B was about 500lb (226kg) heavier than its predecessor: the overall design had been strengthened to carry increased weight.

The wing-surface radiators were constructed with 24-gauge duralumin sheet, with a thin water space between the two sheets. The seams acted as baffles, allowing water to flow parallel to the structure ribs from front to back. They were limited by wing area to handling only 40,000 BTUs (British thermal units) per minute, enough to cool an engine of about 1,000hp. When the surface radiators were filled with almost boiling water before the flight they expanded nearly 1/2in (1.27cm), allowing extra water capacity. This increased capacity, along with radiators on the floats, allowed the system to cool the 2,600hp engine. An ingenious elastic framework prevented the outer skin from buckling. The S.6B floats were 24ft (7.315m) long, only 1ft (0.31m) shorter than the fuselage.

Oil capacity was increased by adding an oil tank to the fairing behind the pilot's head, and cooling efficiency was increased some 40 percent by passing the hot oil through radiators on the fuselage sides. The top surfaces of the floats were also covered with radiators similarly built to those on the wing, and assembled in five sections on each float, which created a complicated pipe system. Access doors were provided next to each pipe connection. The floats and radiators were produced simultaneously, so matching could only be done on paper. But when they were assembled, they fit perfectly, which said something for the sheet-metal formers.

The torque from full power had an effect of suddenly transferring about 500lb (226kg) of force to the port float. To counteract this, the starboard float carried most of the fuel. Fuel was pumped up into a small pressure tank and gravity-fed into the induction system below it.

Fairey Aviation Co. Ltd. developed a new propeller type for increased high-speed efficiency. The 8.5ft (2.59m) diameter was 1ft (0.31m) smaller than the 1929 propellers, and the blades were almost in a stalled condition at takeoff. The S.6B, production number S-1595, was fitted with a 9.2ft (2.788m) diameter propeller and the takeoff problem was eliminated.

Two S.6Bs were built. They were given serial numbers S-1595 and S-1596, and carried race No. 1 and 7, respectively. S.6A N-248 carried race No. 4.

The modified contest rules imposed new problems for the R engine. Inevitably more power was needed, and it was more than just desirable that the fuel and oil consumption should be reduced. Tests for establishing the best approach began with the 1929 engine. The tests probed various modifications on the supercharger diffuser vanes and increased rpm to increase air-intake volume. But the increase in rpm brought about a staggering increase in oil consumption—to about 65.21gal (247ltr) per hour. This was prohibitive in terms of storage space since about 120gal (454.25ltr) would be used during each contest. Also, flight trim would change as the oil was consumed.

The answer lay in the piston rings. There were three compression rings and one oil scraper ring. The first approach was to use tighter and harder compression rings, in hopes of holding higher compression and blocking any oil passage. But this had no effect on oil consumption. They then tried two oil wiper rings, modifications of the breather system, improved scavenging, and a new pump with greater capacity. It brought the oil consumption down to 15.59gal (59ltr) per hour at maximum power.

The exhaust valves were running red hot and causing pre-ignition. This problem was cured by using internally sodium-cooled valves that had been developed in the United States by Samuel D. Heron. But Rolls-Royce modified the design to put the sodium in the hollow valve stem, leaving only the valve face solid. It

Ground crews prepare the M.C.72 for flight at Lake Garda. The machine's absolute speed record stood for 5-1/2 years before being beat by a Heinkel and then a Messerschmitt. Even though these German aircraft were landplanes and had benefitted from much newer technology, the new record was only 28.5mph faster than the M.C.72's. *A. Coccon*

transferred heat up the stem to areas where liquid-cooled valve guides dissipated heat. Engine modifications included new connecting rods to handle the higher loads. Almost every component down to the bolts and nuts was analyzed. Rolls-Royce also called on fuel expert F. Rodwell Banks of the Ethyl Export Corp. to analyze the fuel. He established the mixture of diluting the 100 percent benzol with leaded gasoline. With this fuel, the engine produced 2,800hp, but some cylinder bolts showed signs of failure and via more testing, Rolls-Royce settled on 2,600hp, about 700hp more than the 1929 engine.

American Efforts

In America, Lt. Al Williams resigned his commission in order to devote full time to the 1931 contest. But through 1930, he could not get a backing group together and no project was started. However, when the French and Italian request for delay looked like it might come about, the US Navy had contracted for development of an engine for a racing aircraft for the contest the next year. A telegraph message from Washington, D.C. to the RAeC stated that the United States was preparing an entry for the 1932 Schneider contest. The US

Navy knew that the Schneider Trophy contest was held every two years, so they either were expecting a postponement or were planning for 1933.

The Race Approaches

By August 11 the RAF High Speed Flight team was out at sunrise taking advantage of the first day of good weather. It was the third day of flyable weather in Calshot in five weeks. Both Supermarine S.6Bs had been delivered. Flt. Lt. F. W. Long flew the first flight in the afternoon. The S.6Bs were to be flown mostly for testing and other machines were to be used for practice flights. At about 2:40pm, the pilots were grouped for publicity photos.

N-247 and N-248 had each undergone some of the changes that were incorporated in the S.6B. One would be available as the third entry and the second would be held for back-up. N-247 incurred buckling of the aft fuselage caused by rudder oscillation from harmonics setting up at high speed. A mass lead balance was placed on the rudder and ailerons to dampen out the harmonics oscillations. The fix worked and also provided a change for the S.6B.

On August 18, Jerry Brinton became a victim of the floatplane's instability on takeoff. He was attempting his first flight in S.6A N-247. Team leader A. H. Orlebar was on the pontoon giving him final instructions and running through the checklist. He told him to close the throttle and hold the stick in full-back position if he got into trouble or started porpoising. Brinton taxied out and did a short run to get the feel of the left swing and early bouncing before getting up on the step. He began his takeoff. Orlebar was timing his run when the porpoising started. The nose rose steeply, then the tail went up and the machine fell back onto the water, bouncing off at a steep angle and dropping back and bouncing even higher to about 40–50ft (12.2–15.2m). Then it plunged into the water with its nose steeply downward, tearing off the floats, which then let the machine sink into the water.

The fast tide-changing currents defeated all efforts to get down into the cockpit and all the best rescuers could do was to grapple the submerged wreck and tow it back to Calshot where a crane lifted it onto a ramp. Brinton had died instantly with a broken neck. N-248 was still being repaired from the Lieutenant Hope accident and now N-247 would require complete rebuilding to be serviceable.

The two S.6Bs were low on flying time, one with about 90min and the other about 50min. Before the contest they would need new engines. The erosion characteristics of the fuel loosened the fuel tanks' sealing compound and clogged the fuel filters, causing intermittent engine cutout in flight. However, it was analyzed as excess material breaking loose and so the mechanics just kept cleaning the filters until the excess sealing compound had all broken loose.

On August 19 the weather closed in again, leaving few opportunities for any kind of flying. Then on August 26, the weather did an about-face and dawned as a true summer day. But haze, gusts of wind, changing tide, and a glut of shipping limited flying to trainers until afternoon and early evening. Flt. Lt. J. N. Boothman made a flight in the Gloster IVB in the morning, but the sea conditions were not good. The Fairey Firefly went up in the afternoon to check out conditions and gave the OK at about 3:00pm. An S.6B was towed to the other side of Southampton waters and the S.5 was run up on the slipway. F/O L. S. Snaith was first off in the S.5, and then the Gloster VI was moved onto the slipway and run up by Flt. Lt. W. F. Dry. Then Flt. Lt. G. H. Stainforth climbed into the cockpit, and as the machine was being set to launch, the engine quit.

Boothman tried in vain to get the S.6B into the air but the sea traffic was too heavy. After an hour, the S.6B was towed back to its moorings. In the late afternoon, Orlebar flew out on the course in an Armstrong-Whitworth Atlas to check conditions and gave the OK signal. Again the S.6B was towed out and the Gloster VI was run up. Stainforth then went off the slipway with the Gloster VI in a cloud of spray and took off into the gradually darkening sky. At about 7:00pm Boothman took off for his second flight in an S.6B. He stayed up about 30min and landed during the rapidly approaching dusk.

Then after four unsuitable days, on August 31 flight again resumed. All team members but Snaith flew around the course. Two pilots narrowly missed some kites flown by boys near the West Wittering turning point, and a group of boats carrying curious onlookers cluttered the takeoff area.

From September 1 through September 5 no flying was possible except in some of the hack machines. During this period the two S.6Bs underwent modifications to bring the C.G. forward.

On Wednesday, September 2, at 7:00am the weather showed some promise and Orlebar ordered two S.6s, one Gloster VI (N-249), and one S.5 to prepare for flight. But the heavy, persistent rain returned before they were able to get airborne and practice was abandoned. They were ready to fly again on the sixth, which turned out to be a good flying day. Pilots were briefed by Orlebar to keep the stick back all the way during takeoff and landing. At 8:40am, S.5 N-219 with Stainforth in the cockpit flew for about 15min. Coming in for a long glide with the float heels well down just dipping into the water and settling in up to the step, he gave an exhibition on how a racing seaplane ought to be put down on the water. Boothman was next to go out in N-220. Boothman had to dart around all sorts of watercraft from steamers to sailing yachts. His takeoff run must have been a record for shortness; after 12min he landed again on The Solent. Next was Flt. Lt. F. W. Long in the Fleetwing to again check out the water on the course. He reported it to be suitable, so the S.6A, and the two S.6Bs were taken out to Lee-on-Solent. Halfway out a decision was made to change the propeller on S.6B S-1595, and they brought it back. The change was accomplished in 20min.

The order of flying at this point was as follows: First, Long in S.6A N-248, then Stainforth in S.6B S-1596, and third Snaith in S.6B S-1595 with the new propeller. Orlebar rode out with them in his motor launch. Both S.6Bs showed great improvement on takeoff with the new C.G. This was the first flight of N-246 since it was returned from Woolston after rebuild from Hope's accident. It was also the first time Orlebar didn't make the first flight. The A had larger floats than those used in 1929, but they were still smaller than the new B floats. Long took off at 12:15pm. He stayed aloft for about 15min, which was a normal practice flight time. At 12:50pm Stainforth took S-1596 and practiced turns with different degrees of bank. A battery of binoculars fol-

Francesco Agello sitting on a float of the record-breaking machine in front of the hangars in Milan, Italy. The record of 440.68mph (709.2km/h) still stands today for seaplanes. *A. Coccon*

lowed every move. He stayed in the air for 20min. The weather took a turn, with some rain squalls to stop flying for the rest of the day.

The Grand Finale

Arrangements were made on the mainland to accommodate 20,000 cars and 500,000 people at Portsmouth and South-Sea for the contest. The city of Portsmouth provided a number of enclosures along the 4mi (6.44km) of South-Sea front and the South Parade Pier. Cars and people were also being accommodated at Lee-on-Solent, Gasport, Hayling Island, and West Wittering. Folders with such information were given out by the RAeC. The contest was also viewed by thousands on various boats anchored in the eight selected areas, including some large ocean vessels. The RAeC had had to gamble on which Saturday to pick, and were also limited by the tides.

On September 9 at Calshot there was a general feeling of disappointment that the French and Italians were not coming. When there are no rivals to beat, the sporting side of the contest vanished. None of the RAF team wanted to win the trophy with a fly-over. The Air Ministry had stated that if the first machine to start performs to the satisfaction of the committee, no other machine would start. The plan was that Boothman would fly S.6B S-1595 around the course and substantially beat

the previous records. If he failed, Snaith would repeat the attempt in S.6A N-248, and if a third attempt was needed, Long would be ready in the other S.6B, S-1596.

Although public enthusiasm was considerable, the news that only one aircraft was to fly the course was greeted with the expected negative expression of an inglorious final victory. Yet there was a feeling that history was being made, and that an event so integral to the sport of aviation was about to end. The end may have been mourned by other nations wishing for one more chance, but to Britain, the glory, nevertheless, was there.

Saturday morning, September 12, dawned with reasonable weather, bringing out spectators by the thousands. Flying had been very active for the five good-weather days up to Friday and on that day only Snaith flew in the S.6A, for 18min; Long took one of the S.6Bs up for 15min. Then all concentrated on preparations for the race, except for Boothman flying one of the S.5s at about 11:00am. On Saturday the fly-over was to begin at 12:30pm. The machines were out on their pontoon barges ready to be towed to their takeoff position and launch. But the weather forecasters predicted deteriorating weather by 11:00am (they missed it by 1hr). Orlebar made a final check of the course in one of the hack machines, and when he returned, towing of the pontoon barges to takeoff position had already begun. He had to order them returned to their moorings. A strong wind was picking up, and the sea at St. Helens Point was already heavy with swells and whitecaps. It was too rough for floatplanes. Then at 11:00am it began to rain, and at 1:00pm the fly-over was delayed until the next day, weather permitting.

The crowds dispersed to find a place to dry themselves, and the machines on their pontoons were brought back to Calshot and unloaded on the ramp, where they were rolled into the hangars for cover. The delay caused the toughest luck for a party of 600 Rolls-Royce employees who had left Derby by special train at 2:00 Saturday morning. Then after sitting all day in the wet weather they had to go back to Derby on the train without seeing a contest.

On Sunday, September 13, the crowd was rewarded for their patience. The weather was perfect, the air crystal clear, and visibility was

15mi (42.325km). So from the southern beaches of Southampton, the progress of flight could be visible around the entire course. By 11:00am the beaches were filled from one end to the other with people sunbathing, swimming, wading on the shores, and picnicking while waiting for the show to begin.

Communications between the officials and those aboard HMS *Homeric,* where the official press was accommodated, were sketchy at best. There were loud speakers aboard, but announcements bore little resemblance to what was happening. One couldn't tell what was official and what was a commentary. The RAeC wanted to start at 8:00am, but the Royal Navy would not allow it until noon because the course couldn't be cleared of shipping before then. Because the record attempt was not listed as part of the Schneider contest, the Navy did not keep the 1.86mi (3km) course cleared for Stainforth and thus high-mast sailing vessels plus ocean liners were moving through his line of flight.

Between 9:00 and 10:00am, before the tide was full, the two S.6Bs and S.6A were launched from the ramp and towed out to their pontoons. A fleet of service and civil motorboats loaned for the occasion dashed out to patrol the course and the *Medea* took up station at the starting line. At 10:25am Orlebar and Sqdn. Ldr. L. M. Bailey took off in the Atlas to have a look at the course, landing a few times to test the water surface. When they came down at Calshot, Boothman and Snaith went up in the same machine for one last look. There still was a breeze, but it wouldn't interfere with the contest. At 11:00am Long went around the course in a Fairey Firefly. While this was going on the racers were being towed to the starting line on their pontoons. Just before midday the pilots headed out to the pontoons. The engine of S-1595 was started, final checks were made, and then just after 1:00pm the S.6B was launched from the pontoon with Boothman in the cockpit.

The plan of order-of-flight was announced. Boothman would fly S.6B S-1595 over the course and better the average of the 1929 record. If he failed to achieve it satisfactorily, Orlebar would send up Snaith. Long was to be ready with S.6B S-1596 as needed. At approximately 4:00pm Stainforth was to fly the

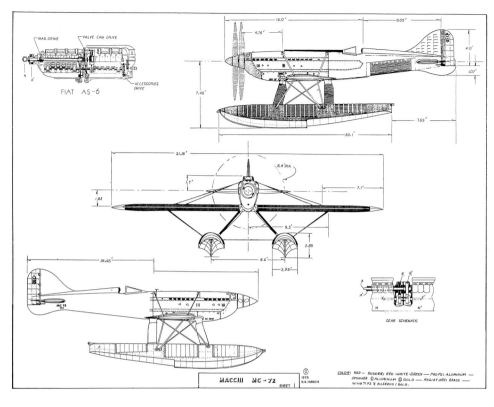

MACCHI MC-72 SHEET 1

COLOR: RED — RUDDER: RED-WHITE-GREEN — PROPS: ALUMINUM — SPINNER ①ALUMINUM ②GOLD — RADIATORS: BRASS — WING TIPS & AILERONS: GOLD.

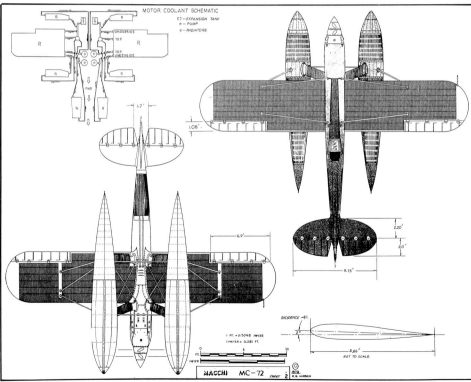

MACCHI MC-72 SHEET 2

1.86mi (3km) speed record course in S-1596. Boothman had been with the High Speed Flight team almost two years and specialized in experimenting with methods to round sharp turns.

The starting gun boomed from HMS *Medea* at 1:02pm and Boothman took off northward into the wind, cleanly and confidently. He gained altitude in a graceful turn and came back with a 160mph (257.6km/h) glide and landed close to his takeoff point, but facing southward. He thus completed the most dangerous or worrisome part of the contest—landing with a full load. The 2min taxi test was rather slow for about 1min, 15sec, and then he increased speed for 40sec, accelerating into a takeoff run, crossing the Ryde pier start line on the water, and then lifting off smoothly.

Boothman used about 800yd (732m) radius for his turns, mathematically the fastest that could be made. What was very noticeable was the consistency of his lap speeds. However, after several laps there was a gradual drop in speed. If the outside air temperature exceeded 62.6deg (17deg C) it was impossible to use full throttle without overheating the engine. The normal water temperature was 190–194deg (88–90deg C) for takeoff and the maximum temperature not to exceed was 203deg (95deg C). Therefore, the water temperature was the governing factor for maximum speed. Boothman was to fly a set water temperature maximum and to throttle back when it was reached. On the first lap and a half, the water temperature remained at 190deg (88deg C), and the S.6B flew wide open. By the sixth lap the machine wanted to fly left wing low due to trim change as fuel and oil was consumed.

Boothman's lap speeds around the course were as follows:

Lap No.	Mph	Km/h
1	343.1	522.05
2	342.7	551.41
3	340.0	547.06
4	338.3	544.33
5	339.6	546.42
6	339.4	546.09
7	337.7	543.36
Average	340.1	542.96

After rounding the Ryde Middle pylon on the last lap, Boothman came across the finish line with a burst of full throttle. The ships anchored in the eight reserved areas let loose with all the noisemaking they could, drowning out the cheering from the hundreds of thousands of spectators on land. After landing, he was taken onboard the *Medea* and given a colossal round of cheers, congratulated by RAeC officials, and subjected to a picture-taking session. Back at Calshot, Boothman got another rousing welcome.

Between the Schneider Trophy contest flight and the attempt on the speed records, Snaith gave the assembled public a display of aerobatics in the Fairey Firefly training machine. He rolled and looped the seaplane as though it was an aerobatic landplane. The Firefly was a fast fighter with a Rolls-Royce Kestrel engine. Snaith did one show off the Hampshire coast and then another off the IOW.

At 4:00pm, Stainforth flew S-1596 after the absolute world speed records. As he taxied into the wind, he had to throttle back to correct for porpoising, but then pushed it up on the step and made an excellent takeoff. He surveyed the course and then started his runs. Long and an official FAI observer were at 1,300ft (396.24m) with a sealed barograph in the Atlas to monitor altitude for the rules. They were also a guide for Stainforth. He made four runs from Ryde pier to Spithead Forts. The difference in up-wind and down-wind runs was 14mph (22.54km/h) during the first pair and 13mph (20.93km/h) in the second pair. Stainforth's runs were timed as follows:

Run No.	Mph	Km/h
1	373.85	601.64
2	388.0	625.99
3	369.87	595.0
4	383.81	617.69
Average	378.65	610.61

The figures were submitted to the FAI for homologation.

Tests were being carried out on various types of propellers in September. On the twenty-ninth, Stainforth flew S-1595 with a new spring engine and an exotic fuel—30 percent benzol, 60 percent methanol, 10 percent ace-

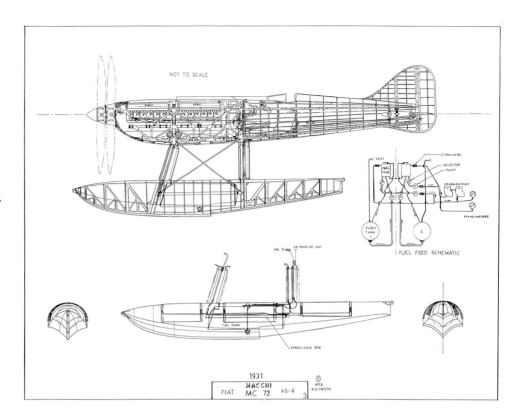

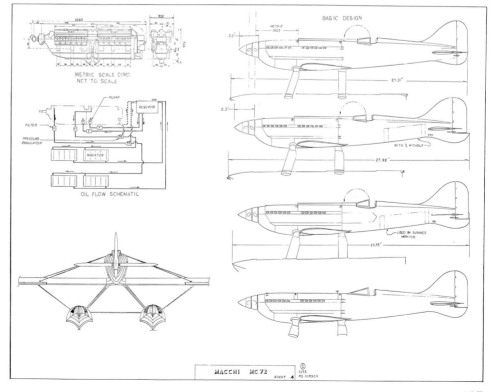

Head-on view of the lone remaining M.C.72 after World War II in Milan. It is being refurbished for museum display. The first M.C.72 crashed into Lake Garda on August 2, 1931, killing Lt. Giovanni Monti. Another M.C.72 was crashed on a speed-record attempt on September 10, 1931, killing pilot Bellini. Both crashes were attributable to the problems caused by a lean fuel-air mixture at high speeds.

tone, and one part per thousand of tetraethyl lead—which developed 2,530hp. He was the first person to travel faster than 400mph (644km/h) by setting a new record of 401.5mph (646.415km/h). It was the final effort for the British. To commemorate their winning the Schneider Trophy and achieving the world speed record, the RAeC held a banquet at Claridge's Hotel on December 9. Presentations were made to members of the Schneider team, Supermarine, and Rolls-Royce. Tickets were sold by the RAeC for £1,1 shilling.

After the contest, Italy continued research with the M.C.72. Fuel expert F. Rodwell Banks was invited by General Crocco to visit the Fiat engine plant in Italy, and he quickly spotted the problems plaguing the machine. The engines tested adequately on bench-test runs. But when in the aircraft traveling at over 400mph with a ram-air intake and maximum rpm, the differential pressure across the carburetor decreased and the mixture became too lean with a net result of violent backfiring into the 7ft (2.13m) induction system full of explosive mixture. This would produce a large bang, blowing up the whole induction system.

Banks demonstrated by simulating ram-air pressure equal to 400mph (644km/h) that indeed the leaning of the mixture was the problem. Using Banks' fuel mixture, Fiat was then able to develop 3,000hp at 3300rpm turning the propellers at 1980rpm.

Then on April 10, 1934, Francesco Agello, set a world speed record of 423.82mph (682.07km/h) on Lake Garda in the M.C.72. Eighteen months later he raised it to 440.68mph (709.20km/h). That record stands today for propeller-driven seaplanes and it wasn't until 1939 that it was beaten by the Heinkel 100 V-8 and then again by a Messerschmitt 209 V-1. These machines were designed to establish a speed record and were not combat-capable aircraft. They were very clean landplanes with retractable gear. On March 30, 1939, the Me 209 V-1 with a special DB 601A engine of 2,300hp for short 1min sprints, attained a speed of 469.2mph (754.94km/h) with Fritz Wendel as pilot. The record was only 28.5mph (45.92km/h) faster than the M.C.72. Also, the record speeds around the race course at the Reno Air Races today are only in the vicinity of about 40mph (64.4km/h) faster than the M.C.72's record.

Bibliography

Books

Abate, Rosario, and Giulio Lazzati. *Velilvoli Macchi from 1912-1963*. Aermacchi, 1963.

Andrews, C. E., and Morgan, E. B. *Supermarine Aircraft since 1914*. UK: Putnam, 1981.

Barker, Ralph. *The Schneider Trophy Races*. UK: Chatto & Windos, 1971.

Barnes, C. H. *Short's Aircraft since 1900*. UK: Putnam, 1967.

Bignozzi, G., and Catalanotto, B. *Aerei D'Italia*. Aeroi De Tutoo l'Mondo.

Bowers, Pete. *Curtiss Aircraft 1907-1947*. UK: Putnam, 1979.

British Seaplane Triumph in Schneider Trophy Contest. UK: Real Photographs Co. Ltd., 1945.

Casey, Louis, and Batchelour, John. *Seaplanes & Flying Boats*. New York: Exeter Books.

Demand, Carlo, and Ende, Heiner. *Conquerors of the Air 1903-1905*. New York: Bonanza Books.

Denham, T. S. *Speed*. London: Pilot Press, 1929.

Dural, G. R. *British Flying Boats and Amphibians*. UK: Putnam, 1966.

Foxworth, Thomas. *Speed Seekers*. New York: Doubleday, 1947.

Hunson, Kenneth. *Pioneer Aircraft 1903-1914*. New York: Macmillan, 1969.

Hunt, Leslie. *Veteran and Vintage Aircraft*. Garnstone Press, 1970.

Jackson, A. J. *Avro Aircraft since 1908*. UK: Putnam, 1965.

Jackson, A. J. *Blackburn Aircraft since 1909*. UK: Putnam, 1968.

James, *Derek N. Gloster Aircraft since 1917*. UK: Putnam, 1971.

James, Derek N. *Schneider Trophy Aircraft—1913–1931*. UK: Putnam, 1972.

Jane's Historical Aircraft, 1902-1916. New York: Doubleday, 1973.

King, H. F. *Sopwith Aircraft*. UK: Putnam, 1980.

Kinnert, Reed. *Racing Planes and Air Races*. California: Aero Publishers, 1967.

Lewis, Peter. *British Racing and Record Breaking Aircraft*. UK: Putnam; 1971.

Mason, F. K. *Hawker Aircraft since 1920*. UK: Putnam, 1968.

Monday, David. *The Schneider Trophy*. UK: Robert Hale & Co.

O'Neil, Paul. *The Epic of Flight—Barnstormers and Speed Kings*. Time-Life Books.

O'Neil, Paul. *The Epic of Flight*. Time-Life Books.

Palmer, Henry R., Jr. *The Story of the Schneider Trophy Race*. Superior Publishing Co., 1962.

Penrose, Harold. *British Aviation 1915-1919*. New York: Funk & Wagnalls, 1969.

Penrose, Harold. *British Aviation, The Pioneer Years*. USA: Aero Publishers.

Robertson, Bruce. *Sopwith—The Man and His Aircraft*. UK: Fountain Press.

Roseberry, C. R. *Glenn Curtiss, Pioneer of Flight*. New York: Doubleday, 1972.

Science of Preflight Aeronautics. Columbia University. New York: Macmillan.

Sunderman, J. F. *Early Air Pioneers, 1862-1935.* New York: Fiauldin Watts

Taylor, H. A. *Fairey Aircraft since 1915.* UK: Putnam, 1974.

Taylor, Michael J. H. *Great Moments in Aviation.* USA: Mallard Press, 1989.

Tempo, Ali Nel. *I Veliouli Macchi 1912-1963.* Milano, Italy.

Villard, Harry Serrano. *Contact.* New York: Bonanza Books.

Periodicals, Articles, and Papers

AAHS, Vol. 11, No. 1, 1966

Aero Digest—1923–1932

Aerofan—September 1984

Aero Modeller—pp.238–242

Aeronautica—Vol. 7, 1955

Aeroplane–1913–1914, 1920–1927, 1929 and 1931

Aircraft Design—Vol. II, C.H.L. Needham, 1939

Aircraft Engine Mechanics Manual, C. D. Moors, 1940

Airplane Service Manual, Lt. Col. V. W. Page, Chapters 23 and 24, 1938

Airplanes and Engines, P. H. Sumner, 1939

Airways—October 1929

Alata International—November 1965

Ali Nuove—March 1959

Aviation—1923-1932

Aviation Engine Examiner—Maj. V. W. Page 1931

Designs of Airscrews for Schneider Trophy Race—1927, P. A. Ralli

Engineering Aerodynamics, Capt. W. S. Diehl USN, 1936

Epoca—Di Armando Sivestri, Italy

Flight—1911–1914, 1919–1932

Historical Brief (IAS). Hist Branch—Jack Canary

Italian Aviation Research Branch of Air Britain—May 1972

L` Aeronautique—pp. 303–304, 358–364, 1927

Les Aeroplanes—1910—1920

L` Idrocorsa Da Coppa Schneider—S.I.A.I. Savoia 5-50, Franco Bugada

NACA Technical Memo No. 691, by Giovanni Pegna

Profile Publications, No. 39

Properties and Strengths of Materials—Vol. III, J. D. Haddon, 1933

Racing Seaplanes—F. Holroyd, February 27, 1930

Schneider Trophy Engine Design, Capt. G. S. Wilkinson, 1927

Schneider Trophy Machine Design—1927, R. J. Mitchell

Take Off—Nos. 18, 19, 20, 21

The Airplane Engine, L. S. Marks, McGraw-Hill, New York, 1922

The Schneider Cup Race—1925, Maj. J. S. Buchanan, January 21, 1926

The Schneider Trophy, 1929—Flight Lieutenant Waghorn

Vitesse a L` Italienne, pp. 8-11

Wy'scig O Puchar Schneidbra, pp. 173-195

Zur Luftartgeschechte—Die Schnellen Der Zwanziger Jahre

Index